PostgreSQL Query Optimization

The Ultimate Guide to Building Efficient Queries

Second Edition

Henrietta Dombrovskaya
Boris Novikov
Anna Bailliekova

Apress®

PostgreSQL Query Optimization: The Ultimate Guide to Building Efficient Queries,
Second Edition

Henrietta Dombrovskaya
DRW Holdings, Chicago, IL, USA

Boris Novikov
Database expert, Helsinki, Finland

Anna Bailliekova
UrbanFootprint, Milwaukee, Wisconsin, USA

ISBN-13 (pbk): 979-8-8688-0068-9
https://doi.org/10.1007/979-8-8688-0069-6

ISBN-13 (electronic): 979-8-8688-0069-6

Managing Director, Apress Media LLC: Welmoed Spahr
Acquisitions Editor: Shaul Elson
Development Editor: Laura Berendson
Project Manager: Jessica Vakili

Cover designed by Straive

Distributed to the book trade worldwide by Springer Science+Business Media New York, 1 New York Plaza, Suite 4600, New York, NY 10004-1562, USA. Phone 1-800-SPRINGER, fax (201) 348-4505, e-mail orders-ny@springer-sbm.com, or visit www.springeronline.com. Apress Media, LLC is a California LLC and the sole member (owner) is Springer Science + Business Media Finance Inc (SSBM Finance Inc). SSBM Finance Inc is a **Delaware** corporation.

For information on translations, please e-mail booktranslations@springernature.com; for reprint, paperback, or audio rights, please e-mail bookpermissions@springernature.com.

Apress titles may be purchased in bulk for academic, corporate, or promotional use. eBook versions and licenses are also available for most titles. For more information, reference our Print and eBook Bulk Sales web page at http://www.apress.com/bulk-sales.

Any source code or other supplementary material referenced by the author in this book is available to readers on GitHub. For more detailed information, please visit https://www.apress.com/gp/services/source-code.

Paper in this product is recyclable

Table of Contents

About the Authors

Henrietta Dombrovskaya is a database researcher and developer with over 40 years of academic and industrial experience. She holds a PhD in computer science from the University of Saint Petersburg, Russia. At present, she is a database architect at DRW Holdings, Chicago, Illinois. She is an active member of the PostgreSQL community, a frequent speaker at the PostgreSQL conference, and the local organizer of the Chicago PostgreSQL User Group. Her research interests are tightly coupled with practice and are focused on developing efficient interactions between applications and databases.

Boris Novikov's experience includes leading postgraduate research groups and advising dozens of PhD students while partnering and collaborating with industrial clients. His research interests are in the broad area of information management and include design, development, and tuning of databases, applications, and database management systems (DBMSs). He also has interests in distributed scalable systems for stream processing and analytics.

Anna Bailliekova is Senior Data Engineer at UrbanFootprint, where she works on data platform tools and cloud ops for geospatial applications. Previously, she worked in data engineering at Zendesk and held a variety of DBA and BI roles at Epic. Her writing can be found in the newsletter *Better Streets MKE*. She received her undergraduate degree with college honors in political science and computer science from Knox College in Galesburg, Illinois.

About the Technical Reviewer

Tom Kincaid is Vice President of Database Development at EnterpriseDB. Tom has been developing, deploying, and supporting database systems and enterprise software for over 25 years. Prior to joining EnterpriseDB, Tom was General Manager of 2ndQuadrant in North America where he oversaw all aspects of 2ndQuadrant's dynamic and growing business for Postgres products, training, support, and professional services. He worked directly with companies from all industries and of all sizes helping them successfully make Postgres part of their mission-critical operations.

Tom has overseen the design and delivery of Postgres training solutions as well as the deployment of PostgreSQL both at Fortune 500 financial institutions and at military facilities all over the world. Teams Tom has managed have delivered major features that have become part of the PostgreSQL open source database.

Tom is also the founder and one of the organizers of the Boston PostgreSQL User Group.

Acknowledgments

It takes many people to bring a book into the world, most of whose names do not appear on the cover. Firstly, we want to thank Jonathan Gennick, who came up with the idea of this book and navigated it through the first edition. Without his initiative, this book wouldn't exist. We're also grateful to the entire team at Apress who have supported this endeavor across two editions.

The contributions of Tom Kincaid as the technical reviewer cannot be overstated. His careful, thorough, and thoughtful feedback improved the content, organization, and usability of the text. This book is more precise, more understandable, and more comprehensive, thanks to Tom. We're grateful that he returned for the second edition, graciously taking another close read. Any remaining issues are, of course, our own responsibility.

After the first edition of this book was released, we heard from many people regarding issues in the postgres_air database, topics readers wished were covered, and passages that could have been more clear. This second edition incorporates many of their suggestions. We are grateful to everyone who took the time to read the book closely and share their comments and suggestions with us. In particular, Hannu Krosing provided thorough, detailed, and specific feedback on postgres_air, and Egor Rogov provided many helpful suggestions for making the book more understandable and clear.

—Henrietta Dombrovskaya, Boris Novikov, Anna Bailliekova

Thank you to Jeff Czaplewski, Alyssa Ritchie, and Greg Nelson, who spent hours, days, and weeks making No-ORM (NORM) work with Java. My time at EDB was a chance to work with and learn from the best of the Postgres best. My colleagues at DRW—both application and database administrator (DBA) teams—have given me new opportunities to push the limits of Postgres.

—Henrietta Dombrovskaya

ACKNOWLEDGMENTS

I'd like to thank Andy Civettini for teaching me how to write and talk about technical topics in an accessible way and for years of academic and professional encouragement. My colleagues at UrbanFootprint challenge and inspire me every day. Finally, John, Nadia, and Kira Bailliekova have each supported me and sacrificed for the sake of this book; I am endlessly grateful to them.

—Anna Bailliekova

Introduction

"Optimization" is a broad enough term to encompass performance tuning, personal improvement, and marketing via social engine and invariably evinces high hopes and expectations from readers. As such, it is prudent to begin not by introducing what is covered, but rather, why this book exists and what will not be covered, to avoid disappointing readers who approach it with inappropriate expectations. Then, we proceed with what this book is about, the target audience, what is covered, and how to get the most use out of it.

Why We Wrote This Book

Like many authors, we wrote this book because we felt we could not *not* write it. We are educators and practitioners; as such, we see both how and what computer science students are taught in class and what knowledge they lack when they enter the workforce. We do not like what we see and hope this book will help bridge this gap.

When learning about data management, most students never see a real production database, and even more alarming, many of their professors never see one, either. While lack of exposure to real-life systems affects all computer science students, the education of future database developers and database administrators (DBAs) suffers the most. Using a small training database, students can learn how to write syntactically correct SQL and perhaps even write a SELECT statement that accurately retrieves desired data. However, learning to write performant queries requires a production-sized dataset. Moreover, it might not be evident that performance might present a problem if a student is working with a dataset that can easily fit into the computer's main memory and return a result in milliseconds regardless of the complexity of the query.

In addition to lacking exposure to realistic datasets, students often don't use DBMSs that are widely used in industry. While the preceding statement is true in relation to many DBMSs, in the case of PostgreSQL, it is even more frustrating. PostgreSQL originated in an academic environment and is maintained as an open source project, making it an ideal database for teaching relational theory and demonstrating database internals. However, so far, few academic institutions have adopted PostgreSQL for their educational needs.

As PostgreSQL is rapidly developing and becoming a more powerful tool, more and more businesses are choosing it over proprietary DBMSs, in part to reduce costs. More and more IT managers are looking for employees who are familiar with PostgreSQL. More and more potential candidates learn to use PostgreSQL on their own and miss opportunities to get the most out of it.

We hope that this book will help all interested parties: candidates, hiring managers, database developers, and organizations that are switching to PostgreSQL for their data needs.

What Won't Be Covered

Often, when users start to complain that "everything is slow" or nightly backups finish in broad daylight and everyone seems to be saying that "the database needs to be optimized," conversations are almost exclusively focused on database configuration parameters and occasionally on underlying Linux parameters. It is often assumed that as soon as the correct values for parameters are chosen and the database instance has been restarted, all the world's problems will be solved.

Countless times, we have worked with customers expecting magical incantations and cheat codes. Countless times, these customers have expressed a deep disappointment when the "wizards" to whom they have appealed suggest looking for the queries that are executed most often or check for missing indexes. After listening politely to all our suggestions, they kept asking: So can you suggest *any other parameter changes*?

Indeed, it is tempting to be able to solve every problem at once. That temptation leads to the popular belief that there is a sort of dark magic and secret codes, a button hidden under a desk somewhere that makes the database run faster.

Since we are aware of these misconceptions, we want to be transparent from the very beginning. The following is the list of topics that are often discussed in books about optimization but will not be covered in this book and why:

- *Server optimization* – With the mass migration to various cloud environments and existing organizational structures, database developers are unlikely to have a say in how servers are configured.

- *PostgreSQL configuration parameters* – In this second edition of the book, we do cover this topic. However, it comprises a relatively small portion of the book, as their impact on performance is overrated, as we will demonstrate, and usually, database developers do not have the necessary privileges to alter them (with a few exceptions).

- *Distributed systems* – We do not have enough industrial experience with them.

- *Transactions* – Their impact on performance is very limited (although we will cover some cases when they can have a major impact).

- *New and cool features* – These change with every new release, and our goal is to cover the fundamentals.

- *Magic, rituals, cheat codes, etc.* – We are not proficient in these approaches to optimization.

There are plenty of books available that cover all of the topics listed previously, except the last, but this book is not one of them. Instead, we focus on everyday challenges database developers face: when that one application page keeps timing out, when a customer is kicked out of the application just before the "Contract Signed" page, when the CEO dashboard is showing an hourglass instead of yesterday's product KPI, or when procuring more hardware is not an option.

Everything we are presenting in this book has been tested and implemented in an industrial environment, and though it may look like magic, we will explain any query performance improvement or lack thereof.

Target Audience

Most of the time, a book about optimization is viewed as a book for DBAs. Since our goal is to prove that optimization is more than just building indexes, we hope that this book will be beneficial for a broader audience.

This book is for IT professionals working in PostgreSQL who want to develop performant and scalable applications. It is for anyone whose job title contains the words "database developer" or "database administrator" or who is a backend developer charged with programming database calls. It is also useful to system architects involved in the overall design of application systems running against a PostgreSQL database.

What about report writers and business intelligence specialists? Unfortunately, large analytical reports are most often thought of as being slow by definition. However, if a report is written without considering how it will perform, the execution time might end up being not just minutes or hours, but years! For most analytical reports, execution time can be significantly reduced by using simple techniques covered in this book.

What Readers Will Learn

In this book, the readers will learn how to

- Identify optimization goals in OLTP (Online Transaction Processing) and OLAP (Online Analytical Processing) systems

- Read and understand PostgreSQL execution plans

- Identify indexes that will improve query performance

- Optimize full table scans

- Distinguish between long queries and short queries

- Choose the right optimization technique for each query type

- Avoid the pitfalls of ORM frameworks

At the end of the book, we present the *Ultimate Optimization Algorithm*, which guides a database developer through the process of producing the most performant query.

The Postgres Air Database

Throughout this book, examples are built on one of the databases of a virtual airline company called Postgres Air. This company connects over 600 virtual destinations worldwide, offers about 32,000 direct virtual flights weekly, and has over 100,000 virtual members in its frequent flyer program and many more passengers every week. The company fleet consists of virtual aircraft.

Please note that all data provided in this database is fictional and provided for illustrative purposes only. Although some data appears very realistic (especially descriptions of airports and aircraft), they cannot be used as sources of information about real airports or aircraft. All phone numbers, email addresses, and names are generated.

To install the training database on your local system, please refer to the GitHub repo: *github.com/Hettie-d/postgres_air*.

The README.md file contains the link to the data directory and detailed installation instructions.

In addition, after you restore the data, you will need to run the script in Listing 1 to create several indexes.

Listing 1. Initial set of indexes

```
SET search_path TO postgres_air;
CREATE INDEX flight_departure_airport ON flight(departure_airport);
CREATE INDEX flight_scheduled_departure ON flight  (scheduled_departure);
CREATE INDEX flight_update_ts ON flight  (update_ts);
CREATE INDEX booking_leg_booking_id ON booking_leg  (booking_id);
CREATE INDEX booking_leg_update_ts ON booking_leg  (update_ts);
CREATE INDEX account_last_name ON account (last_name);
```

We will use this database schema to illustrate the concepts and methods that are covered in this book. You can also use this schema to practice optimization techniques.

This schema contains data that might be stored in an airline booking system. We assume that you have booked a flight online, at least once, so the data structure should be easily understood. Of course, the structure of this database is much simpler than the structure of any real database of this kind.

Anyone who books a flight needs to create an account, which stores login information, first and last names, and contact information. We also store data about frequent flyers, which might or might not be attached to an account. A person who makes a booking can book for several passengers, who might or might not have their accounts in the system. Each booking may include several flights (legs). Before the flight, each traveler is issued a boarding pass with a seat number.

The Entity-Relationship (ER) diagram for this database is presented in Figure 1.

- *airport* stores information about airports and contains the airport's three-character (IATA) code, name, city, geographical location, and time zone.

- *flight* stores information about flights between airports. For each flight, the table stores a flight number, arrival and departure airports, scheduled and actual arrival and departure times, aircraft code, and flight status.

- *account* stores login credentials, the account holder's first and last names, and possibly a reference to a frequent flyer program membership; each account may potentially have multiple phone numbers, which are stored in the *phone* table.

- *frequent_flyer* stores information about membership in the frequent flyer program.

- *booking* contains information about booked trips; each trip may have several booking legs and several passengers.

- *booking_leg* stores individual legs of bookings.

- *passenger* stores information about passengers, linked to each booking. Note that a passenger ID is unique to a single booking; for any other booking, the same person will have a different passenger ID.

- *aircraft* provides the aircraft's description, and the *seat* table stores seat maps for each of the aircraft types.

- Finally, the *boarding_pass* table stores information about issued boarding passes.

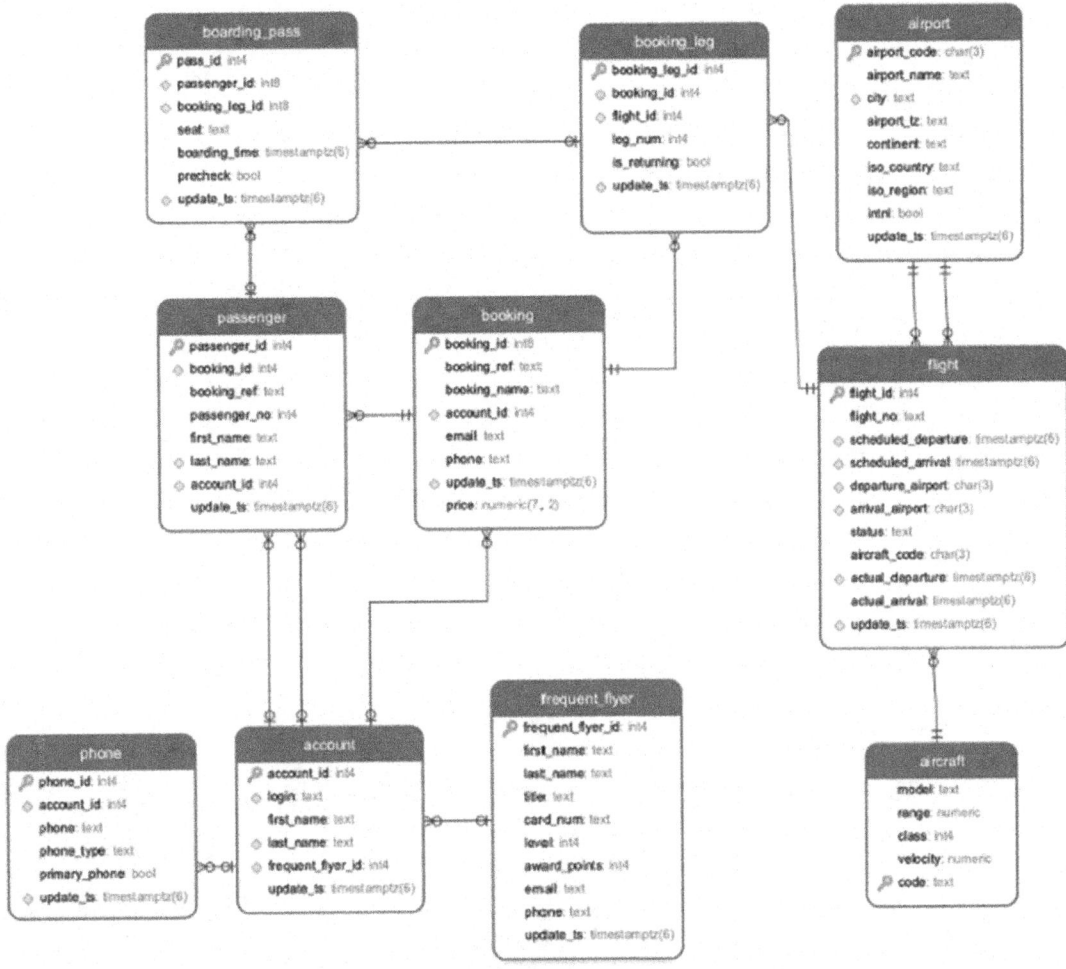

Figure 1. *ER diagram of the booking schema*

CHAPTER 1

Why Optimize?

This chapter covers why optimization is an important part of database development. You will learn the differences between declarative languages, like SQL, and imperative languages, like Java, which may be more familiar, and how these differences affect programming style. We also demonstrate that optimization applies not only to database queries but also to database design and application architecture.

What Do We Mean by Optimization?

While the majority of people think about database optimization as choosing the best system configuration parameters, in the context of this book, optimization means any transformation that improves system performance. This definition is purposely generic, since we want to emphasize that optimization is not a separate development phase. Quite often, database developers try to "just make it work" first and optimize later. We do not think that this approach is productive. Writing a query without having any idea of how long it will take to run creates a problem that could have been avoided altogether by writing it correctly way from the start. We hope that by the time you finish this book, you'll be prepared to optimize in precisely this fashion: as an integrated part of query development.

We will demonstrate some specific techniques; however, the most important thing is to understand how a database engine processes a query and how a query planner decides what execution path to choose. When we teach optimization in a classroom setting, we often say, "Think like a database!" Look at your query from the point of view of a database engine, and imagine what it has to do to execute that query; imagine that you have to do it yourself instead of the database engine doing it for you. By thinking about the scope of work, you can avoid imposing suboptimal execution plans. This is discussed in more detail in subsequent chapters.

© Henrietta Dombrovskaya, Boris Novikov, Anna Bailliekova 2024
H. Dombrovskaya et al., *PostgreSQL Query Optimization*, https://doi.org/10.1007/979-8-8688-0069-6_1

If you practice "thinking like a database" long enough, it will become a natural way of thinking, and you will be able to write queries correctly right away, often without the need for future optimization.

Why It Is Difficult: Imperative and Declarative

Why isn't it enough to write a SQL statement that returns a correct result? That's what we expect when we write application code. Why is it different in SQL, and why is it that two queries that yield the same result may drastically differ in execution time? The underlying source of the problem is that SQL is a *declarative language*. That means that when we write a SQL statement, we describe the result we want to get, but we do not specify *how* that result should be obtained. By contrast, in an *imperative language*, we specify *what* to do to obtain a desired result—that is, the sequence of steps that should be executed.

As discussed in Chapter 2, the *database optimizer* chooses the best way of doing it. What is best is determined by many different factors, such as storage structures, indexes, and data statistics.

Let's look at a simple example: find the flights, including their departure and arrival airports, that are scheduled to arrive on October 14, 2023. Now, let's consider the queries in Listings 1-1 and 1-2.

Listing 1-1. A query selecting flights with the comparison operators

```
SELECT
        flight_id
        ,departure_airport
        ,arrival_airport
FROM flight
WHERE scheduled_arrival >='2023-10-14'
     AND scheduled_arrival <'2023-10-15';
```

Listing 1-2. A query selecting flights by casting to date

```
SELECT
        flight_id
        ,departure_airport
```

```
        ,arrival_airport
FROM flight
WHERE scheduled_arrival ::date='2023-10-14' ;
```

These two queries look almost identical and should yield identical results. However, the execution time will be different because the work done by the database engine will be different. In Chapter 5, we will explain why this happens and how to choose the best query from a performance standpoint.

Thinking imperatively is natural for humans. Generally, when we think about accomplishing a task, we think about the steps that we need to take. Similarly, when we think about a complex query, we think about the sequence of conditions we need to apply to achieve the desired result. However, if we force the database engine to follow this sequence strictly, the result might not be optimal.

For example, let's try to find out how many people with frequent flyer level 4 fly out of Chicago for Independence Day. If at the first step you wanted to select all frequent flyers with level 4, you might write something like this:

```
SELECT * FROM frequent_flyer WHERE level =4;
```

Now that you have found all the records with level=4, you can use them to find the corresponding accounts. The query will look like this:

```
SELECT * FROM account WHERE frequent_flyer_id IN (
        SELECT frequent_flyer_id FROM frequent_flyer WHERE level =4
);
```

Great, you found accounts. On the next step, you want to find all bookings made by these accounts:

```
WITH level4 AS (SELECT * FROM account WHERE
frequent_flyer_id IN (
        SELECT frequent_flyer_id FROM frequent_flyer WHERE level =4
)
SELECT * FROM booking WHERE account_id IN
(SELECT account_id FROM level4);
```

But that's not it! Remember, the original goal was to find frequent flyers who traveled to Chicago on July 3. Continuing to build the query imperatively, we can come up with the code presented in Listing 1-3.

Listing 1-3. Imperatively constructed query

```
WITH bk AS (
WITH level4 AS (SELECT *
                FROM account
                WHERE frequent_flyer_id IN (
                            SELECT frequent_flyer_id
                                FROM frequent_flyer
                                WHERE level =4
                            )
                )
    SELECT * FROM booking WHERE account_id IN
            (SELECT account_id FROM level4
            )
        )
SELECT * FROM bk WHERE bk.booking_id IN
    (SELECT booking_id FROM booking_leg WHERE
        leg_num=1 AND is_returning IS false
        AND flight_id IN (
                    SELECT flight_id
                    FROM flight
                    WHERE departure_airport IN ('ORD', 'MDW')
                        AND scheduled_departure:: DATE='2023-07-04')
    )
```

Now, imagine that in addition, you need to calculate the actual number of travelers. One way to do this would be with the query in Listing 1-4.

Listing 1-4. Calculating a total number of passengers

```
WITH bk_chi AS (
    WITH bk AS (
        WITH level4 AS (SELECT *
                    FROM account
                    WHERE frequent_flyer_id IN (
                                SELECT frequent_flyer_id
                                FROM frequent_flyer
```

```
                                WHERE level =4
                                )
                        )
                SELECT * FROM booking WHERE account_id IN
                        (SELECT account_id FROM level4
                        )
                )
        SELECT * FROM bk WHERE bk.booking_id IN
            (SELECT booking_id FROM booking_leg WHERE
                leg_num=1 AND is_returning IS false
                AND flight_id IN (
                            SELECT flight_id
                            FROM flight
                            WHERE departure_airport IN ('ORD', 'MDW')
                                AND scheduled_departure:: DATE='2023-07-04')
            )
        )
SELECT count(*) FROM passenger WHERE booking_id IN (
                                SELECT booking_id FROM bk_chi)
```

With a query constructed like this, you are not letting the query planner choose the best execution path, because the sequence of actions is hard-coded. Although the preceding query is written in a declarative language, it is imperative by nature.

Instead, to write a declarative query, simply specify what you need to retrieve from the database, as shown in Listing 1-5.

Listing 1-5. Declarative query to calculate the number of passengers

```
SELECT count(*)
FROM booking bk
JOIN booking_leg bl ON bk.booking_id=bl.booking_id
JOIN flight f ON f.flight_id=bl.flight_id
JOIN account a ON a.account_id=bk.account_id
JOIN frequent_flyer ff ON ff.frequent_flyer_id=a.frequent_flyer_id
JOIN passenger ps ON ps.booking_id=bk.booking_id
WHERE level=4
  AND leg_num=1
```

```
AND is_returning IS false
AND departure_airport IN ('ORD', 'MDW')
AND scheduled_departure >= '2023-07-04'
AND scheduled_departure <'2023-07-05'
```

This way, you allow the database to decide which order of operations is best, which may vary depending on the distribution of values in the relevant columns.

You may want to run these queries after all required indexes are built in Chapter 5.

Optimization Goals

So far, we have implied that a performant query is a query that is executed quickly. However, that definition is neither precise nor complete. Even if, for the moment, we consider reduction of execution time as the sole goal of optimization, the question remains: What execution time is "good enough"? For a monthly general ledger of a big corporation, completion within one hour may be an excellent execution time. For a daily marketing analysis, minutes might be great. For an executive dashboard with a dozen reports, refresh within ten seconds may be the best time we can achieve. For a function called from a web application, even a hundred milliseconds can be alarmingly slow.

In addition, for the same query, execution time may vary at different times of day or with different database loads. In some cases, we might be interested in average execution time. If a system has a hard timeout, we may want to measure performance by capping the maximum execution time. There is also a subjective component in response time measurement. Ultimately, a company is interested in user satisfaction. Most of the time, user satisfaction depends on response time, but it is also a subjective characteristic.

However, beyond execution time, other characteristics may be taken into account. For example, a service provider may be interested in maximizing system throughput. A small startup may be interested in minimizing resource utilization without compromising the system's response time. We know one company that increased the system's main memory to keep the execution time fast. Their goal was to make sure that the whole database could fit into main memory. That worked for a while until the database grew bigger than any main memory configuration available.

How do we define optimization goals? We use the familiar SMART goal framework. SMART goals are

- Specific

- Measurable

- Achievable (attainable)

- Result-based (relevant)

- Time-bound (time-driven)

Examples of SMART goals are presented in Table 1-1.

Table 1-1. *SMART goal examples*

Characteristic	Bad Example	Good Example
Specific	All pages should respond fast.	Each function execution should be completed before a system-defined timeout.
Measurable	Customers shouldn't wait too long to complete their application.	Response time of the registration page should not exceed four seconds.
Achievable	Daily data refresh time in the data warehouse should never increase.	When source data volume grows, the daily data refresh time should grow not more than logarithmically.
Result-based	Each report refresh should run as fast as possible.	Refresh time for each report should be short enough to avoid lock waits.
Time-bound	We will optimize as many reports as we can.	By the end of the month, all financial reports should run in under 30 seconds.

Optimizing Processes

It is essential to bear in mind that a database does not exist in a vacuum. A database is the foundation for multiple, often independent applications and systems. For any user (external or internal), overall system performance is the one they experience and the one that matters.

At the organization level, the objective is to improve the performance of the whole system. It might be response time or throughput (essential for the service provider) or, most likely, a balance of both. Nobody is interested in database optimizations that have no impact on overall performance.

Database developers and DBAs often tend to over-optimize any bad query that comes to their attention, just because it is bad. At the same time, their work is often isolated from both application development and business analytics. This is one reason optimization efforts may appear to be less productive than they could be. A SQL query cannot be optimized in isolation, outside the context of its purpose and the environment in which it is executed.

Since queries might not be written declaratively, the original purpose of a query might not be evident. Finding out the business intent of what is to be done might be the first and the most critical optimization step. Moreover, questions about the purpose of a report might lead to the conclusion that it is not needed at all. In one case, questioning the purpose of the most long-running reports allowed us to cut the total traffic on the reporting server by 40%.

Optimizing OLTP and OLAP

There are many ways to classify databases, and different database classes may differ in both performance criteria and optimization techniques. Two major classes are *OLTP* (Online Transaction Processing) and *OLAP* (Online Analytical Processing). OLTP databases support applications, and OLAP databases support BI and reporting. Through the course of this book, we will emphasize different approaches to OLTP and OLAP optimization. We will introduce the concepts of *short* queries and *long* queries and explain how to distinguish one from the other.

Hint   It does not depend on the length of the SQL statement.

In the majority of cases, in OLTP systems we are optimizing short queries and in OLAP systems both short and long queries.

Database Design and Performance

We have already mentioned that we do not like the approach of "first write, then optimize" and that this book's goal is to help you write queries right right away. When should a developer start thinking about performance of the query they are working on? The answer is the sooner, the better. Ideally, optimization starts from requirements. In practice, this is not always the case, although gathering requirements is essential.

To be more precise, gathering requirements allows us to come up with the best database design, and database design can impact performance.

If you are a DBA, chances are, from time to time, you get requests to review new tables and views, which means you need to evaluate someone else's database design. If you do not have any exposure to what a new project is about and the purpose of the new tables and views, there is not much you can do to determine whether the proposed design is optimal. The only thing you may be able to evaluate without going into the details of the business requirements is whether the database design is normalized. Even that might not be obvious without knowing the business specifics.

The only way to evaluate a proposed database design is to ask the right questions. The right questions include questions about what real-life objects the tables represent. To illustrate that statement, let's look at the following example: in this database, we need to store user accounts, and we need to store each account holder's phone number(s). Two possible designs are shown in Figures 1-1 and 1-2, respectively.

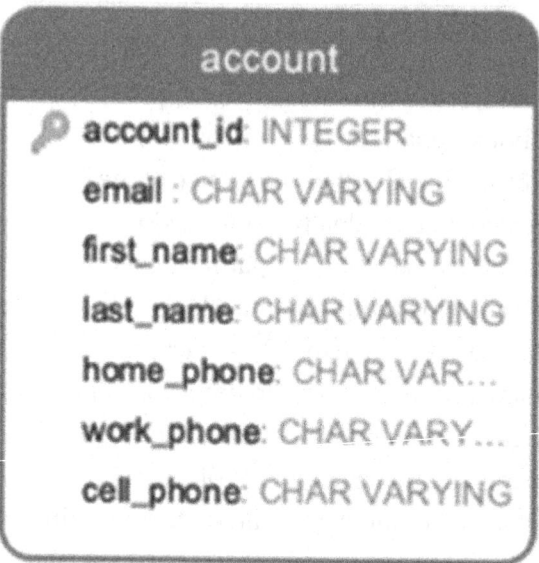

Figure 1-1. *Single-table design*

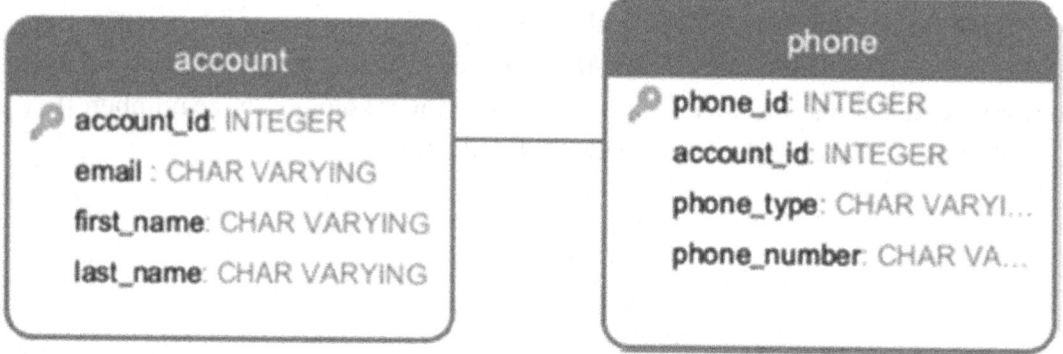

Figure 1-2. *Two-table design*

Which of the two designs is the right one? It depends on the intended usage of the data. If phone numbers are never used as search criteria and are selected as a part of an account (to be displayed on the customer support screen), if UX has fields labeled with specific phone types, then a single-table design is more appropriate.

However, if we want to search by phone number regardless of type, having all phones in a separate table will make the search more performant.

Also, users are often asked to indicate which phone number is their primary phone. It is easy to add one Boolean attribute `is_primary` to the two-table design, but it will be more complicated in the one-table design. An additional complication might arise when somebody does not have a landline or a work phone, which happens often. On the other hand, people often have more than one cell phone, or they might have a virtual number, like Google Voice, and they might want to record that number as the primary number to reach them. All these considerations are in favor of the two-table design.

Lastly, we can evaluate the frequency of each use case and how critical response time is in each case.

Application Development and Performance

We are talking about application development, not just the database side of development because once again, database queries are not executed by themselves—they are parts of applications. Traditionally, optimizing the individual queries is viewed as "optimization," but we are going to take a broader approach.

Quite often, although each database query executed by an application returns results in less than 0.1 seconds, an application page response time may amount to ten seconds or more. Technically speaking, optimization of such processes is not a "database optimization" in its traditional meaning, but there is a lot a database developer can do to improve the situation. We cover a relevant optimization technique in Chapters 10 and 13.

Other Stages of the Lifecycle

The life of an application does not end after release in production, and the optimization is a continuous process as well. Although our goal should be to optimize long-term, it is hard to predict how exactly the system will evolve. It is a good practice to continually keep an eye on the system performance, not only on the execution times but on trends.

A query may be very performant, and one might not notice that the execution time started to increase because it is still within acceptable limits and no automated monitoring system will be alerted.

Query execution time may change because data volume increased or the data distribution changed or execution frequency increased. In addition, we expect new indexes and other improvements in each new PostgreSQL release, and some of them may be so significant that they prompt rewriting original queries.

Whatever the cause of the change is, no part of any system should be assumed to be optimized forever.

PostgreSQL Specifics

Although the principles described in the previous section apply to any relational database, PostgreSQL, like any other database, has some specifics that should be considered. If you have some previous experience in optimizing other databases, you might find a good portion of your knowledge does not apply. Do not consider this a PostgreSQL deficiency; just remember that PostgreSQL does lots of things differently.

For former Oracle users, the most important distinction they should be aware of is that PostgreSQL does not cache queries; it only caches the data in the shared buffers. When Oracle would produce a generic execution plan, which will be available for multiple connections, PostgreSQL will generate a new execution plan each time the query is executed. Even though all the necessary data is already in the main memory, the query itself must be executed. This difference in behavior might drastically decrease application performance after conversion to Oracle. Later in this book, we will discuss the ways to address this problem.

The absence of the cached query plans leads to another important distinction: the difference between the execution of parameterized queries and dynamic SQL. Chapter 13 of this book is dedicated to the use of dynamic SQL, an option that is often overlooked.

Another important PostgreSQL feature you should be aware of is that PostgreSQL does not have optimizer hints. If you previously worked with a database like Oracle, which does have the option of "hinting" to the optimizer, you might feel helpless when you are presented with the challenge of optimizing a PostgreSQL query. However, here is some good news: PostgreSQL does not have hints by design. The PostgreSQL core team believes in investing in developing a query planner that is capable of choosing the best execution path without hints. As a result, the PostgreSQL optimization engine is one of the best among both commercial and open source systems. Many strong database internal developers have been drawn to Postgres because of the optimizer. In addition,

Postgres has been chosen as the founding source code base for several commercial databases partly because of the optimizer. With PostgreSQL, it is even more important to write your SQL statements declaratively, allowing the optimizer to do its job.

With PostgreSQL, it is especially important to be aware of new features and capabilities added with each release. In recent years, Postgres has had over 180 of them each year. Many of these features are around optimization. We are not planning to cover them all; moreover, between the writing of this chapter and its publication, there will indubitably be more. PostgreSQL has an incredibly rich set of types and indexes, and it is always worth consulting recent documentation to check whether a feature you wanted might have been implemented.

More PostgreSQL specifics will be addressed later in the book.

Summary

Writing a database query is different from writing application code using imperative languages. SQL is a declarative language, which means that we specify the desired outcome, but do not specify an execution path. Since two queries yielding the same result may be executed differently, utilizing different resources and taking a different amount of time, optimization and "thinking like a database" are core parts of SQL development.

Instead of optimizing queries that are already written, our goal is to write queries correctly from the start. Ideally, optimization begins at the time of gathering requirements and designing the database. Then, we can proceed with optimizing both individual queries and the way the database calls from the application are structured. But optimization does not end there; in order to keep the system performant, we need to monitor performance throughout the system's lifecycle and continually seek opportunities to optimize it.

CHAPTER 2

Theory: Yes, We Need It!

In order to write performant queries, database developers need to understand how queries are processed by the database engine. And to do that, we need to know the basics of relational theory. If the word "theory" sounds too dry, we can call it "the secret life of a database query." In this chapter, we will take a look at this "secret life," explaining what happens to a database query between the moment you click "Execute" or press Enter and the moment you see the result set returned from the database.

As discussed in the previous chapter, a SQL query specifies what results are needed or what must be changed in the database but does not specify how exactly to execute the requested action. It is the job of the database engine to convert the source SQL query into executable code and execute it. This chapter covers the operations used by the database engine as it interprets a SQL query and their theoretical underpinning.

Query Processing Overview

In order to produce query results, PostgreSQL performs the following steps:

- Compile and transform a SQL statement into an expression consisting of high-level logical operations, known as a logical plan.

- Optimize the logical plan and convert it into an execution plan.

- Execute (interpret) the plan and return results.

Compilation

Compiling a SQL query is similar to compiling code written in an imperative language, such as Java or Python. The source code is parsed, and an internal representation is generated. However, the compilation of SQL statements has two essential differences.

© Henrietta Dombrovskaya, Boris Novikov, Anna Bailliekova 2024
H. Dombrovskaya et al., *PostgreSQL Query Optimization*, https://doi.org/10.1007/979-8-8688-0069-6_2

First, in an imperative language, the definitions of identifiers are usually included in the source code, while definitions of objects referenced in SQL queries are mostly stored in the database. Consequently, the meaning of a query depends on the database structure: for example, an object with the same name could be a table in one database, a view in another one, and a function in yet another one.

Second, the output of an imperative language compiler is usually (nearly) executable code, such as byte code for a Java virtual machine. In contrast, the output of a query compiler is an expression consisting of high-level operations that remain declarative— they do not give any instruction on how to obtain the required output. A possible order of operations is specified at this point, but not the manner of executing those operations.

Optimization and Execution

The instructions on how to execute the query appear at the next phase of query processing, optimization. The optimizer performs two kinds of transformations: it replaces logical operations with their execution algorithms and possibly changes the logical expression structure by changing the order in which logical operations will be executed.

Neither of these transformations is straightforward; a logical operation can be computed using different algorithms, and the optimizer tries to choose the best one. The same query may be represented with several equivalent expressions producing the same result but requiring a significantly different amount of computational resources for execution. The optimizer tries to find a logical plan and physical operations that minimize required resources, including execution time. This search requires sophisticated algorithms that are out of scope for this book. However, we do cover how an optimizer estimates the amount of resources needed for physical operations and how these resources depend on the specifics of how data is stored and the amount of data stored.

The output of the optimizer is an expression containing physical operations. This expression is called a (physical) execution plan. For that reason, the PostgreSQL optimizer is called the query planner.

Finally, the query execution plan is interpreted by the query execution engine, frequently referred to as the executor in the PostgreSQL community, and output is returned to the client application.

Let's take a closer look at each step of query processing and the operations each uses.

Relational, Logical, and Physical Operations

To go deeper into how SQL is understood by the database engine, we must at last confront this chapter's titular concern: theory. Many modern database management systems, including PostgreSQL, are called relational because they are based on relational theory.[1] Despite some bad press (that theory is dry, incomprehensible, or irrelevant), understanding a small part of relational theory is essential to master optimization—specifically, relational operations. To be more precise, we will need to understand how relational operations correspond to logical operations and the query language used in queries. The previous section covered three steps of query processing at a high level; this section describes each level in more detail, starting with descriptions of relational operations.

Some readers may think the material covered here is trivial and find it already familiar, while others may feel that this is introducing an unnecessary complication. For now, hang in there and trust that this is building a foundation for what comes next.

Relational Operations

The central concept of relational theory is a *relation*. For our purposes, we view a relation as a table, although academics may quibble that this elides some subtle but important differences.

Any relational operation takes one or more relations as its arguments and produces another relation as its output. This output can be used as an argument for another relational operation producing yet another relation that, in turn, can become an argument. This way, we can build complex expressions and represent complex queries. The possibility to construct complex expressions makes the set of relational operations (called *relational algebra*) a powerful query language.

Moreover, expressions in relational algebra can be used to define additional operations.

---

[1] C. J. Date, *An Introduction to Database Systems*; J. Ullman, *Principles of Database Systems, Second Edition*

The first three operations to be discussed are *filter, project,* and *product.*

Figure 2-1. *Filter*

The *filter* operation (represented in Figure 2-1) is often called selection and is called restriction in relational theory. We prefer to use the term *filter* to avoid confusion with the SQL SELECT statement, while the term *restriction* has too deep of mathematical origins. This operation accepts a single relation as an argument and includes in its output all tuples (or rows) satisfying the condition specified as a filtering condition, for example:

```
SELECT *
 FROM flight
 WHERE departure_airport='LAG'
     AND (arrival_airport='ORD'
         OR arrival_airport='MDW')
     AND scheduled_departure BETWEEN '2023-05-27' AND
                                     '2023-05-28'
```

Here, we start from the relation flight and apply restrictions on the values of arrival_airport, departure_airport, and scheduled_departure attributes. The result is a set of records, that is, also a relation.

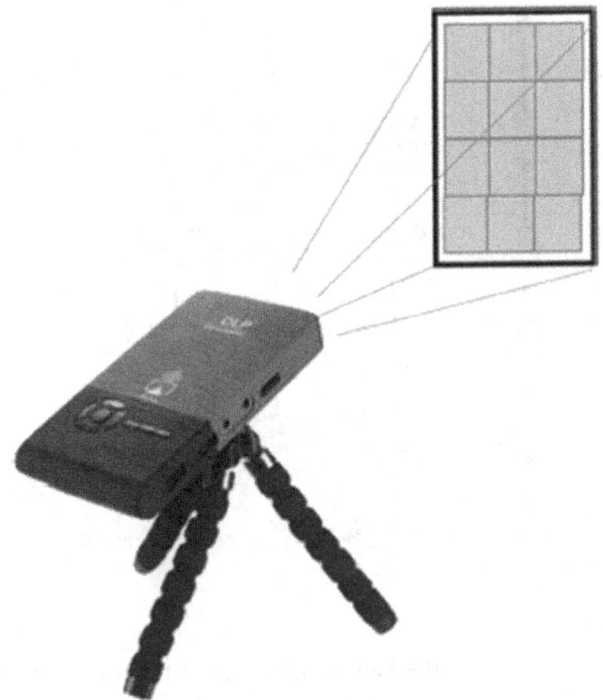

Figure 2-2. *Project*

The *project* operation (represented in Figure 2-2) similarly takes a single relation as an argument and removes some attributes (columns). The relational project operation also removes duplicates from the output, while the SQL project operation does not, for example:

```
SELECT city, zip FROM address
```

when executed in PostgreSQL will return as many rows as there are records in the `address` table. But if we perform the relational operation `project`, it would leave one record for each zip code. To achieve the same result in PostgreSQL, we would need to add the *distinct* keyword:

```
SELECT DISTINCT city, zip FROM address
```

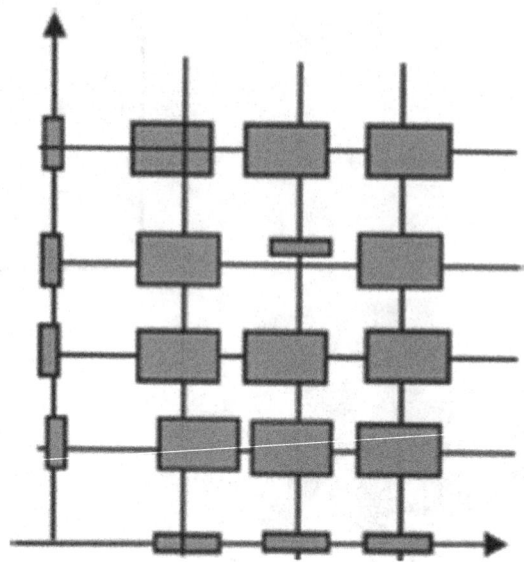

Figure 2-3. *Product*

The *product* operation (also called a Cartesian product and represented by Figure 2-3) produces the set of all pairs of rows from its first and second arguments. It is very difficult to find a real-life, useful example of a product, but let's imagine we want to find all possible flights that might exist (from any airport in the world to any airport in the world). The product operation will look like this:

```
SELECT
        d.airport_code AS departure_airport
        a.airport_code AS arrival_airport
FROM    airport a,
        airport d
```

Now that we have covered these primary relational operations, you may feel cheated: Where is the join operation? We know that join operations are essential. The answer is hidden in plain sight: a join operation can be expressed as a product followed by filtering. From a relational theory point of view, a join operation is redundant. This is a perfect example of how a declarative language works; the formal definition is one way (but not the only way) to find the result of a join. If we compute a Cartesian product of two relations and then apply a filter, we will obtain the desired result. But hopefully, no database engine would use this approach on a larger dataset; it could literally take years! In Chapter 3, we will discuss how joins can be implemented more efficiently than straightforward computation based on the formal definition.

Relational operations also include grouping, union, intersection, and set difference.

The last piece of relational theory that we need for optimization is *equivalence rules*. All relational operations satisfy several equivalence rules, including

- *Commutativity* – JOIN(R,S) = JOIN (S,R)

Commutativity means that the order of two relations is not important. If we have two relations, R and S, then R JOIN S will produce the same result as S JOIN R.

- *Associativity* – JOIN(R, JOIN(S,T) = JOIN(JOIN(R,S), T)

Associativity means that if we have three relations, R, S, and T, we can choose to first perform R JOIN S and then JOIN T to the result, or we can first perform S JOIN T and then JOIN R to the result of the first JOIN, and the results will be equivalent in both cases.

- *Distributivity* – JOIN(R, UNION(S,T)) = UNION(JOIN(R,S),
  JOIN(R, T))

Distributivity means that if we are joining a relation with a UNION of two other relations, the result will be the same as when we perform two joins, R JOIN S and R JOIN T separately, and then UNION the results.

The equivalence rules listed in the preceding text are just examples among dozens. Why is it important to know about these rules? For efficiency, it might be better to execute operations in a different order than they are listed in. There will be multiple examples of such transformations in subsequent chapters. Equivalences ensure that a query may be represented with several different expressions, providing the impetus for an optimizer.

Logical Operations

The set of logical operations needed for representation of SQL queries includes all relational operations, but the semantics is different. As noted earlier, the SQL project operation does not remove duplicates. An additional operation for removal of duplicates is included.

Other additional operations are needed to represent SQL constructs that cannot be expressed in relational theory, for example, left, right, and full outer joins produce a result that is not a relation (but still is a SQL table).

Many equivalence rules are also valid for logical operations. For any relatively complex query, an optimizer can choose the best from a huge number of expressions. More information about relational theory can be found in the resources found in the end notes.

Queries as Expressions: Thinking in Sets

Writing declarative queries is not an easy task for humans. People are more familiar with actions than with rules or conditions. Thinking in sets[2] makes it easier: we can think about actions on tables and operations on tables, rather than on individual objects (or rows).

All logical operations mentioned earlier can be easily expressed in SQL. These operations accept tables as arguments, both tables stored in the database and tables that are the result output of previous operations.

A PostgreSQL expression written as a SQL query will be processed by the optimizer and will mostly likely be replaced with another, equivalent expression, using the equivalence rules discussed earlier.

Since the result of any relational operation is a relation, it can be passed directly to the next relational operation, without the need for intermediate storage. Some database developers choose to create temporary tables to store intermediate results, but such practices can produce unneeded computational overhead and block the optimizer.

In more theoretical words, the previous paragraph states that the ability of an optimizer to produce an efficient execution plan depends on two factors:

- A rich set of equivalences provides for a large space of equivalent expressions.

- Relational operations produce no side effects, such as temporary tables—that is, the only thing produced is the result of the operation.

---

[2] Joe Celko, *Joe Celko's Thinking in Sets: Auxiliary, Temporal, and Virtual Tables in SQL* (The Morgan Kaufmann Series in Data Management Systems)

Operations and Algorithms

In order to make a query executable, logical operations must be replaced with physical operations (also called algorithms). In PostgreSQL, this replacement is performed by the query planner, and the overall execution time of a query depends on which algorithms are chosen and whether they are chosen correctly.

When we move from the logical to the physical level, mathematical relations are transformed into tables that are stored in the database, and we need to identify ways to retrieve data from the tables. Any stored data must be extracted with one of the *data access algorithms* discussed in the next chapter. Usually, data access algorithms are combined with operations consuming their results.

More complex logical operations, such as join, union, and grouping, can be implemented with several alternative algorithms. Sometimes a complex logical operation is replaced with multiple physical operations.

These algorithms are discussed in detail in Chapter 3.

Summary

The database engine interprets SQL queries by parsing them into a logical plan, transforming the results, choosing algorithms to implement the logical plan, and finally executing the chosen algorithms. The logical operations used by the database engine are based on operations derived from relational theory, and understanding these is crucial to thinking like a database.

CHAPTER 3

Even More Theory: Algorithms

By now, those of you who are diligently reading this book without skipping chapters might be impatient. We are already in Chapter 3, and we are still talking about theory! When are we going to get to write code?

Very soon! This chapter covers the last part of query processing, and by the end, we will have all the pieces we need to understand execution plans.

Chapter 2 covered relational operations and stated that we need physical operations, or algorithms, to execute queries. Mapping these algorithms to logical operations is not straightforward; sometimes, a complex logical operation is replaced with multiple physical operations, or several logical operations are merged into a single physical operation.

This chapter describes those algorithms, starting from algorithms for data retrieval and then proceeding to algorithms for more complex operations.

Understanding these algorithms will allow us to go back to execution plans and get a better grasp of their components. Thus, we will be only one step away from our goal: learning how to tune queries.

Algorithm Cost Models

Chapter 1 mentioned several ways of measuring the performance of a system, including response time, cost, and user satisfaction. These metrics are external to the database, and although external metrics are the most valuable, they aren't available to the query optimizer.

Instead, the optimizer uses internal metrics based on the amount of computing resources needed to execute a query or a single physical operation within a plan. The most important resources are those that affect execution time, namely, CPU cycles and I/O accesses (read/write disk blocks). Other resources, such as memory or disk space, have an indirect impact on execution time; for example, the amount of available memory will influence the ratio of CPU cycles and I/O accesses. The distribution of memory is almost always controlled by configuration parameters and will be covered in Chapter 10.

These two primary metrics, CPU cycles and number of I/O operations, are not directly comparable. However, in order to compare query execution plans, the optimizer has to combine them into a single cost function: the lower the cost, the better the plan. For several decades, the number of I/O operations was the dominating component of the cost because rotating hard drives are orders of magnitude slower than CPUs. This is not necessarily the case for modern hardware, so the optimizer must be tuned to use the correct ratio. This is also controlled via server parameters.

A cost model of a physical operation estimates the resources needed to execute the operation. In this book we outline simplified cost models that are easy to understand but are still useful in understanding how more sophisticated cost models work. Specifically, we'll estimate the amount of resources needed for an algorithm as the number of low-level operations to be performed for each row or each block of tables used as an input or produced as an output of an algorithm. For example, we count the number of block accesses but do not distinguish if the access actually requires an I/O operation. In our simplified models, an access to a block is an access, whether it requires I/O or the block is already on the buffer pool of the operating system.

Generally, the cost depends on the tables given as arguments to the operation. To represent cost models, we'll use simple formulas with the following notation: for any table or relation R, TR and BR denote the number of rows in the table and the number of storage blocks occupied by the table, respectively. Additional notation will be introduced as needed.

The following section discusses physical operations, outlining algorithms and cost models for each. As the relative speed of CPU and external storage may vary in a wide range, CPU costs and I/O costs are considered separately. Two logical operations discussed in the previous chapter, project and filter, are not included. These are typically combined with the operation that precedes them, because they can be applied independently to a single row, without depending on other rows in the argument table.

Of course, the project and filter are not free in terms of cost that is proportional to the number of processed rows. However, in most cases these costs are negligible, so we do not include these costs into cost models of other algorithms.

Data Access Algorithms

To begin executing a query, the database engine must extract stored data. This section concerns algorithms used to read data from database objects. In practice, these operations are often combined with their following operation in the query execution plan. This is advantageous in cases where it is possible to save execution time by avoiding reading that will be subsequently filtered out.

The efficiency of such operations depends on the ratio of rows that are retained to the total rows in the stored table. This ratio is called *selectivity*. The choice of algorithm for a given read operation depends on the selectivity of filters that can be simultaneously applied.

Storage Structures

It should come as no surprise that data is stored in files that reside on hard drives. Any file used for database objects is divided in blocks of the same length; by default, PostgreSQL uses blocks containing 8192 bytes each. A block is the unit that is transferred between the hard drive and the main memory, and the number of I/O operations needed to execute any data access is equal to the number of blocks that are being read or written.

Database objects consist of logical items (table rows, index records, etc.). PostgreSQL allocates space for these items in blocks. Several small items can reside in the same block; items that don't fit within a single block use a separate storage mechanism. The generic structure of a block is shown in Figure 3-1.

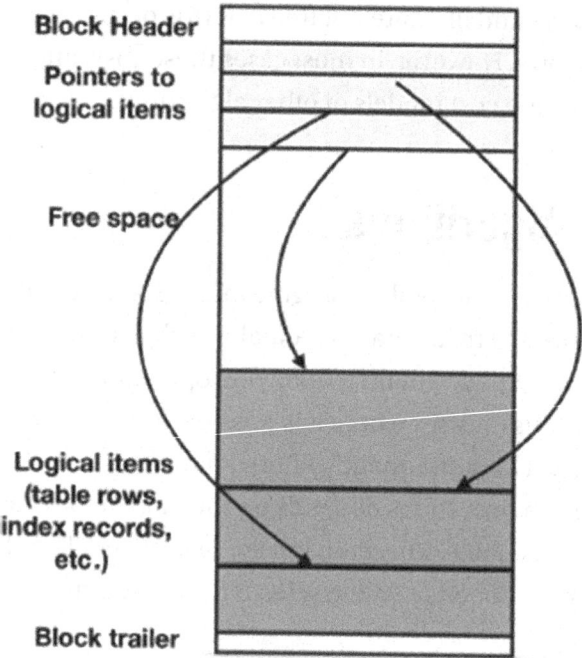

Figure 3-1. *The generic block structure in PostgreSQL*

The allocation of items to blocks also depends on the type of the database object. Table rows are stored using a data structure called a heap: a row can be inserted in any block that has sufficient free space, without any specific ordering. Other objects (e.g., indexes) may use blocks differently.

Full Scan

In a full scan, at times referred to as a sequential scan, the database engine consecutively reads all of the rows in a table and checks the filtering condition for each row. To estimate the cost of this algorithm, we need a more detailed description, as shown in the pseudocode in Listing 3-1.

Listing 3-1. Pseudocode for a full-scan data access algorithm

```
FOR each block IN a_table LOOP
      read block;
      FOR each row IN block LOOP
            IF filter_condition (row)
```

```
        THEN output (row)
        END IF;
    END LOOP;
END LOOP;
```

The number of I/O accesses is BR; the total number of iterations of the inner loop is TR. We also need to estimate the cost of operations producing the output. This cost depends on selectivity, denoted as S, and is equal to S * TR. Putting all these parts together, we can estimate the cost of a full scan as

$$c_1 * BR + c_2 * TR + c_3 * S* TR$$

where constants c_1, c_2, and c_3 represent properties of hardware.

A full scan can be used with any table; additional data structures are not needed. Other algorithms depend on the existence of indexes on the table, described in the following.

Index-Based Table Access

Note that until we got to physical operations, we did not even mention data access algorithms. We do not need to "read" relations—they are abstract objects. If we follow the idea that relations are mapped to tables, there is no other way to retrieve data than to read the whole table into the main memory. How else will we know which rows of data contain which values? But relational databases wouldn't be such a powerful tool for data processing if we stopped there. All relational databases, including PostgreSQL, allow for building additional, redundant data structures, making data access dramatically faster than a simple sequential read.

These additional structures are called indexes.

How indexes are built will be covered later in this chapter; for now, we need to understand two facts about indexes. First, they are "redundant" database objects; they do not store any additional information that can't be found in the source table itself.

Second, indexes provide additional data access paths; they allow us to determine what values are stored in the rows of a table without actually reading the table—this is how index-based access works. And, as mentioned previously, this happens entirely invisibly to the application.

If a filtering condition (or conditions) is encapsulated by an index on a table, the index can be used to access data from that table.

To get a table row from a pointer, the block containing this row must be read. The underlying data structure of a table is a *heap*, that is, rows are stored unordered. Their order is not guaranteed, nor does it correspond to properties of the data. Depending on the index selectivity, PostgreSQL utilizes one of two methods. The first is an index scan; the second depends on a bitmap index scan, followed by a bitmap heap scan.

An index entry includes addresses of the records that match the indexed value; this address contains the block address and the offset of the record within the block. In an index scan, the database engine reads each entry of the index that satisfies the filter condition and retrieves blocks in index order. Because the underlying table is a heap, multiple index entries might point to the same block. If an index has a low selectivity, these situations are rare, and there are high chances that no block will be read (or rather attempted to read) more than once. However, the situation is different when the selectivity is high or multiple indexes are used or the filtering condition differs from equal. In these cases, a bitmap index scan will be used. This method builds a heap bitmap in memory. The whole bitmap is a single bit array, with as many bits as there are heap blocks in the table being scanned.

Each index used to satisfy a selection criterion is used sequentially. To perform a bitmap index scan, first, a bitmap is created with all entries initially set to 0 (false). Whenever an index entry that matches the search condition is found, the bit corresponding to the heap block indicated by the index entry is set to 1 (true). The second and any additional bitmap index scans do the same thing with the indexes corresponding to the additional search conditions. Once all bitmaps have been created, the engine performs a bitwise logical AND operation to find which blocks contain requested values for all selection criteria, producing a final candidate list. This means that blocks that satisfy only one of the two criteria in a logical AND never have to be accessed. An illustration is shown in Figure 3-2.

Block#	1	2	3	4	5	6	7	8	9	10	11	12	13	14	15	16
Index 1	0	1	0	0	0	1	0	0	1	0	0	0	0	0	0	1
Index 2	0	0	1	0	0	1	0	0	0	1	0	0	1	0	0	1
Logical AND ⇓																
	0	0	0	0	0	1	0	0	0	0	0	0	0	0	0	1

Figure 3-2. *Using bitmaps for table access through multiple indexes*

After the final candidate list is computed, the candidate blocks are read sequentially using a `bitmap heap scan` (a heap scan based on a bitmap), and for each block, the individual records are examined to recheck the search conditions. Note that requested values may reside in different rows in the same block. The bitmap ensures that relevant rows will not be missed, but does not guarantee that all scanned blocks contain a relevant row. This explanation elides some implementation details for the sake of brevity and clarity. The actual implementation is more sophisticated and handles various edge cases.

The cost model of index-based access is much more complex than a full scan. Informally, it can be described this way: For small values of selectivity, rows satisfying the filtering conditions will most likely be located in different blocks and, consequently, the cost is proportional to the number of result rows. For larger values of selectivity, the number of processed blocks approaches the total number of blocks. In the latter case, the cost becomes higher than the cost of a full scan because resources are needed to access the index.

Index-Only Scan

Data access operations do not necessarily return entire rows. If some columns are not needed for the query, these columns can be skipped as soon as a row passes filtering conditions (if any). More formally, this means that the logical project operation is combined with data access. This combination is especially useful if an index used for filtering contains every column needed for the query.

In this algorithm, data is read from the index and any remaining filtering conditions are applied, if necessary. Usually there is no need to access table data, but sometimes additional checks are needed—this will be discussed in detail in Chapter 5.

The cost model for an index-only scan is similar to the model for index-based table access except that there's no need to actually access table data. For small values of selectivity, the cost is approximately proportional to the number of returned rows. For large values of selectivity, the algorithm performs an (almost) full scan of the index. The cost of an index scan is usually lower than the cost of a full table scan because it contains less data.

Comparing Data Access Algorithms

The choice of the best data access algorithm depends mostly on query selectivity. The relationship of cost to selectivity for different data access algorithms is shown in Figure 3-3. We intentionally omitted all numbers on this chart as they depend on hardware and table size, while the qualitative comparison does not.

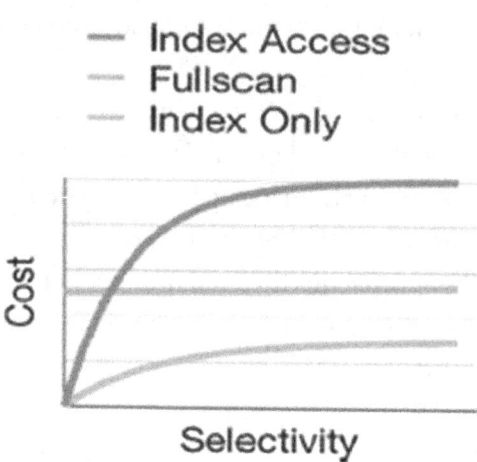

Figure 3-3. *Relationship of cost and query selectivity for different data access algorithms*

The cost function for a full scan is linear and is almost horizontal because the growth is due to generation of output. Typically, the cost of output generation is negligible in comparison with other costs for this algorithm.

The cost function of index-based table access starts from (almost) 0 and grows quickly with the growth of selectivity. The growth slows down for large values of selectivity, where the cost is significantly higher than the cost of a full scan.

The most interesting point is the intersection of the two functions: for smaller values of selectivity, index-based access is preferable, while a full scan is better for larger values of selectivity. The position of the intersection depends on hardware and may depend on the size of the table. For relatively slow rotating drives, index-based access is preferable only if selectivity does not exceed 2–5%. For SSDs or virtual environments, this value can be higher. On older spinning disk drives, random block access can be an order of magnitude slower than sequential access, so the additional overhead of indexes is higher for a given proportion of rows.

The line representing an index-only scan is the lowest, meaning that this algorithm is always preferable if it is applicable (i.e., all needed columns are in the index).

The query optimizer estimates both the selectivity of a query and the selectivity of the intersection point for this table and this index. The query shown in Listing 3-2 has a range filtering condition that selects a significant portion of the table.

Listing 3-2. A range filtering query executed with a full table scan

```
SELECT
    flight_no,
    departure_airport,
    arrival_airport
FROM flight
WHERE scheduled_departure BETWEEN
'2023-05-15'  AND  '2023-08-31';
```

In this case, the optimizer chooses a full scan.

However, a smaller range in the same query (see Listing 3-3) results in index-based table access.

Listing 3-3. Range filtering with index-based table access

```
SELECT
    flight_no,
    departure_airport,
    arrival_airport
FROM flight
WHERE scheduled_departure BETWEEN
'2023-08-12'  AND  '2023-08-13';
```

In reality, the job of a query optimizer is much more complex: filtering conditions can be supported with multiple indexes with different values of selectivity. Multiple indexes can be combined to produce a block bitmap with fewer number of blocks to be scanned. As a result, the number of choices available to the optimizer is significantly larger than three algorithms.

Thus, there are no winners and losers among data access algorithms. Any algorithm can be a winner under certain conditions. Further, the choice of algorithm depends on storage structures and statistical properties of the data. The database maintains metadata known as statistics for tables including metrics such as column cardinality, sparseness, etc. Usually these statistics are not known during application development and may change throughout the application lifecycle. Therefore, the declarative nature of the query language is essential for system performance. More specifically, as the table statistics change or if other costing factors are adjusted, a different execution plan can be chosen for the same query.

Index Structures

This section briefly explores the most common index structures, such as trees and hash indexes, and touches on some PostgreSQL specifics.

We show how to estimate the scale of improvement for different types of indexes and how to detect cases when index usage won't provide any performance benefits.

What Is an Index?

One might assume that any person who works with databases knows what an index is. Alas, a surprising number of people, including database developers and report writers and, in some cases, even DBAs, use indexes, even create indexes, with only a superficial understanding of what indexes are and how they are structured. To avoid misunderstanding, we'll begin with a definition of what we mean by an index.

There are many types of indexes, so it is foolhardy to search for structural properties to recognize an index. Instead, we define an index based on its usage. A data structure is called an index if it is

- A redundant data structure

- Invisible to the application

- Designed to speed up data selection based on certain criteria

---

The redundancy means that an index can be dropped without any data loss and can be reconstructed from data stored elsewhere (in the tables, of course). Invisibility means that an application cannot detect if an index is present or absent. That is, any query produces the same results with or without an index. And finally, an index is created with the hope (or confidence) that it improves performance of a specific query or (even better!) several queries.

The performance improvement does not come for free. As an index is redundant, it must be updated when table data are updated. That produces some overhead for update operations that is sometimes not negligible. In particular, PostgreSQL indexes may have an outsized impact on vacuum operations. However, many database textbooks overestimate this overhead. Modern high-performance DBMSs use algorithms that reduce the cost of index updates, so usually, it is beneficial to create several indexes on a table.

Although index structures can differ significantly among index types, the speed-up is achieved due to a fast check of some filtering conditions specified in a query. Such filtering conditions specify certain restrictions on table attributes.

Figure 3-4 shows how an index can speed up the access to the specific table rows.

The right part of Figure 3-4 shows a table, and the left represents an index that can be viewed as a special kind of a table. Each row of the index consists of an index key and a pointer to a table row. The value of an index key usually is equal to the value of a table attribute. The example in Figure 3-4 has airport code as its value; hence, this index supports search by airport code.

A column can have the same value in multiple rows of a table. If this column is indexed, the index must contain pointers to all rows containing this value of an index key. That is, a key may be logically associated with a list of pointers to rows rather than a single pointer.

In PostgreSQL, for some of the index types, an index contains multiple records, that is, the index key is repeated for every pointer to a table row.

Figure 3-4 explains how to reach the corresponding table row when an index record is located; however, it does not explain why an index row can be found much faster than a table row. Indeed, this depends on how the index is structured, and this is exactly what is discussed in the following subsections.

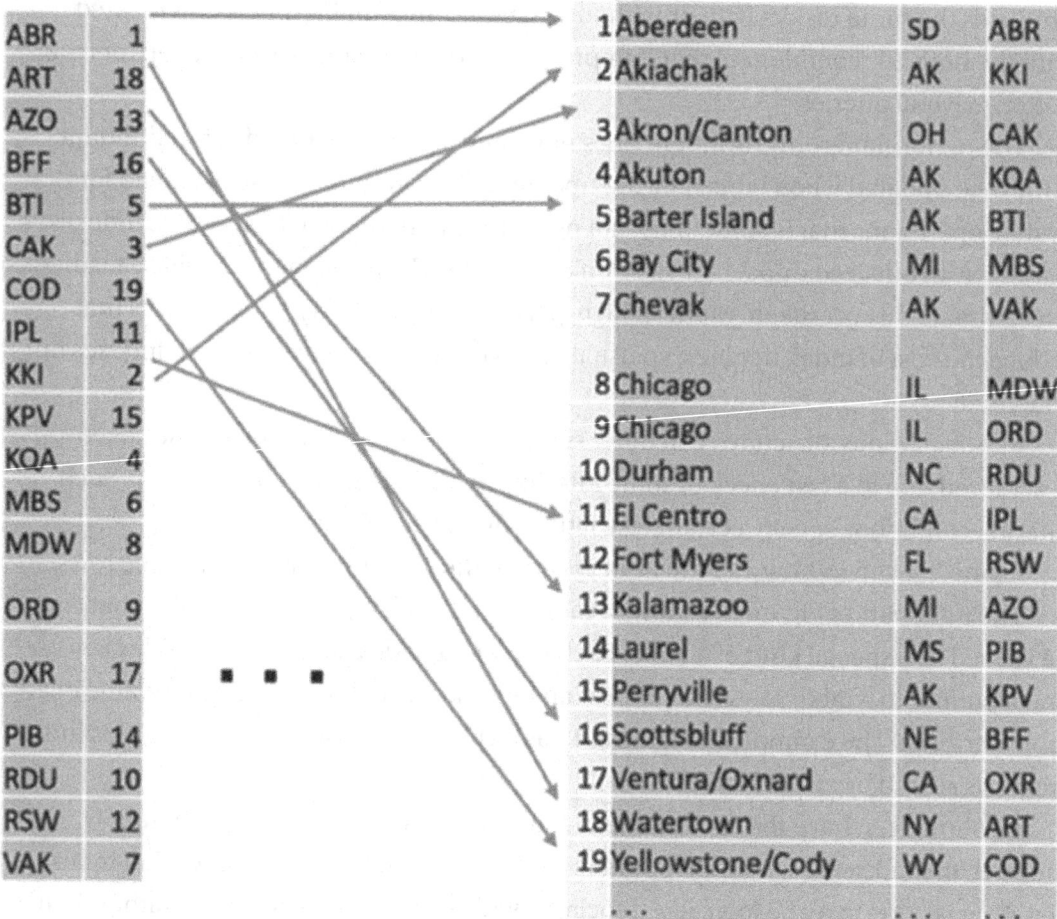

Figure 3-4. *Index access to table rows*

B-Tree Indexes

The most common structure of an index is a B-tree. The structure of a B-tree is shown in Figure 3-5; airport codes are the index keys. The tree consists of hierarchically organized nodes that are associated with blocks stored on a disk.

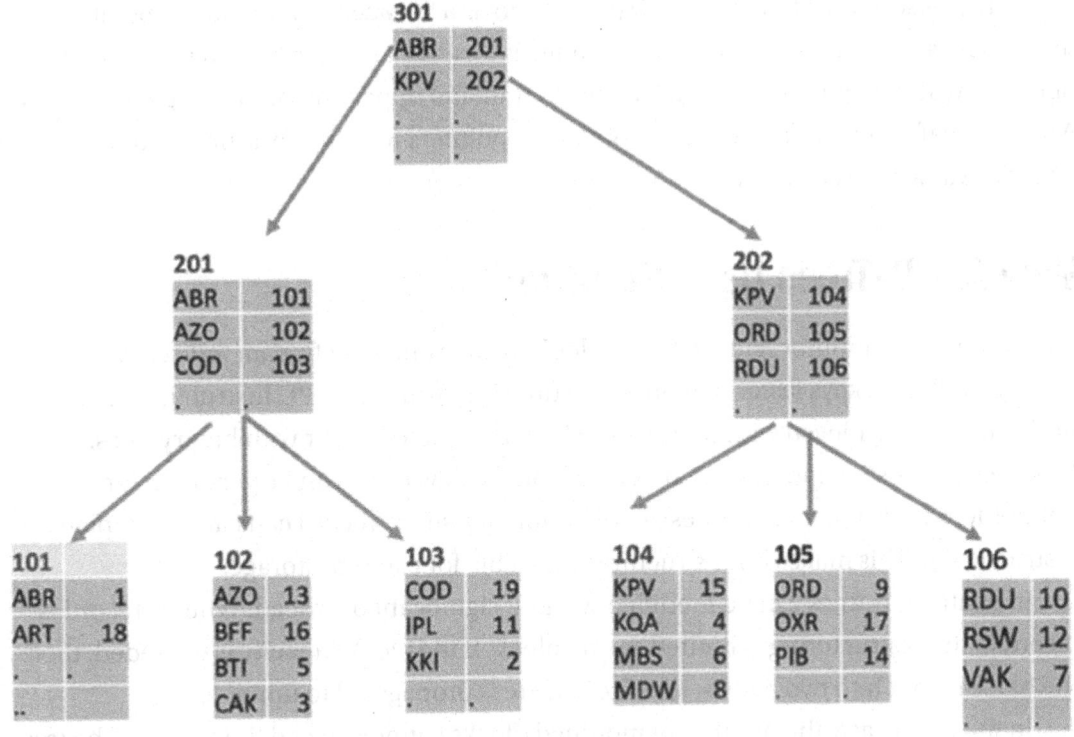

Figure 3-5. *An example of a B-tree*

The leaf nodes (shown in the bottom row in Figure 3-5) contain index records exactly like those in Figure 3-4; these records contain an index key and a pointer to a table row. Non-leaf nodes (located at all levels except the bottom) contain records that consist of the smallest key (in Figure 3-5, the lowest alphanumeric value) in a block located at the next level and a pointer to this block. All records in all blocks are ordered, and at least half of the block capacity is used in every block.

Any search for a key K starts from the root node of the B-tree. During the block lookup, the largest key P not exceeding K is found, and then the search continues in the block pointed to by the pointer associated with P until the leaf node is reached, where a pointer refers to table rows. The number of accessed nodes is equal to the depth of the tree. Of course, the key K is not necessarily stored in the index, but the search finds either the key or the position where it could be located.

B-trees also support range search (expressed as a between or inequality operations in SQL). As soon as the lower end of the range is located, all index keys in the range are obtained with a sequential scan of leaf nodes until the upper end of the range is reached. A scan of leaf nodes is also needed to obtain all pointers if the index is not unique (i.e., an index value may correspond to more than one row).

Why Are B-Trees Used So Often?

We know from computer science that no lookup algorithm can find an index key among N different keys faster than in $\log N$ time (measured in CPU instructions). This performance is achieved with binary search on an ordered list or with binary trees. However, the cost of updates (such as insertions of new keys) can be very high for both ordered lists and binary trees: an insertion of a single record can cause complete restructuring. This makes both structures unusable for external storage.

In contrast, B-trees can be modified without significant overhead. When a record is inserted, the restructuring is limited to one block. If the block capacity is exceeded, then the block is split into two blocks, and the update is propagated to upper levels.

In the worst case, the number of modified blocks cannot exceed the depth of the tree.

To estimate the cost of a B-tree search, we need to calculate the depth. If each block contains f pointers, then the number of blocks at each level is f times larger than in the previous one. Consequently, the depth of a tree containing N records is $\log N / \log f$. This formula gives the number of block accesses needed for a single key search. The number of CPU instructions is limited for each block, and usually binary search is used inside a block.

Consequently, the CPU cost is only slightly worse than the best that is theoretically possible. Block size in PostgreSQL is 8 Kb. An 8 Kb block can fit dozens of index records; consequently, an index with six to seven levels can accommodate billions of index records.

The depth of the tree is critical for performance of the index. After a split of an overfull block, each of new blocks is at least half-filled. As a result, the depth of the tree does not grow significantly, and the index remains efficient. Theoretically, blocks that are not sufficiently filled should be merged. However, none of actual implementations (including PostgreSQL) do the merge. Consequently, a large number of deletions may result in too large depth and degrade the performance. To avoid the degradation, the index should be rebuilt.

In PostgreSQL, a B-tree index can be created for any ordinal data type; that is, for any two distinct values of the data type, one value is less than the other. This includes user-defined types.

Other Kinds of Indexes

PostgreSQL offers a variety of index structures supporting several data types and several classes of search conditions.

A *hash index* uses a hash function to calculate the address of an index block containing an index key. This type of index has better performance than a B-tree index for equality conditions. However, this index is completely useless for range queries. The cost estimation for hash index search does not depend on index size (in contrast with logarithmic dependency for B-trees).

An *R-tree index* supports a search on spatial data. An index key for an R-tree always represents a rectangle in a multidimensional space. A search returns all objects having a non-empty intersection with the query rectangle. The structure of an R-tree is similar to the structure of a B-tree; however, splitting overflowed nodes is much more complicated. R-tree indexes are efficient for a small number of dimensions (typically, two to three).

Other types of indexes available in PostgreSQL are useful for full text search, search in very large tables, and much more. Additional details on these topics are covered in Chapter 14. Any of these indexes can be relatively easily configured for user-defined data types. However, we do not discuss indexes on user-defined types in this book.

Combining Relations

The real power of relational theory and SQL databases relies on combining data from several tables.

In this section, we describe algorithms for operations that combine data, including a Cartesian product, joins, union, intersection, and even grouping. Surprisingly, most of these operations can be implemented with almost identical algorithms. For this reason, we discuss algorithms rather than the operations they implement. We will use the names R and S for input tables when describing these algorithms.

Nested Loops

The first algorithm is for a Cartesian product, that is, the set of all pairs of rows from the input tables. The easy way to calculate the product is to loop over table R and, for each row of R, loop over S. The pseudocode for this simple algorithm is presented in Listing 3-4, and the graphical representation of the algorithm is shown in Figure 3-6.

Listing 3-4. Pseudocode for nested loops

```
FOR row1 IN table1 LOOP
      FOR row2 IN table2 LOOP
          INSERT output row
      END LOOP
END LOOP
```

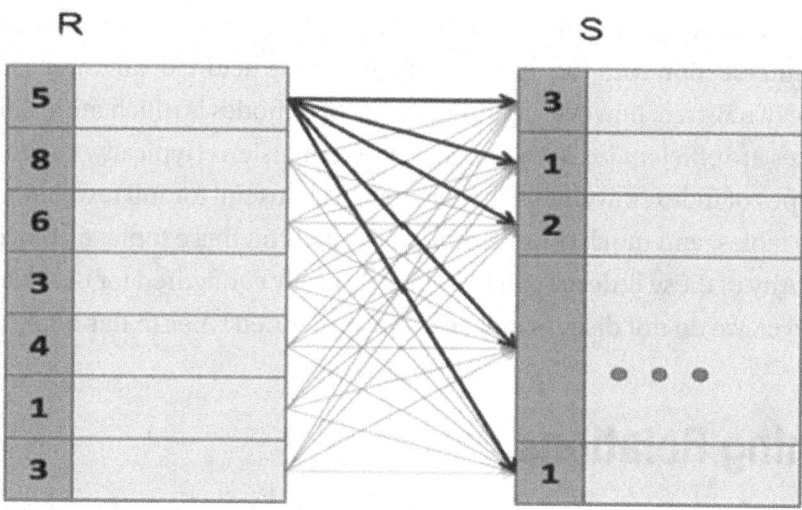

Figure 3-6. *Nested loop algorithm*

The time needed for this simple algorithm is proportional to the product of the sizes of the input tables: rows(R) * rows(S).

A remarkable theoretical fact states that any algorithm that calculates a Cartesian product cannot perform better; that is, any algorithm's cost will be proportional to the product of the sizes of its inputs or higher. Of course, some variations of this algorithm may perform better than others, but the cost remains proportional to the product.

Slight modifications of the nested loop algorithm can calculate nearly any logical operation that combines data from two tables. The pseudocode in Listing 3-5 implements the join operation.

Listing 3-5. Nested loop algorithm for a join operation

```
FOR row1 IN table1 LOOP
    FOR row2 IN table2 LOOP
  IF match(row1,row2) THEN
      INSERT output row
      END IF
  END LOOP
END LOOP
```

Observe that a nested loop join is a straightforward implementation of the abstract definition of a join, as a Cartesian product followed by a filter. As the nested loop join processes all pairs of rows from the input, the cost remains the same, although the size of the output is smaller than in the case of a Cartesian product.

In practice, one or both input tables are stored tables, rather than the result of preceding operations. If this is the case, a join algorithm can be combined with data access.

Although the processing cost remains the same, variations of the nested loop algorithm combined with a full scan execute nested loops on blocks of input tables and another level of nested loops on rows contained in these blocks. More sophisticated algorithms minimize the number of disk accesses by loading multiple blocks of the first table (outer loop) and processing all rows of these blocks with a single pass over S.

These algorithms can work with any join conditions. However, the majority of joins we will ever need to execute are equi-joins, that is, the join condition requires that some attributes of R are equal to the corresponding attributes of S.

The nested loop join algorithm can also be combined with index-based data access if the table S has an index on attributes used in the join condition. For equi-joins, the inner loop of the index-based nested loop algorithm shrinks to few rows of S for each row of R. The inner loop can even vanish completely if the index on S is unique, for example, the join attribute of S is its primary key.

The index-based nested loop algorithm is usually the best choice if the number of rows in R is also small. However, index-based access becomes inefficient if the number of rows to be processed becomes high, as discussed in Chapter 2.

It is possible to formally prove that there does not exist an algorithm more performant for Cartesian products and joins with arbitrary conditions than nested loops. However, the important question is whether there exists a better algorithm for any specific types of join conditions. The next section shows this is true for equi-joins.

Hash-Based Algorithms

The output of an equi-join consists of pairs of rows from R and S that have equal values on the join attributes. The idea of the hash join algorithm is simple: if the values are equal, then the hash values are also equal.

The algorithm partitions both input tables according to values of the hash function and then joins rows in each bucket independently. The schema of this algorithm is shown in Figure 3-7.

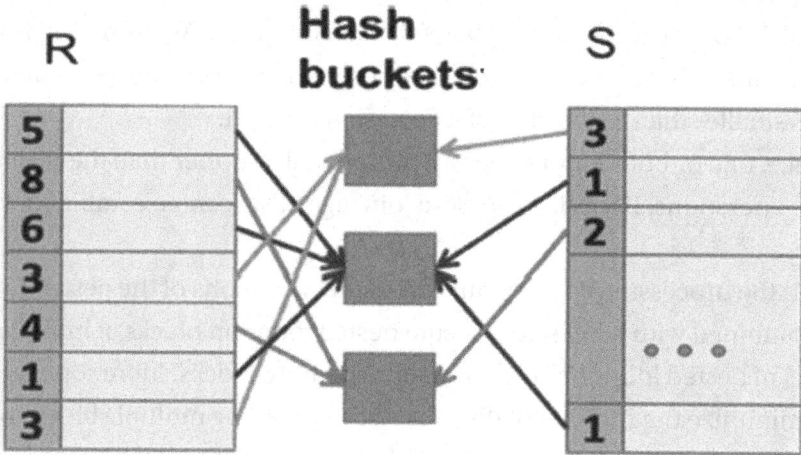

Figure 3-7. *Hash join algorithm*

The basic version of the hash join algorithm includes two phases:

1. During the *build* phase, all tuples of R are stored in buckets according to the values of the hash function.

2. In the *probe* phase, each row of table S is sent to an appropriate bucket. If matching rows of table R are in the bucket, output rows are produced.

The easiest way to find matching rows in the bucket is to use nested loops (actually loop over all rows in the bucket for each row of S).

The two phases of the hash-based algorithm are shown as separate physical operations in the execution plan.

The cost of a hash join can be approximately estimated with the following formula, where JA is the join attribute:

```
cost(hash,R,S)=size(R)+size(S)+size(R)*size(S)/size(JA)
```

The first and second terms in this formula approximate the cost of a single pass over all the rows of R and S. The last term represents the size of the join result to be produced. Of course, the cost of output is the same for all join algorithms, but we did not need to include it in the nested loop algorithm cost estimation because it is smaller than the cost of nested loops.

This formula shows that a hash-based algorithm is significantly better than nested loops for large tables and a large number of different values of the join attribute. For example, if the join attribute is unique in one of the input tables, then the last term will be equal to just the size of the other table.

The basic hash join algorithm works if all buckets produced at the build phase can fit into main memory. Another variation, called hybrid hash join, joins tables that cannot fit into main memory. The hybrid hash join partitions both tables so that partitions of one table can fit and then executes a basic algorithm for each pair of corresponding partitions. The cost of a hybrid hash join is higher because partitions are stored temporarily on the hard disk and both tables are scanned twice. However, the cost is still proportional to the sum of the sizes, rather than the product.

Sort-Merge Algorithm

Another algorithm (called sort-merge) for equi-joins is schematically shown in Figure 3-8.

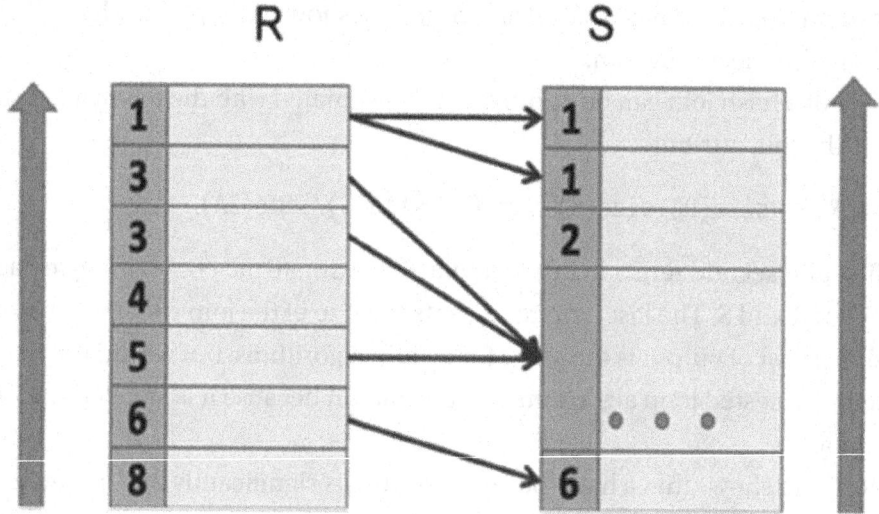

Figure 3-8. *Sort-merge algorithm*

The first phase of the algorithm sorts both input tables in ascending order by the join attribute.

When the input tables are properly ordered, the merge phase scans both input tables once and, for each value of the join attribute, calculates the Cartesian product of rows containing this value of the join attribute. Note that this product is a necessary part of the join result. New rows with the same value attribute cannot appear in the remaining part of input because the input tables are ordered.

The cost of the merge phase can be expressed with the same formula as for a hash join, that is, proportional to the sum of sizes of input and output. The actual cost is somewhat lower because there is no need for the build phase.

The cost of sorting can be estimated with the following formula:

```
Size(R)*log(size(R)) + size(s)*log(size(S))
```

The sort-merge algorithm is especially efficient if one of both input tables is already sorted. This may happen in a series of joins with the same join attribute.

Comparing Algorithms

Just as with data access algorithms, there are no default winners or losers. Any of the algorithms can be the best, depending on the circumstances. The nested loop algorithm is more universal and is the best for small index-based joins; a sort-merge and hash are more efficient for large tables, when applicable.

Summary

Having covered cost models for algorithms, data access algorithms, the purpose and structure of indexes, and algorithms for more complex operations, such as joins, we finally have enough building blocks to move on to the full product of the query planner—an execution plan.

The next chapter covers how to read and understand execution plans and improve them.

CHAPTER 4

Understanding Execution Plans

At long last, it's time to look at execution plans. Before we begin, let's review our theoretical foundations. Chapter 3 explained how logical operations are mapped to their physical execution, covering data retrieval and more complex operations.

In this chapter, understanding these algorithms will enable us to interpret execution plans and get a better grasp of their components.

Putting Everything Together: How an Optimizer Builds an Execution Plan

The output of the PostgreSQL optimizer is an *execution plan*. While a SELECT defines *what* needs to be done, an execution plan defines *how* to execute SQL operations.

The job of the optimizer is to build the best possible physical plan that implements a given logical plan. This is a complex process: sometimes, a complex logical operation is replaced with multiple physical operations, or several logical operations are merged into a single physical operation.

To build a plan, the optimizer uses *transformation rules*, *heuristics*, and cost-based *optimization algorithms*. A *rule* converts a plan into another plan with better cost. For example, filter and project operations reduce the size of the dataset and therefore should be executed as early as possible; a rule might reorder operations so that filter and project operations are executed sooner. An *optimization algorithm* chooses the plan with the lowest cost estimate. However, the number of possible plans (called the *plan space*) for a query containing several operations is huge—far too large for the algorithm to

© Henrietta Dombrovskaya, Boris Novikov, Anna Bailliekova 2024
H. Dombrovskaya et al., *PostgreSQL Query Optimization*, https://doi.org/10.1007/979-8-8688-0069-6_4

consider every single possible plan. After all, time spent choosing the correct algorithm contributes to the total execution time of the query. *Heuristics* are used to reduce the number of plans evaluated by the optimizer.

Reading Execution Plans

To paraphrase Elvis, a little less abstraction, a little more action, please. Let's take a look at an example. The query in Listing 4-1 selects all flights that departed from JFK and arrived at ORD with a scheduled departure between August 10 and August 23, 2023. For each flight, the total number of passengers is calculated.

Listing 4-1. A query selecting the number of passengers on specific flights

```
SELECT f.flight_no,
       f.actual_departure,
       count(passenger_id) passengers
FROM flight f
JOIN booking_leg bl ON bl.flight_id = f.flight_id
JOIN passenger p ON p.booking_id=bl.booking_id
WHERE f.departure_airport = 'JFK'
    AND f.arrival_airport = 'ORD'
    AND f.actual_departure BETWEEN
        '2023-08-10' and '2023-08-13'
GROUP BY f.flight_id, f.actual_departure;
```

A logical plan for this query is shown in Listing 4-2.

Listing 4-2. The logical plan for the query in Listing 4-1

```
project f.flight_no,  f.actual_departure, count(p.passenger_id)[] (
   group [f.flight_no, f.actual_departure] (
      filter [f.departure_airport = 'JFK'] (
         filter [f.arrival_airport = 'ORD'] (
            filter [f.actual_departure >='2023-08-10'](
               filter [f.actual_departure <='2023-08-13' ] (
                  join [bl.flight_id = f.flight_id] (
                     access (flights f),
```

```
join(bl.booking_id=p.booking_id (
access (booking_leg bl),
access (passenger p)
))))))))
```

The logical plan shows which logical operations should be executed, but it does not provide details on how they will be executed. The query planner produces an execution plan for the query, shown in Figure 4-1.

	QUERY PLAN text
1	GroupAggregate (cost=762880.24..762887.73 rows=4 width=24)
2	Group Key: f.flight_id
3	-> Sort (cost=762880.24..762882.72 rows=994 width=20)
4	Sort Key: f.flight_id
5	-> Hash Join (cost=366850.85..762830.75 rows=994 width=20)
6	Hash Cond: (p.booking_id = bl.booking_id)
7	-> Seq Scan on passenger p (cost=0.00..334798.06 rows=16312506 width=8)
8	-> Hash (cost=366849.54..366849.54 rows=105 width=20)
9	-> Hash Join (cost=9371.98..366849.54 rows=105 width=20)
10	Hash Cond: (bl.flight_id = f.flight_id)
11	-> Seq Scan on booking_leg bl (cost=0.00..310506.66 rows=17893566 width=8)
12	-> Hash (cost=9371.93..9371.93 rows=4 width=16)
13	-> Bitmap Heap Scan on flight f (cost=123.95..9371.93 rows=4 width=16)
14	Recheck Cond: (departure_airport = 'JFK'::bpchar)
15	Filter: ((actual_departure >= '2023-08-10 00:00:00-05'::timestamp with time zone) AND (actual_departure <= '2023-08-13 00:00:00-05'::timestamp with
16	-> Bitmap Index Scan on flight_departure_airport (cost=0.00..123.94 rows=11136 width=0)
17	Index Cond: (departure_airport = 'JFK'::bpchar)

Figure 4-1. *Execution plan*

To obtain the execution plan for a query, the EXPLAIN command is run. This command takes any grammatically correct SQL statement as a parameter and returns its execution plan.

We encourage you to run the code examples throughout this book and examine the execution plans. However, a word of caution: Choosing the correct execution plan is a nondeterministic process. The plans that your local database produces might differ slightly from the plans shown in this book. Even when the plans are identical, execution times may vary with differences in hardware and configuration.

Hopefully, looking at Figure 4-1, the value of the preceding chapters is evident—each line represents an operation previously covered, so it's clear what's going on under the hood. Note that, in addition to the names of the algorithms, each line of the execution plan includes several mysterious numbers in parentheses. This mystery can be easily resolved by recalling Chapter 3, which discussed how the costs of different algorithms are calculated.

Specifically, a plan contains the expected number of output rows and the expected average width of output row, which are calculated from database statistics, and estimates of costs, which are calculated based on the previously obtained estimates and configuration parameters. The values of costs include the accumulated cost of all pervious operations. There are two cost estimations for each operation: the first shows the cost needed to produce the first row of output, while the second estimates the cost of the complete result. For example, in Figure 4-1, line 13, 123.95 is the cost of the first row of output and 9371.93 the cost of the complete result. Estimates for the number and width of output rows are needed to estimate the cost of an operation that consumes the output. How costs are estimated will be covered later in this chapter.

It is important to emphasize that all these numbers are approximate. The actual values obtained during execution may differ. If you suspect that the optimizer chose a plan that is not optimal, you might need to look at these estimates. Usually, the error is small for stored tables, but it inevitably accumulates after each operation.

An execution plan is presented as a tree of physical operations. In this tree, nodes represent operations, and arrows point to operands. The tree structure might not be apparent from looking at Figure 4-1. There are multiple tools, including pgAdmin, which can generate a graphical representation of execution plans. Figure 4-2 illustrates what an output might look like. (Different graphic tools may use different iconography; this example is presented for illustrative purposes only.) In fact, this figure represents the execution plan for Listing 4-4, which we discuss later in this chapter.

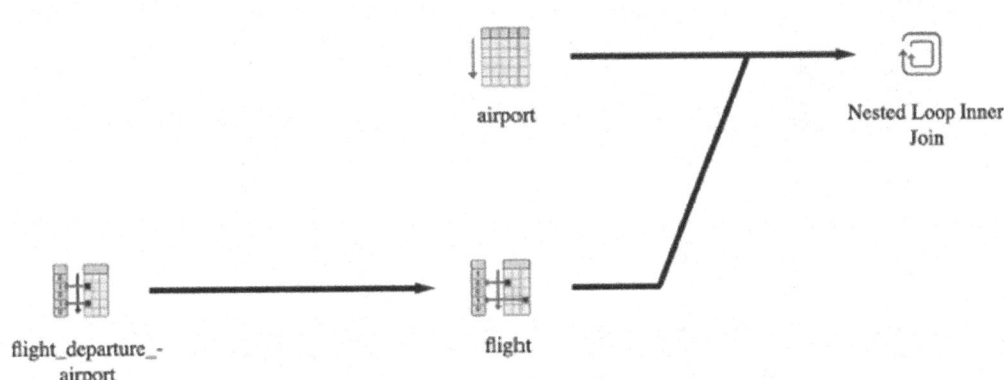

Figure 4-2. *Graphical representation of a simple execution plan (Listing 4-4)*

For more complex queries, the graphical representation of the execution plan may be less helpful—see the graphical representation of the execution plan for Listing 4-1 in Figure 4-3.

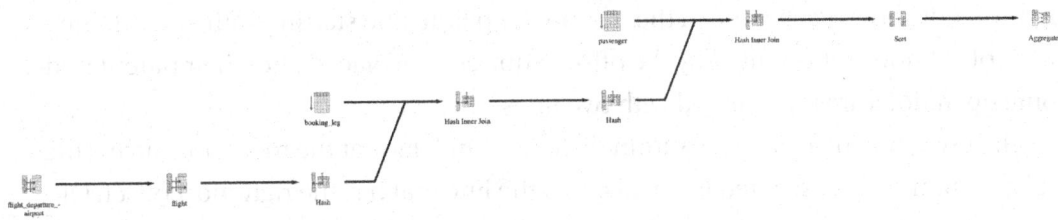

Figure 4-3. *Graphical representation of the execution plan for Listing 4-1*

In such cases, a more compact representation could be more useful, like the one presented in Figure 4-4.

	Node
1.	→ Aggregate
2.	→ Sort
3.	→ Hash Inner Join Hash Cond: (p.booking_id = bl.booking_id)
4.	→ Seq Scan on passenger as p
5.	→ Hash
6.	→ Hash Inner Join Hash Cond: (bl.flight_id = f.flight_id)
7.	→ Seq Scan on booking_leg as bl
8.	→ Hash
9.	→ Bitmap Heap Scan on flight as f Filter: ((actual_departure >= '2023-08-10 00:00:00-05'::timestamp with time zone) AND (actual_departure <= '202: Recheck Cond: (departure_airport = 'JFK'::bpchar)
10.	→ Bitmap Index Scan using flight_departure_airport Index Cond: (departure_airport = 'JFK'::bpchar)

Figure 4-4. *Alternative representation of the same execution plan*

Now, let's get back to the actual output of the EXPLAIN command, shown in Figure 4-1. It shows each node of the tree on a separate line starting with ->, with the depth of the node represented by the offset. Subtrees are placed after their parent node. Some operations are represented with two lines.

The execution of a plan starts from the leaves and ends at the root. This means that the operation that is executed first will be on the line that has the rightmost offset. Of course, a plan may contain several leaf nodes that are executed independently. As soon as an operation produces an output row, this row is pushed up to the next operation. Thus, there is no need to store intermediate results between operations.

In Figure 4-1, execution starts from the last line, accessing the table flight using the index on the departure_airport column. Since several filters are applied to the table and only one of the filtering conditions is supported by the index, PostgreSQL performs a bitmap index scan (covered in Chapter 2). The engine accesses the index and compiles the list of blocks that could contain needed records. Then, it reads the actual blocks from the database using bitmap heap scan, and for each record extracted from the database, it rechecks that rows found via the index are current and applies filter operations for additional conditions for which we do not have indexes: arrival_airport and scheduled_departure.

The result is joined with the table booking_leg. PostgreSQL uses a sequential read to access this table and a hash join algorithm on the condition bl.flight_id = f.flight_id.

Then, the table passenger is accessed via a sequential scan (since it doesn't have any indexes), and once again, the hash join algorithm is used on the p.booking_id = bl.booking_id condition.

The last operation to be executed is grouping and calculating the aggregate function sum(). Sorting determines the flights that satisfy the search criteria. Then, the count of all passengers on each of the flights is performed.

The next section addresses what else can be gleaned from the execution plan and why it is important.

Understanding Execution Plans

Understanding small execution plans is easy. Recall that in Chapter 3 we compared two SELECT statements, Listings 3-2 and 3-3. We stated that for the first one, PostgreSQL would choose a sequential scan, while for the second one it would choose index access. How did we know that? Now, you know the answer: we ran the EXPLAIN command for both statements. The execution plan for Listing 3-2 is presented in Figure 4-5 and the execution plan for Listing 3-3 in Figure 4-6.

	QUERY PLAN text
1	Seq Scan on flight (cost=0.00..18814.67 rows=353801 width=12)
2	Filter: ((scheduled_departure >= '2023-05-15 00:00:00-05'::timestamp with time zone) AND (scheduled_departure <= '2023-08-31 00:00:00-05

Figure 4-5. *Execution plan for Listing 3-3*

	QUERY PLAN text
1	Bitmap Heap Scan on flight (cost=51.87..6611.44 rows=3458 width=12)
2	Recheck Cond: ((scheduled_departure >= '2023-08-12 00:00:00-05'::timestamp with time zone) AND (scheduled_departure <= '2023-08-13 00:(
3	-> Bitmap Index Scan on flight_scheduled_departure (cost=0.00..51.00 rows=3458 width=0)
4	Index Cond: ((scheduled_departure >= '2023-08-12 00:00:00-05'::timestamp with time zone) AND (scheduled_departure <= '2023-08-13 00:

Figure 4-6. *Execution plan for Listing 3-4*

But what is an execution plan is more complex?

Often, when we explain how to read execution plans in the manner described in the preceding text, our audience feels overwhelmed by the size of the execution plan for a relatively simple query, especially given that a more complex query can produce an execution plan of 100+ lines. Even the plan presented in Figure 4-1 might require some time to read. Sometimes, even when each and every single line of a plan can be interpreted, the question remains: "I have a query, and it is slow, and you tell me to look at the execution plan, and it is 100+ lines long. What should I do? Where should I start?"

The good news is that most of the time, you do not need to read the whole plan to understand what exactly makes the execution slow. In this section, we will learn more about interpreting execution plans.

What Is Going On During Optimization?

As mentioned in Chapter 2, the optimizer performs two kinds of transformations: it replaces logical operations with corresponding physical execution algorithms and (possibly) changes the logical expression structure by changing the order in which logical operations are executed.

After the query is parsed and checked for syntactic correctness, the first step is query rewriting. In this step, the PostgreSQL optimizer enhances the code by eliminating subqueries, substituting views with their textual presentation, and so on. It is essential to keep in mind that this step always happens. When the concept of a view is introduced, SQL textbooks often suggest that "views can be used like tables," which is misleading. In most cases, views are substituted by their source code. However, "most of the time" does not mean "always." Chapter 7 discusses views, how the optimizer processes them, and their potential performance pitfalls.

The next step after query rewrite is what we usually call optimization, which includes the following:

- Determining the possible orders of operations

- Determining the possible execution algorithms for each operation

- Comparing the costs of different plans

- Selecting the optimal execution plan

Many SQL developers presume that PostgreSQL executes queries accessing (and joining) tables in the same order they appear in the FROM clause.

However, the order of joins is *not* preserved most of the time—the database does not expect these instructions. In subsequent chapters, we will discuss in more detail what influences the order of operations. For now, let's consider how to evaluate an execution plan.

Why Are There So Many Execution Plans to Choose From?

We've noted several times that one SQL statement can be executed in many ways, using different execution plans. In fact, there could be hundreds, thousands, or even millions of possible ways to execute one statement! This chapter gives some sense of where these numbers are coming from. Plans may vary in

- Order of operations

- Algorithms used for joins and other operations (e.g., nested loops, hash join)

- Data retrieval methods (e.g., index usage, full scan)

Formally speaking, the optimizer finds the best plan by computing the costs for all possible plans and then comparing the costs. But since we know that there are three basic algorithms to execute each join, even a simple SELECT on three tables can generate nine possible execution plans; given the 12 possible join orders, there are 108 possible plans (3 * 3 * 12 = 108). If we then consider all the potential data retrieval methods for each table, there are several thousand plans to compare.

Fortunately, PostgreSQL does not check every possible plan.

The cost-based optimization algorithm relies on the optimality principle: a sub-plan of an optimal plan is optimal for the corresponding subquery. A plan can be considered a composition of multiple component pieces, or sub-plans. A sub-plan is a plan that includes any operations of the original plan as a root node and all its descendant nodes, that is, all operations that contribute to the input arguments for the operation chosen as a root of the sub-plan. The optimizer builds the optimal plan starting from the smallest sub-plans (i.e., data access to single tables) and gradually produces more complex sub-plans, including more operations with only a few checks of cost on each step. The algorithm is exhaustive in the sense that the optimal plan will be built, despite the fact that a significant portion of possible plans will not be tried.

For example, in the preceding example, once the optimizer selects the correct data retrieval algorithm for one of the three tables, it will not consider any plans that do not use this optimal algorithm.

Still, the number of produced sub-plans can be huge. The `geqo_threshold` configuration parameter specifies the maximum number of joins in a query for which the near-exhaustive search of the best join sequence is performed. If the number of tables exceeds the maximum, the joins order is determined by heuristics. Heuristics cut out parts of the plan space that are unlikely to contain optimal plans, reducing the number of plans examined by the optimization algorithm. While this feature helps the optimizer select an execution plan more quickly, it can also affect performance negatively: there is a risk that the best execution plan will be accidentally dropped before the cost comparison.

Although heuristics may cut out the optimal plan, the algorithm builds the best of the remaining plans.

Now, let's take a closer look at how these costs are calculated.

How Are Execution Costs Calculated?

In Chapter 3, we discussed ways to measure the performance of database algorithms. We talked about internal metrics and established that the costs of algorithms are measured in the number of I/O operations and CPU cycles. Now, we are going to apply this theory to practice.

The cost of each execution plan depends on

- Cost formulas of algorithms used in the plan

- Statistical data on tables and indexes, including distribution of values

- System settings (parameters and preferences), such as `join_collapse_limit` or `cpu_index_tuple_cost`

Chapter 3 covered the formulas to calculate cost for each algorithm. Each of these formulas depends on the size of the table(s) used, as well as on the expected size of the result set. And finally, users can alter the default cost for operations with system settings. The choice of an optimal plan can be implicitly controlled by changes in the optimizer parameters that are used during the cost estimation. Thus, all three pieces of information factor into the calculation of the cost of execution plans.

This is counterintuitive; often, SQL developers have the subconscious expectation that the "best possible plan" exists and, moreover, that it is the same for all "similar" queries. However, due to the factors listed in the preceding list, the optimizer may produce different execution plans for nearly identical SQL queries or even for the same query. How can this happen? The optimizer chooses the plan with the best cost estimation. However, there may be several plans with only slightly different costs. The cost estimation depends on the database statistics that are gathered from random samples. The statistics gathered yesterday may slightly differ from those gathered today. Due to these slight changes, a plan that was the best yesterday can become second best today. Of course, statistics may also change as a result of insertions, updates, and deletions.

Let's look at some examples. Listings 4-3 and 4-4 present two queries, which appear almost identical. The only difference is in the filtering value. However, the execution plans presented in Figures 4-7 and 4-8 are markedly different.

Listing 4-3. Simple SELECT with one condition

```
SELECT flight_id,
            scheduled_departure
FROM flight f
JOIN airport a ON departure_airport=airport_code
            AND iso_country='US'
```

	QUERY PLAN 🔒
	text
1	Hash Join (cost=20.09..25467.60 rows=144636 width=12)
2	Hash Cond: (f.departure_airport = a.airport_code)
3	-> Seq Scan on flight f (cost=0.00..23642.76 rows=683176 width=16)
4	-> Hash (cost=18.33..18.33 rows=141 width=4)
5	-> Seq Scan on airport a (cost=0.00..18.33 rows=141 width=4)
6	Filter: (iso_country = 'US'::text)

Figure 4-7. *Execution plan for Listing 4-3*

Listing 4-4. The same SELECT as Listing 4-3, with a different search value

```
SELECT flight_id,
              scheduled_departure
FROM flight f
JOIN airport a ON departure_airport=airport_code
                        AND iso_country='CZ'
```

	QUERY PLAN text	
1	Nested Loop (cost=40.40..3347.29 rows=1026 width=12)	
2	-> Seq Scan on airport a (cost=0.00..18.33 rows=1 width=4)	
3	Filter: (iso_country = 'CZ'::text)	
4	-> Bitmap Heap Scan on flight f (cost=40.40..3318.67 rows=1029 width=16)	
5	Recheck Cond: (departure_airport = a.airport_code)	
6	-> Bitmap Index Scan on flight_departure_airport (cost=0.00..40.14 rows=1029 width=0)	
7	Index Cond: (departure_airport = a.airport_code)	

Figure 4-8. *Execution plan for Listing 4-4*

What causes this difference? Figure 4-9 gives a clue: The first query selects a significant portion of all airports, and using an index won't improve performance. The second query, by contrast, will select only one airport, and in this case index-based access will be more efficient.

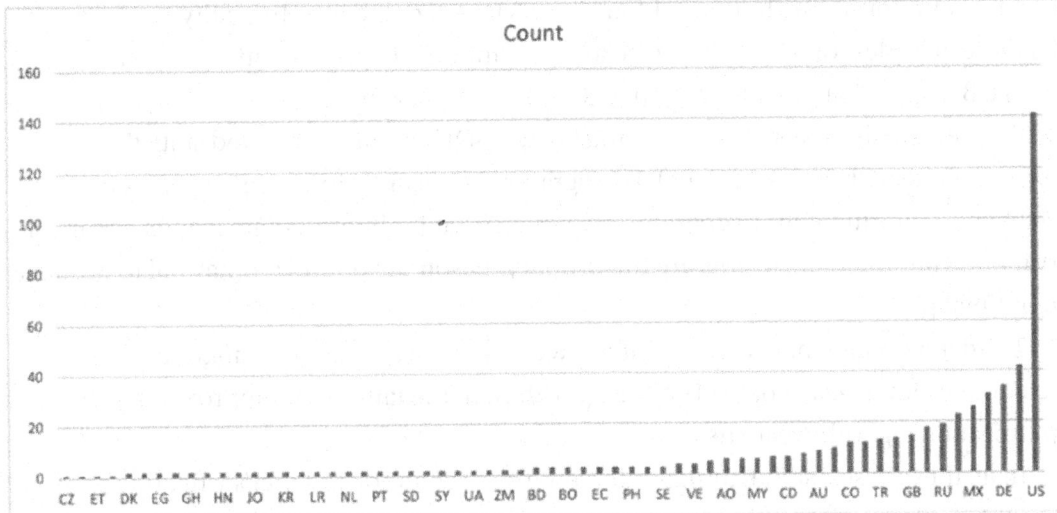

Figure 4-9. *A histogram of value distribution*

This example also explains why keeping the database statistics up to date is so important. If the query planner won't be aware of such uneven distribution, it might choose an execution plan that would be far from optimal. The ANALYZE command recalculates statistics for a table that is passed as a parameter and updates statistics on the table's indexes. PostgreSQL has a special mechanism to update statistics automatically, and we will discuss it in more detail in Chapter 8. However, if you are following the examples from this book and replay them on your local copy, you should manually run ANALYZE after building new indexes.

How Can the Optimizer Be Led Astray?

But how can we be sure that the plan the optimizer has selected is indeed the best possible plan? Is it even possible to find the best execution plan? We spent quite a bit of time explaining that the optimizer does the best possible job if we leave it alone and don't interfere. If that's true, what is the rest of the book about? The reality is that no optimizer is perfect, even the PostgreSQL query planner.

First, while the optimization algorithm is mathematically correct—it finds the plan with the best cost estimation—those cost estimates are intrinsically imprecise. The simple formulas explained in Chapter 3 are valid only for a uniform distribution of data, but a uniform distribution seldom occurs in real databases. In reality, optimizers use more complex formulas, but these are also imperfect approximations of reality. As George Box said, "All models are wrong, but some are useful."

Second, database systems, including PostgreSQL, maintain detailed statistics of stored data (usually in histograms). Histograms significantly improve estimates of selectivity. Unfortunately, histograms cannot be used for intermediate results. Errors in estimating intermediate results are the primary reason the optimizer may fail to produce an optimal plan.

Third, an optimal plan may be cut out with heuristics, or a query might be too complex for an exact optimization algorithm. In the latter case, approximate optimization algorithms are used.

In all these cases, some human intervention is required, and that's what this book is about! Now that we know what's going on during optimization, we can fix it if something doesn't work quite right.

In spite of these potential hiccups, optimizers work well in the majority of cases. However, humans observe the behavior of the system and therefore have more information available than the optimizer and can use this additional knowledge to help the optimizer do its job even better.

Summary

This chapter covered execution plans: how they are generated and how to read and understand them. We also learned about cost-based optimization and factors that impact the cost of execution plans.

Although cost-based optimizers usually do a good job, sometimes they need help, and now we are well equipped to provide it. Subsequent chapters will go over multiple examples of queries that require some human intervention to achieve better performance.

CHAPTER 5

Short Queries and Indexes

Chapter 4 took a deep dive into understanding execution plans. Now, we turn to what to do once the EXPLAIN command has been run and an execution plan is returned. Where do we start if our goal is to improve the query execution plan?

The first step is to identify whether the query is a short query or a long query. This chapter focuses on optimizing short queries. You will learn how to identify short queries, what optimization technique to use with short queries, and why indexes are critically important for this query type. We also discuss different types of indexes available in PostgreSQL and when each index type can be used.

Before proceeding with this chapter, let's create several additional indexes:

```
SET search_path TO postgres_air;
CREATE INDEX flight_arrival_airport ON flight  (arrival_airport);
CREATE INDEX booking_leg_flight_id ON booking_leg  (flight_id);
CREATE INDEX flight_actual_departure ON flight  (actual_departure);
CREATE INDEX boarding_pass_booking_leg_id ON boarding_pass  (booking_
leg_id);
CREATE INDEX booking_update_ts ON booking  (update_ts);
```

Don't forget to run ANALYZE on all the tables for which you build new indexes:

```
ANALYZE  flight ;
ANALYZE  booking_leg;
ANALYZE  booking;
ANALYZE boarding_pass;
```

© Henrietta Dombrovskaya, Boris Novikov, Anna Bailliekova 2024
H. Dombrovskaya et al., *PostgreSQL Query Optimization*, https://doi.org/10.1007/979-8-8688-0069-6_5

What Makes a Query "Short"?

The term *short query* has come up multiple times, without a formal definition. What is a short query? First, it has nothing to do with the length of the SQL query. Take a look at the two queries shown in Listings 5-1 and 5-2, for example. The query in Listing 5-1 contains only four lines of code, but it represents a *long query*. Listing 5-2 contains many more lines but is a short query.

Listing 5-1. Long query example

```
SELECT
      d.airport_code AS departure_airport,
      a.airport_code AS arrival_airport
FROM  airport a,
      airport d
```

Listing 5-2. Short query example

```
SELECT
      f.flight_no,
      f.scheduled_departure,
       boarding_time,
       p.last_name,
       p.first_name,
       bp.update_ts as pass_issued,
       ff.level
  FROM flight f
   JOIN booking_leg bl ON bl.flight_id = f.flight_id
   JOIN passenger p ON p.booking_id=bl.booking_id
   JOIN account a on a.account_id =p.account_id
   JOIN boarding_pass bp on bp.passenger_id=p.passenger_id
   LEFT OUTER JOIN frequent_flyer ff on ff.frequent_flyer_id=a.frequent_
   flyer_id
   WHERE f.departure_airport = 'JFK'
                AND f.arrival_airport = 'ORD'
```

```
                AND f.scheduled_departure BETWEEN
                    '2023-08-05' AND '2023-08-07'
```

Second, it is not defined by the size of the result set. The query in Listing 5-3 yields only one line; however, it is a long query.

Listing 5-3. Long query that produces one row

```
SELECT
    avg(flight_length),
    avg (passengers)
FROM (SELECT
                flight_no,
                scheduled_arrival -scheduled_departure AS flight_length,
                count(passenger_id) passengers
        FROM flight f
        JOIN booking_leg bl ON bl.flight_id = f.flight_id
        JOIN passenger p ON p.booking_id=bl.booking_id
        GROUP BY 1,2) a
```

So what is a short query?

A query is short when the number of rows needed to compute its output is small, no matter how large the involved tables are. Short queries may read every row from small tables but read only a small percentage of rows from large tables.

The most important part of the preceding definition is the difference between *needs* and *accesses*. A poor execution plan for a short query may read and/or process many more rows than needed for final output. Although a certain amount of redundant processing is unavoidable, our goal is to reduce it.

How small is a "small percentage"? Unsurprisingly, it depends on system parameters, application specifics, actual table sizes, and possibly other factors. Most of the time, however, it means less than 10%. Later in this chapter, a case study will show how to identify this border line.

By contrast, the output of a long query depends on a significant fraction of rows in a large table or several large tables.

Our taxonomy of queries is similar to the commonly accepted distinction between OLTP and OLAP queries. All OLTP queries are short. However, many modern applications require queries that return hundreds of rows but still are short.

Why is Listing 5-1 a long query? Because all the rows from the airport table are required to obtain the result. Why is Listing 5-2 a short query? Because data from just a couple of flights is needed, out of about 200,000. Why isn't Listing 5-3 short? Because data from every booking in the system is required to calculate the results.

When we optimize a short query, we know that in the end, we select a relatively small number of records. This means that the optimization goal is to reduce the size of the result set as early as possible. If the most restrictive selection criterion is applied in the first steps of query execution, further sorting, grouping, and even joins will be less expensive. Looking at the execution plan, there should be no table scans of large tables. For small tables, a full scan may still work, as shown in Figure 3-2 in Chapter 3.

Choosing Selection Criteria

It might seem easy to make sure that the most restrictive selection criteria are applied first; however, this isn't always straightforward. To acknowledge the obvious, this chapter is called "Short Queries and Indexes" for a reason: you can't select a subset of records quickly from a table if there is no index supporting the corresponding search. That's why short queries require indexes for faster execution. If there is no index to support a highly restrictive query, in all likelihood, one needs to be created.

Index Selectivity

Chapter 3 introduced the concept of *query selectivity*. The same concept can be applied to indexes: the smaller the number of records that correspond to one value of the index, the lower the index's selectivity value. We do not want to create indexes with high selectivity; as we saw in Chapter 3, index-based data retrieval in this case will take *more* time than a sequential scan. Since the PostgreSQL optimizer predetermines the cost of each access method, this index would never be used, so performance wouldn't be compromised. However, it is still undesirable to add a database object that requires storage space and extra time to update, but doesn't provide any benefit.

A database table might have multiple indexes on different columns, each with different selectivity. The best performance possible for a short query occurs when the most restrictive indexes (i.e., indexes with the lowest selectivity) are used.

Let's look at the query in Listing 5-4. Can you tell which filtering criterion is the most restrictive?

Listing 5-4. Index selectivity

```
SELECT *
FROM flight
WHERE departure_airport='LAX'
                AND update_ts BETWEEN '2023-08-13' AND '2023-08-15'
                AND status='Delayed'
                AND scheduled_departure BETWEEN '2023-08-13' AND
                '2023-08-15'
```

Delayed status might be the most restrictive, because ideally, on any given day, there are many more on-time flights than delayed flights.

In our training database, we have a flight schedule for six months, so limiting it by two days might not be very restrictive. On the other hand, usually the flight schedule is posted well in advance, and if we are looking for flights where the timestamp of the last update is relatively close to the scheduled departure, it most likely indicates that these flights were delayed or canceled.

Another factor that may be taken into consideration is the popularity of the airport in question. LAX is a popular airport, and for Listing 5-4, a restriction on update_ts will be more restrictive than on departure_airport. However, if we change the filtering on departure_airport to FUK, the airport criterion will be more restrictive than selection based on update_ts.

If all the search criteria are indexed, there is no cause for concern; the way multiple indexes can work together will be covered in a moment. But if the most restrictive criterion is not indexed, the execution plan may be suboptimal, and likely, an additional index is needed.

Unique Indexes and Constraints

The better (lower) the selectivity of an index, the faster the search. Thus, the most efficient indexes are unique indexes.

An index is *unique* if for each indexed value there is exactly one matching row in the table.

There are several different ways to create a unique index. First, PostgreSQL automatically creates a unique index to support any primary key or unique constraint on a table.

What is the difference between a primary key and a unique constraint? A common misconception among SQL developers is that a primary key has to be an incrementing numeric value and that each table "has" to have a primary key. Although it often helps to have a numeric incremental primary key (called a *surrogate key*), a primary key does not have to be numeric, and moreover, it does not have to be a single-attribute constraint. It is possible to define a primary key as a combination of several attributes; it just has to satisfy two conditions: the combination must be UNIQUE and NOT NULL for all of the participating attributes. In contrast, unique constraints in PostgreSQL allow for NULL values.

A table can have a single primary key (though a primary key is not required) and multiple unique constraints. Any non-null unique constraint can be chosen to be a primary key for a table; thus, there is no programmatic way to determine the best candidate for a table's primary key. For example, the table booking has a primary key on booking_id and a unique key on booking_ref—see Listing 5-5.

Listing 5-5. A primary key and a unique constraint

```
ALTER TABLE booking
    ADD CONSTRAINT booking_pkey PRIMARY KEY (booking_id);
ALTER TABLE booking
    ADD CONSTRAINT booking_booking_ref_key UNIQUE (booking_ref);
```

Since booking_ref is a non-null attribute, we could choose either booking_id or booking_ref to be the primary key.

As shown in the ER diagram in Chapter 1, the column frequent_flyer_id in the table account is nullable and also unique:

```
ALTER TABLE account
    ADD CONSTRAINT account_freq_flyer_unq_key UNIQUE (frequent_flyer_id);
```

It is also possible to create a unique index without formally defining a unique constraint. All you have to do is to add the keyword unique to the index creation statement:

```
CREATE UNIQUE INDEX account_freq_flyer ON
account (frequent_flyer_id);
```

If we create this index after data was already inserted into this table, CREATE UNIQUE INDEX will validate the uniqueness of values, and if any duplicates are found, the index won't be created. For any subsequent inserts and updates, the uniqueness of new values will be validated as well.

What about foreign keys? Do they automatically create any indexes? A common misconception is the belief that the presence of a foreign key necessarily implies the presence of an index on the child table. This is not true.

A *foreign key* is a referential integrity constraint; it guarantees that for each non-null value in the child table (i.e., the table with the foreign key constraint), there is a matching unique value in the parent table (i.e., the table it is referencing).

For example, there is a foreign key constraint on the flight table that ensures that each arrival airport matches an existing airport code:

```
ALTER TABLE flight
    ADD CONSTRAINT arrival_airport_fk FOREIGN KEY (arrival_airport)
    REFERENCES airport (airport_code);
```

This constraint does not automatically create an index; if searches by arrival airport are slow, the index must be explicitly created:

```
CREATE INDEX flight_arrival_airport
    ON flight (arrival_airport);
```

Chapter 3 mentioned that unique indexes make nested loops efficient. If you refer to Figure 3-7, you will realize what happens when an index is present.

The nested loop join algorithm can also be combined with index-based data access if the table S has an index on attributes used in the join condition. For natural joins, the inner loop of the index-based nested loop algorithm shrinks to few rows of S for each row of R. The inner loop can even vanish completely if the index on S is unique, for example, the join attribute of S is its primary key.

Often, this is misunderstood to mean that nested loops are always efficient when joining on a primary/foreign key. However, as mentioned earlier, this is true only if the column in the child table—that is, the foreign key—is indexed.

Is it a best practice to always create an index on a column that has a foreign key constraint? Not always. An index should only be created if the number of distinct values is large enough. Remember, indexes with high selectivity are unlikely to be useful. For example, the `flight` table has a foreign key constraint on `aircraft_code`:

```
ALTER TABLE flight
    ADD CONSTRAINT aircraft_code_fk FOREIGN KEY (aircraft_code)
    REFERENCES aircraft (code);
```

This foreign key constraint is necessary because for each flight, there must be a valid aircraft assigned. In order to support the foreign key constraint, a primary key constraint was added to the `aircraft` table. That table, however, has only 12 rows. Therefore, it is not necessary to create an index on the `aircraft_code` column of the `flight` table. This column has only 12 distinct values, so an index on that column will not be used.

To illustrate this statement, let's look at the query in Listing 5-6. This query selects all fights departing from JFK airport between August 14 and 16, 2023. For each flight, we select the flight number, scheduled departure, aircraft model, and number of passengers.

Listing 5-6. A join by a primary/foreign key without an index

```
SELECT
    f.flight_no,
    f.scheduled_departure,
    model,
    count(passenger_id) passengers
FROM flight f
JOIN booking_leg bl ON bl.flight_id = f.flight_id
```

```
JOIN passenger p ON p.booking_id=bl.booking_id
JOIN aircraft ac ON ac.code=f.aircraft_code
WHERE f.departure_airport ='JFK'
      AND f.scheduled_departure BETWEEN
          '2023-08-14' AND '2023-08-16'
GROUP BY 1,2,3
```

The execution plan for this query is shown in Figure 5-1, and it is massive.

	QUERY PLAN text
1	GroupAggregate (cost=398695.75..398727.72 rows=1260 width=52)
2	Group Key: f.flight_no, f.scheduled_departure, ac.model
3	-> Sort (cost=398695.75..398699.62 rows=1550 width=48)
4	Sort Key: f.flight_no, f.scheduled_departure, ac.model
5	-> Hash Join (cost=2615.33..398613.61 rows=1550 width=48)
6	Hash Cond: (p.booking_id = bl.booking_id)
7	-> Seq Scan on passenger p (cost=0.00..334807.39 rows=16313439 width=8)
8	-> Hash (cost=2613.26..2613.26 rows=165 width=48)
9	-> Nested Loop (cost=222.22..2613.26 rows=165 width=48)
10	-> Hash Join (cost=221.78..609.05 rows=6 width=48)
11	Hash Cond: ((f.aircraft_code)::text = ac.code)
12	-> Bitmap Heap Scan on flight f (cost=220.51..607.47 rows=105 width=20)
13	Recheck Cond: ((scheduled_departure >= '2023-08-13 00:00:00-05'::timestamp with time zone) AND (scheduled_departure <= '2023-08-15 0(
14	-> BitmapAnd (cost=220.51..220.51 rows=105 width=0)
15	-> Bitmap Index Scan on flight_scheduled_departure (cost=0.00..100.88 rows=6845 width=0)
16	Index Cond: ((scheduled_departure >= '2023-08-13 00:00:00-05'::timestamp with time zone) AND (scheduled_departure <= '2023-08-1
17	-> Bitmap Index Scan on flight_departure_airport (cost=0.00..119.33 rows=10521 width=0)
18	Index Cond: (departure_airport = 'JFK'::bpchar)
19	-> Hash (cost=1.12..1.12 rows=12 width=64)
20	-> Seq Scan on aircraft ac (cost=0.00..1.12 rows=12 width=64)
21	-> Index Scan using booking_leg_flight_id on booking_leg bl (cost=0.44..333.19 rows=85 width=8)
22	Index Cond: (flight_id = f.flight_id)

Figure 5-1. *A plan with a sequential scan of a small table*

The only part of this plan we are interested in now is this:

```
Hash  (cost=1.12..1.12 rows=12 width=64)
    -> Seq Scan on aircraft ac (cost=0.00..1.12 rows=12
```

The PostgreSQL optimizer accesses table statistics and is able to detect that the size of the aircraft table is small and index access won't be efficient. In contrast, as we observed earlier in this chapter, the index on the departure_airport field of the flight table proved to be useful due to its low selectivity.

Indexes and Non-equal Conditions

Chapter 3 described the structure of B-tree indexes, how they are built, and how they are used for searches. What follows is a demonstration of their practical application.

The previous section relates to simple B-tree indexes. As noted in Chapter 3, they can support searches by equality, greater than, less than, and between conditions: all the searches that require comparison and ordering. The majority of searches in an OLTP system fall into this category, but there are also a nontrivial number of cases when search criteria are more complex.

Indexes and Column Transformations

What is a column transformation? A column transformation occurs when the search criteria are on some modifications of the values in a column. For example, `lower(last_name)` (converting the last_name value to lowercase) and `update_ts::date` (casting timestamp with time zone to date) are column transformations.

How do column transformations affect index use? Quite simply, B-tree indexes on the attribute cannot be used. Recall from Chapter 3 how a B-tree is built and how a search on a B-tree is performed: in each node, the value of the attribute is compared to the value in the node. The transformed value is not recorded anywhere, so there is nothing to compare it to. Thus, if there is an index on last name

```
CREATE INDEX account_last_name
  ON account (last_name);
```

...the following search won't be able to take advantage of the index:

```
SELECT *
FROM account
WHERE lower(last_name)='daniels';
```

How do we solve this problem? A search like this might be needed because passengers may enter their last names with different cases. If you believe that covering the most common cases is sufficient, you could modify the search criterion like so:

```
SELECT *
FROM account
WHERE last_name='daniels'
```

```
    OR last_name='Daniels'
    OR last_name ='DANIELS'
```

The execution plan for this query is shown in Figure 5-2.

	QUERY PLAN text	
1	Bitmap Heap Scan on account (cost=14.45..506.31 rows=143 width=53)	
2	Recheck Cond: ((last_name = 'daniels'::text) OR (last_name = 'Daniels'::text) OR (last_name = 'DANIELS'::text))	
3	-> BitmapOr (cost=14.45..14.45 rows=143 width=0)	
4	-> Bitmap Index Scan on account_last_name (cost=0.00..4.78 rows=48 width=0)	
5	Index Cond: (last_name = 'daniels'::text)	
6	-> Bitmap Index Scan on account_last_name (cost=0.00..4.78 rows=48 width=0)	
7	Index Cond: (last_name = 'Daniels'::text)	
8	-> Bitmap Index Scan on account_last_name (cost=0.00..4.78 rows=48 width=0)	
9	Index Cond: (last_name = 'DANIELS'::text)	

Figure 5-2. *An execution plan with "like" operator rewrite*

A better solution would be to create an (additional) *functional* index:

```
CREATE INDEX account_last_name_lower
  ON account (lower(last_name));
```

When a functional index is built, PostgreSQL applies the function to the values of the column (or columns) and then places these values in the B-tree. Similar to a regular B-tree index, where the nodes contain the values of the column, in a functional index, a node contains the value of the function. In our case, the function is lower(). After the index is created, query #1 in Listing 5-7 won't use a sequential scan but will be able to utilize the new index. The corresponding execution plan is shown in Figure 5-3.

Listing 5-7. Different search conditions use different indexes

```
---#1
SELECT * FROM account WHERE lower(last_name)='daniels';
---#2
SELECT * FROM account WHERE last_name='Daniels';
---#3
SELECT * FROM account WHERE last_name='daniels';
---#4
SELECT * FROM account WHERE lower(last_name)='Daniels';
```

Note that an index on the `last_name` column is still necessary if we want a search on a case-specific value to be supported by an index (e.g., query #2). Also, it's worth mentioning that if the table account contains one record with last_name ='Daniels' and another record with last_name='DANIELS', query #1 will return both, query #2 will return only the first record, and queries #3 and #4 won't return either of them.

	QUERY PLAN
	text
1	Bitmap Heap Scan on account (cost=5.25..382.20 rows=107 width=53)
2	Recheck Cond: (lower(last_name) = 'daniels'::text)
3	-> Bitmap Index Scan on account_last_name_lower_pattern (cost=0.00..5.22 rows=107 width=0)
4	Index Cond: (lower(last_name) = 'daniels'::text)

Figure 5-3. *A plan that uses a functional index*

Note   Sometimes, an additional index is not needed.

Should a functional index be created every time we need to search using a column transformation? Not necessarily. However, it is important to recognize a column transformation, which can be subtle.

For example, let's look at the following SELECT statement:

```
SELECT *
FROM flight
WHERE scheduled_departure ::date
BETWEEN '2023-08-17' AND '2023-08-18'
```

At first glance, it appears we are using the column `scheduled_departure` as a selection criterion, and since there is an index on this column, it should be used. However, the plan in Figure 5-4 diverts to a sequential scan.

	QUERY PLAN
	text
1	Seq Scan on flight (cost=0.00..22230.56 rows=3416 width=71)
2	Filter: (((scheduled_departure)::date >= '2023-08-17'::date) AND ((scheduled_departure)::date <= '2023-08-18'::date))

Figure 5-4. *A plan that does not use the index due to the column transformation*

Why doesn't PostgreSQL use the index? Because when the timestamp is converted to a date, a column transformation has been performed.

So is an additional functional index on `scheduled_departure::date` needed? Not necessarily. What does this selection criterion mean? It means that we want to select flights that depart on these two specific dates, no matter the time of day. This means that the flight could depart any time between midnight of August 17, 2023, and midnight of August 19, 2023. In order to make the existing index work, the selection criteria can be modified to

```
SELECT *
FROM flight
WHERE scheduled_departure >='2023-08-17'
      AND  scheduled_departure <'2023-08-19'
```

Figure 5-5 shows how the execution plan has changed.

	QUERY PLAN text
1	Bitmap Heap Scan on flight (cost=121.38..9057.81 rows=8288 width=71)
2	Recheck Cond: ((scheduled_departure >= '2023-08-17 00:00:00-05'::timestamp with time zone) AND (scheduled_departure < '2023-08-19 00:00:00-05'::timesta
3	-> Bitmap Index Scan on flight_scheduled_departure (cost=0.00..119.30 rows=8288 width=0)
4	Index Cond: ((scheduled_departure >= '2023-08-17 00:00:00-05'::timestamp with time zone) AND (scheduled_departure < '2023-08-19 00:00:00-05'::timesta

Figure 5-5. *An execution plan that uses the index*

Looking at the execution plan, you can see that the cost estimate for a plan with index-based access is more than twice less than a sequential scan (13857.42 vs. 30474). What is more important, the execution time supports this observation: 0.5 seconds for index-based access vs. 1.5 seconds for a sequential scan.

Pay very close attention to this example. When you read about this example in a book, the preceding paragraph looks obvious. However, numerous SQL developers and report writers use similar search conditions over and over again. One frequent use case is changes made to a table today. Ninety-five percent of the time, this condition is written as `update_ts::date=CURRENT_DATE`, which successfully blocks the use of an index on the `update_ts` column. To take advantage of the index, this criterion should be written as

```
update_ts>= CURRENT_DATE
```

or, if it is possible for values of this timestamp to be in the future, the condition should be written as

```
WHERE update_ts>= CURRENT_DATE AND update_ts< CURRENT_DATE +1
```

Let's examine another example where column transformation often remains unnoticed. Let's say today is August 17, 2023. We are looking for flights that have departed or are scheduled to depart today. We know that for flights that have not yet departed, the `actual_departure` column may be null.

The `coalesce()` function in PostgreSQL allows us to use a different value when the first argument is null. Thus, `coalesce(actual_departure, scheduled_departure)` will return `actual_departure` if it is not null and `scheduled_departure` otherwise. Both the `scheduled_departure` and `actual_departure` columns are indexed, and you might expect these indexes to be used. For example, look at the execution plan for the following SQL statement shown in Figure 5-6:

```
SELECT *
FROM flight
WHERE coalesce(actual_departure, scheduled_departure)
      BETWEEN '2023-08-17' AND '2023-08-18'
```

| | QUERY PLAN |
	text
1	Seq Scan on flight (cost=0.00..18814.67 rows=3416 width=71)
2	Filter: ((COALESCE(actual_departure, scheduled_departure) >= '2023-08-17 00:00:00-05'::timestamp with time zone) AND (COALESCE(actual_departure

Figure 5-6. *A plan with a sequential scan, when indexes are present*

Why aren't any indexes utilized? Because `coalesce()` is a function, which modifies column values. Should we create another functional index? We can, but it is not really necessary. Instead, we can rewrite this SQL statement as shown in Listing 5-8, which will result in the execution plan in Figure 5-7.

Listing 5-8. Query that uses both indexes

```
SELECT * FROM flight
WHERE (actual_departure
    BETWEEN '2023-08-17' AND '2023-08-18')
    OR (actual_departure IS NULL
        AND scheduled_departure BETWEEN '2023-08-17' AND '2023-08-18')
```

	QUERY PLAN text
1	Bitmap Heap Scan on flight (cost=67.75..7271.32 rows=2395 width=71)
2	Recheck Cond: (((actual_departure >= '2023-08-17 00:00:00-05'::timestamp with time zone) AND (actual_departure <= '2023-08-18 00:00:00-05'::timestamp with time
3	Filter: (((actual_departure >= '2023-08-17 00:00:00-05'::timestamp with time zone) AND (actual_departure <= '2023-08-18 00:00:00-05'::timestamp with time zone)) OI
4	-> BitmapOr (cost=67.75..67.75 rows=4169 width=0)
5	-> Bitmap Index Scan on flight_actual_departure (cost=0.00..4.43 rows=1 width=0)
6	Index Cond: ((actual_departure >= '2023-08-17 00:00:00-05'::timestamp with time zone) AND (actual_departure <= '2023-08-18 00:00:00-05'::timestamp with tii
7	-> Bitmap Index Scan on flight_scheduled_departure (cost=0.00..62.11 rows=4169 width=0)
8	Index Cond: ((scheduled_departure >= '2023-08-17 00:00:00-05'::timestamp with time zone) AND (scheduled_departure <= '2023-08-18 00:00:00-05'::timestam

Figure 5-7. *Execution plan for the query from Listing 5-8*

Indexes and the *like* Operator

Another group of search conditions that are not a straightforward comparison of column value constants are searches using the like operator. For example, the query

```
SELECT * FROM account
    WHERE lower(last_name) like 'johns%';
```

will yield all accounts for which the last name begins with "johns." In the postgres_air schema, the list of returned last names is

```
"Johnson"
"Johns"
"johns"
"Johnston"
"JOHNSTON"
"JOHNS"
"JOHNSON"
"johnston"
"johnson"
```

The only problem with this query is that it won't utilize the functional index we created in the previous section, because B-tree indexes do not support searches with the "like" operator. Once again, if we check the execution plan for this query, we will see a sequential scan of the account table.

How can we solve this problem and avoid a scan?

75

One possible solution is to rewrite the query, replacing `like` with two conditions:

```
SELECT * FROM account
  WHERE (lower(last_name) >='johns' and lower(last_name) < 'johnt')
```

The execution plan for this query is shown in Figure 5-8, and we can see that this plan uses an existing index.

	QUERY PLAN
◢	text
1	Bitmap Heap Scan on account (cost=83.20..3905.42 rows=2222 width=53)
2	Recheck Cond: ((lower(last_name) >= 'johns'::text) AND (lower(last_name) < 'johnt'::text))
3	-> Bitmap Index Scan on account_last_name_lower (cost=0.00..82.64 rows=2222 width=0)
4	index Cond: ((lower(last_name) >= 'johns'::text) AND (lower(last_name) < 'johnt'::text))

Figure 5-8. *The plan for a rewritten query that uses an index*

A better solution would be to create a *pattern search* index:

```
CREATE INDEX account_last_name_lower_pattern
  ON account (lower(last_name) text_pattern_ops);
```

Why is this index necessary? Because comparison of text values depends on the *locale*, a set of rules about character ordering, formatting, and similar things that vary by language and country. Although some may think what we have in US English is the universal order of things, it is not. The only locale that would allow us to use a B-tree index is a "C" locale, which is a standards-compliant default locale. Only strict ASCII characters are valid in this locale.

To see which locale was defined when the database was created, you need to run the command

```
SHOW LC_COLLATE;
```

And if you reside in the United States, there's a good chance you will see

```
"en_US.UTF-8"
```

This newly created index will be utilized by queries that use the `like` operator. The new execution plan for our original query is shown in Figure 5-9, and we can see that it takes advantage of the new index.

	QUERY PLAN
	text
1	Bitmap Heap Scan on account (cost=83.61..3894.73 rows=3889 width=53)
2	Filter: (lower(last_name) ~~ 'johns%'::text)
3	-> Bitmap Index Scan on account_last_name_lower_pattern (cost=0.00..82.64 rows=2222 width=0)
4	Index Cond: ((lower(last_name) ~>=~ 'johns'::text) AND (lower(last_name) ~<~ 'johnt'::text))

Figure 5-9. *An execution plan with a pattern index*

Using Multiple Indexes

In Figure 5-7, we see an execution plan that uses two indexes on the same table—flight. The discussion of index-based access in Chapter 3 was primarily concerned with the case of a single index. What happens when there is more than one available? How exactly does PostgreSQL use them efficiently?

The answer is in the word bitmap, as seen in the execution plan. Creating in-memory bitmaps allows the optimizer to use multiple indexes on one table to speed up data access. Let's look at the query with three filtering criteria for one table, all of which are supported by indexes.

Listing 5-9. A query with three filters on one table

```
SELECT
      scheduled_departure ,
      scheduled_arrival
FROM flight
WHERE departure_airport='ORD'
      AND arrival_airport='JFK'
      AND scheduled_departure BETWEEN '2023-07-03' AND '2023-07-04';
```

The execution plan for this query is shown in Figure 5-10.

	QUERY PLAN text
1	Bitmap Heap Scan on flight (cost=328.84..332.86 rows=1 width=16)
2	Recheck Cond: ((scheduled_departure >= '2023-07-03 00:00:00-05'::timestamp with time zone) AND (scheduled_departure <= '2023-07-04 00:00:00-05'::t
3	-> BitmapAnd (cost=328.84..328.84 rows=1 width=0)
4	-> Bitmap Index Scan on flight_scheduled_departure (cost=0.00..52.12 rows=3570 width=0)
5	Index Cond: ((scheduled_departure >= '2023-07-03 00:00:00-05'::timestamp with time zone) AND (scheduled_departure <= '2023-07-04 00:00:00-0
6	-> Bitmap Index Scan on flight_arrival_airport (cost=0.00..125.31 rows=11318 width=0)
7	Index Cond: (arrival_airport = 'JFK'::bpchar)
8	-> Bitmap Index Scan on flight_departure_airport (cost=0.00..150.91 rows=13664 width=0)
9	Index Cond: (departure_airport = 'ORD'::bpchar)

Figure 5-10. Execution plan with multiple index scans on one table

As discussed in depth in Chapter 3, Postgres can use the search results from multiple indexes by creating a bitmap of blocks with matching records in main memory and then OR-ing or AND-ing them. After this process is completed, the only blocks left are the blocks that satisfy all search criteria, and PostgreSQL reads all the records in the remaining blocks to recheck the search conditions.

The blocks will be scanned in physical order, so the index-based ordering will be lost.

Using a bitmap AND and OR of several index-based searches is a very efficient mechanism of applying multiple filters, but not the only one. In the next section, we will discuss another option—creating compound indexes.

Compound Indexes

So far, the indexes shown have been on individual columns. This section discusses indexes built on multiple columns and their advantages.

How Do Compound Indexes Work?

Let's return to the query in Listing 5-9. The result of three search criteria applied to the table flight can be computed by using multiple indexes. Another option would be to create a compound index on all three columns:

```
CREATE INDEX flight_depart_arr_sched_dep ON  flight(
       departure_airport,
        arrival_airport,
        scheduled_departure)
```

With this index, the execution plan would be as shown in Figure 5-11.

	QUERY PLAN text
1	Index Scan using flight_depart_arr_sched_dep on flight (cost=0.42..8.45 rows=1 width=16)
2	Index Cond: ((departure_airport = 'ORD'::bpchar) AND (arrival_airport = 'JFK'::bpchar) AND (scheduled_departure >= '2023-07-03

Figure 5-11. *A plan that uses a compound index*

This new compound index will support searches by departure_airport, by departure_airport and arrival_airport, and by departure_airport, arrival_airport, and scheduled_departure. It will not support, however, the searches by arrival_airport or scheduled_departure.

The query

```
SELECT
      departure_airport,
      scheduled_arrival,
      scheduled_departure
FROM flight
WHERE  arrival_airport='JFK'
      AND scheduled_departure BETWEEN '2023-07-03' AND '2023-07-04'
```

...will produce the execution plan shown in Figure 5-12.

	QUERY PLAN text
1	Bitmap Heap Scan on flight (cost=177.71..400.06 rows=59 width=20)
2	Recheck Cond: ((scheduled_departure >= '2023-07-03 00:00:00-05'::timestamp with time zone) AND (scheduled_(
3	-> BitmapAnd (cost=177.71..177.71 rows=59 width=0)
4	-> Bitmap Index Scan on flight_scheduled_departure (cost=0.00..52.12 rows=3570 width=0)
5	Index Cond: ((scheduled_departure >= '2023-07-03 00:00:00-05'::timestamp with time zone) AND (schedul
6	-> Bitmap Index Scan on flight_arrival_airport (cost=0.00..125.31 rows=11318 width=0)
7	Index Cond: (arrival_airport = 'JFK'::bpchar)

Figure 5-12. *A compound index is not used*

On the other hand, the query

```
SELECT
      scheduled_departure ,
      scheduled_arrival
FROM flight
WHERE departure_airport='ORD' AND arrival_airport='JFK'
      AND scheduled_arrival BETWEEN '2023-07-03' AND '2023-07-04';
```

...will use the compound index, although only for the first two columns, as shown in Figure 5-13.

	QUERY PLAN text
1	Bitmap Heap Scan on flight (cost=6.69..798.54 rows=1 width=16)
2	Recheck Cond: ((departure_airport = 'ORD'::bpchar) AND (arrival_airport = 'JFK'::bpchar))
3	Filter: ((scheduled_arrival >= '2023-07-03 00:00:00-05'::timestamp with time zone) AND (scheduled_arrival <= '20
4	-> Bitmap Index Scan on flight_depart_arr_sched_dep (cost=0.00..6.68 rows=226 width=0)
5	Index Cond: ((departure_airport = 'ORD'::bpchar) AND (arrival_airport = 'JFK'::bpchar))

Figure 5-13. *A plan that uses the compound index for the first two columns*

In general, an index on (X,Y,Z) will be used for searches on X, (X,Y), and (X,Y,Z) and even (X,Z) but not on Y alone and not on YZ. Thus, when a compound index is created, it's not enough to decide which columns to include; their order must also be considered.

Why create compound indexes? After all, the previous section demonstrated that using several indexes together will work just fine. There are two major reasons to create this type of index: lower selectivity and additional data storage.

Lower Selectivity

Remember that the lower the selectivity is, the faster the search is, and when we are optimizing short queries, our goal is to avoid reading a large number of rows at any given point (even if we will be able to filter them out later). Sometimes, none of the individual column values are restrictive enough, and only a certain combination makes a query short.

In the example from the previous section, there are 12,922 flights with departure airport ORD and 10,530 flights that arrive at JFK. However, the number of flights that originate in ORD and land in JFK is only 184.

Using Indexes for Data Retrieval

When all the columns from a SELECT statement are included in a compound index, they may be retrieved without accessing the table. This is called the *index-only-scan* data retrieval method.

All of the execution plans in the previous section still needed to read records from the table after they were located using the index scan, because we still needed the values from columns that were not included in the index.

Let's build one more compound index and include one more column:

```
CREATE INDEX flight_depart_arr_sched_dep_sched_arr
    ON flight (departure_airport,
               arrival_airport,
               scheduled_departure,
               scheduled_arrival );
```

The execution plan of the query will instantaneously convert into an index-only scan as shown in Figure 5-14.

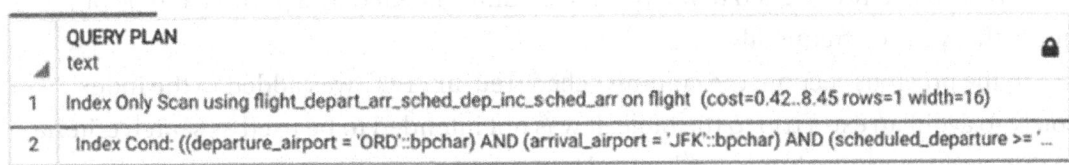

	QUERY PLAN text	🔒
1	Index Only Scan using flight_depart_arr_sched_dep_inc_sched_arr on flight (cost=0.42..8.45 rows=1 width=16)	
2	Index Cond: ((departure_airport = 'ORD'::bpchar) AND (arrival_airport = 'JFK'::bpchar) AND (scheduled_departure >= '...	

Figure 5-14. *A plan with an index-only scan*

Note that once again the search was on the first three columns of the index. If the search did not include the first column of the index, for example

```
SELECT
      departure_airport,
       scheduled_departure ,
       scheduled_arrival
```

```
FROM flight
WHERE arrival_airport='JFK'
        AND scheduled_departure BETWEEN '2023-07-03' AND '2023-07-04'
```

...the execution plan will revert to using several indexes with AND and OR, as shown in Figure 5-15.

	QUERY PLAN text
1	Bitmap Heap Scan on flight (cost=177.71..400.06 rows=59 width=20)
2	Recheck Cond: ((scheduled_departure >= '2023-07-03 00:00:00-05'::timestamp with time zone) AND (scheduled_departure <= '2023
3	-> BitmapAnd (cost=177.71..177.71 rows=59 width=0)
4	-> Bitmap Index Scan on flight_scheduled_departure (cost=0.00..52.12 rows=3570 width=0)
5	Index Cond: ((scheduled_departure >= '2023-07-03 00:00:00-05'::timestamp with time zone) AND (scheduled_departure <= '2
6	-> Bitmap Index Scan on flight_arrival_airport (cost=0.00..125.31 rows=11318 width=0)
7	Index Cond: (arrival_airport = 'JFK'::bpchar)

Figure 5-15. *When a search does not include the first index column, a compound index is not used*

Covering Indexes

Covering indexes were first introduced in PostgreSQL 11. These indexes can be viewed as a continuation of efforts to support the index-only-scan access method. A *covering index* is specifically designed to include the columns needed by a particular type of query that you run frequently.

In the previous section, the column scheduled_arrival was added to the index solely to avoid an extra trip to the table. It was not intended to be used as search criteria. In this case, a covering index can be used instead:

```
CREATE INDEX flight_depart_arr_sched_dep_inc_sched_arr   ON flight
      (departure_airport,
        arrival_airport,
        scheduled_departure)
    INCLUDE (scheduled_arrival);
```

The execution plan for the query

```
SELECT
      departure_airport,
```

```
        scheduled_departure ,
        scheduled_arrival
FROM flight
WHERE arrival_airport='JFK' AND departure_airport='ORD'
      AND scheduled_departure BETWEEN '2023-07-03' AND '2023-07-04'
```

will look like the one shown in Figure 5-16.

	QUERY PLAN text	
1	Index Only Scan using flight_depart_arr_sched_dep_inc_sched_arr on flight (cost=0.42..8.45 rows=1 width=16)	
2	Index Cond: ((departure_airport = 'ORD'::bpchar) AND (arrival_airport = 'JFK'::bpchar) AND (scheduled_departure >= '...	

Figure 5-16. *A plan with an index-only scan of a covering index*

In cases like this one, there is not much difference between including an extra column in the index vs. creating a covering index. However, if more (or wider) columns need to be stored together with the indexed values, a covering index will likely be more compact.

Excessive Selection Criteria

Sometimes, when filtering logic is complex and involves attributes from multiple tables, it is necessary to provide additional, redundant filters to prompt the database engine to use specific indexes or reduce the size of join arguments. This practice is called using excessive selection criteria. The intent is to use this additional filter to preselect a small subset of records from a large table.

For some of these complex criteria, PostgreSQL is able to perform a query rewrite automatically.

For example, the filtering conditions in the query in Listing 5-10 combine values of attributes from the tables `flight` and `passenger`. In earlier versions of PostgreSQL, the engine could not start filtering prior to joining all the tables, because the AND is applied to the columns of different tables.

Listing 5-10. Query with conditions on two tables

```
SELECT
        last_name,
        first_name,
         seat
FROM boarding_pass bp
JOIN booking_leg bl USING (booking_leg_id)
JOIN flight f USING (flight_id)
JOIN booking b USING(booking_id)
JOIN passenger p USING (passenger_id)
WHERE
        (departure_airport='JFK'
         AND scheduled_departure BETWEEN
                 '2023-07-10' AND '2023-07-11'
        AND last_name ='JOHNSON')
OR
(departure_airport='EDW'
 AND scheduled_departure BETWEEN '2023-07-13' AND '2023-07-14'
 AND last_name ='JOHNSTON')
```

However, now the optimizer can perform a complex query rewrite, as shown in Figure 5-17.

	QUERY PLAN text
1	Nested Loop (cost=187.56..61277.24 rows=11 width=15)
2	-> Nested Loop (cost=187.13..61262.37 rows=11 width=19)
3	Join Filter: ((((f.departure_airport = 'JFK'::bpchar) AND (f.scheduled_departure >= '2023-07-10 00:00:00-05'::timestamp with time zone) AND (f.scheduled_departure
4	-> Nested Loop (cost=186.69..55670.30 rows=2184 width=27)
5	-> Nested Loop (cost=186.25..20399.65 rows=1545 width=20)
6	-> Bitmap Heap Scan on flight f (cost=185.82..408.60 rows=59 width=16)
7	Recheck Cond: (((scheduled_departure >= '2023-07-10 00:00:00-05'::timestamp with time zone) AND (scheduled_departure <= '2023-07-11 00:00:00-05':
8	-> BitmapOr (cost=185.82..185.82 rows=59 width=0)
9	-> BitmapAnd (cost=172.53..172.53 rows=56 width=0)
10	-> Bitmap Index Scan on flight_scheduled_departure (cost=0.00..52.91 rows=3649 width=0)
11	Index Cond: ((scheduled_departure >= '2023-07-10 00:00:00-05'::timestamp with time zone) AND (scheduled_departure <= '2023-07-11 00:00:
12	-> Bitmap Index Scan on flight_departure_airport (cost=0.00..119.33 rows=10521 width=0)
13	Index Cond: (departure_airport = 'JFK'::bpchar)
14	-> Bitmap Index Scan on flight_depart_arr_sched_dep_inc_sched_arr (cost=0.00..13.28 rows=2 width=0)
15	Index Cond: ((departure_airport = 'EDW'::bpchar) AND (scheduled_departure >= '2023-07-13 00:00:00-05'::timestamp with time zone) AND (sched
16	-> Index Scan using booking_leg_flight_id on booking_leg bl (cost=0.44..337.98 rows=85 width=12)
17	Index Cond: (flight_id = f.flight_id)
18	-> Index Scan using boarding_pass_booking_leg_id on boarding_pass bp (cost=0.44..22.60 rows=23 width=19)
19	Index Cond: (booking_leg_id = bl.booking_leg_id)
20	-> Index Scan using passenger_pkey on passenger p (cost=0.43..2.53 rows=1 width=16)
21	Index Cond: (passenger_id = bp.passenger_id)
22	Filter: ((last_name = 'JOHNSON'::text) OR (last_name = 'JOHNSTON'::text))
23	-> Index Only Scan using booking_pkey on booking b (cost=0.43..1.35 rows=1 width=8)
24	Index Cond: (booking_id = bl.booking_id)

Figure 5-17. *Execution plan with conditions on two tables with query rewrite*

Note the lines from 8 to 15. PostgreSQL rewrites the logical expression and selects all records from the table `flight` that may be needed for both conditions connected with OR.

In cases like this, the only thing to do is to let PostgreSQL do its job.

However, there are some queries that will run forever without human intervention. Let's look at the query in Listing 5-11. This query looks for flights that were more than one hour delayed (of which there should not be many). For all of these delayed flights, the query selects boarding passes issued after the scheduled departure.

Listing 5-11. Short query with hard-to-optimize filtering

```
SELECT
        bp.update_ts AS boarding_pass_issued,
        scheduled_departure,
        actual_departure,
        status
```

```
FROM flight f
JOIN booking_leg bl USING (flight_id)
JOIN boarding_pass bp USING (booking_leg_id)
WHERE bp.update_ts > scheduled_departure + interval '30 minutes'
      AND f.update_ts >=scheduled_departure -interval '1 hour'
```

This might seem like a contrived example, but it is modeled on production exception reports. Many companies have some sort of exception reporting in place to identify the abnormal system behavior. Crucially, by definition, the output of execution reports should be small. Exception reports, to be useful, should report on conditions that occur relatively rarely—otherwise, they would just be reports on business as usual.

The described situation certainly sounds abnormal, and there should not be many cases like this. However, the execution plan in Figure 5-18 has full scans of large tables and hash joins, even though all the appropriate indexes on all the tables involved exist.

	QUERY PLAN text
1	Hash Join (cost=822656.15..2204168.07 rows=2810405 width=162)
2	Hash Cond: (bp.booking_leg_id = bl.booking_leg_id)
3	Join Filter: (bp.update_ts > (f.scheduled_departure + '00:30:00'::interval))
4	-> Seq Scan on boarding_pass bp (cost=0.00..513696.84 rows=25293684 width=40)
5	-> Hash (cost=654903.74..654903.74 rows=5964513 width=99)
6	-> Hash Join (cost=32574.20..654903.74 rows=5964513 width=99)
7	Hash Cond: (bl.flight_id = f.flight_id)
8	-> Seq Scan on booking_leg bl (cost=0.00..328049.64 rows=17893564 width=32)
9	-> Hash (cost=27058.64..27058.64 rows=227725 width=71)
10	-> Seq Scan on flight f (cost=0.00..27058.64 rows=227725 width=71)
11	Filter: (update_ts >= (scheduled_departure - '01:00:00'::interval))

Figure 5-18. Suboptimal execution plan for a short query

So what went wrong?

Let's go back to the definition of a short query. It seemed very clear in the beginning, but now it becomes a bit trickier. Recall that a query is short if it needs a small number of rows to compute results. Indeed, in this case, the number of rows we need is small, but there is no easy way to find them. So here is the caveat: it is not just that a short query requires a small number of rows, but also that the number of rows in the result of any intermediate operation should also be small. If a query with three joins is short and, after executing the first of the joins, the intermediate result is huge, it means that something is wrong with the execution plan.

As previously discussed, the only way to read a small number of rows from a table is to use an index. However, we do not have any indexes that would support the filtering conditions in the query from Listing 5-11. Moreover, it is not possible to build such an index, because selection criteria from one table depend on values from another table. In this case, there is no way to make a selection before joining, which results in full scans and hash joins.

How can this query be improved? The answer to this question is not directly related to SQL. Chapter 1 stated that database optimization starts from gathering requirements, and this is a case where gathering precise requirements is the best path toward optimization.

Notice that, in the original query, the search space is all the flights since the dawn of time—or at least, for the entire time period captured by the database. However, this is an exception report, which most likely is reviewed on a regular cadence, and, likely, the business owner of this report is interested in recent cases since the last review. Earlier exceptions would have already appeared in previous reports and hopefully have been addressed. The next step would be to connect with the business owner of this report and ask whether a report including only the most recent exceptions suits their needs.

If the answer is *yes*, the excessive selection criterion we just got from business can be applied to the query. Also, we need one more index:

```
CREATE INDEX boarding_pass_update_ts ON postgres_air.boarding_
pass (update_ts);
```

Listing 5-12 shows the modified query, retaining two days of exceptions.

Listing 5-12. Query with added excessive selection criteria

```
SELECT
    bp.update_ts AS boarding_pass_issued,
    scheduled_departure,
    actual_departure,
    status
FROM flight f
```

```
JOIN booking_leg bl USING (flight_id)
JOIN boarding_pass bp USING (booking_leg_id)
WHERE bp.update_ts > scheduled_departure + interval '30 minutes'
  AND f.update_ts >=scheduled_departure -interval '1 hour';
  AND bp.update_ts >='2023-08-13' AND bp.update_ts< '2023-08-14';
```

Now, the search by timestamps will be applied first, as seen in the execution plan in Figure 5-19.

	QUERY PLAN text
1	Nested Loop (cost=664.78..321665.97 rows=3463 width=35)
2	Join Filter: (bp.update_ts > (f.scheduled_departure + '00:30:00'::interval))
3	-> Nested Loop (cost=664.36..307178.01 rows=31168 width=12)
4	-> Bitmap Heap Scan on boarding_pass bp (cost=663.91..89143.01 rows=31168 width=16)
5	Recheck Cond: ((update_ts >= '2023-08-13 00:00:00-05'::timestamp with time zone) AND (update_ts < '2023-08-14 00:00:00-05'::timestan
6	-> Bitmap Index Scan on boarding_pass_update_ts (cost=0.00..656.12 rows=31168 width=0)
7	Index Cond: ((update_ts >= '2023-08-13 00:00:00-05'::timestamp with time zone) AND (update_ts < '2023-08-14 00:00:00-05'::timestar
8	-> Memoize (cost=0.45..7.08 rows=1 width=8)
9	Cache Key: bp.booking_leg_id
10	Cache Mode: logical
11	-> Index Scan using booking_leg_pkey on booking_leg bl (cost=0.44..7.07 rows=1 width=8)
12	Index Cond: (booking_leg_id = bp.booking_leg_id)
13	-> Index Scan using flight_pkey on flight f (cost=0.42..0.45 rows=1 width=31)
14	Index Cond: (flight_id = bl.flight_id)
15	Filter: (update_ts >= (scheduled_departure - '01:00:00'::interval))

Figure 5-19. *Execution plan with excessive selection criteria*

The execution time for this query is less than 200 milliseconds, while the execution time for the original query was 2 minutes and 44 seconds.

A *Memoize* node (lines 8–10) will appear in the execution plan if you run PostgreSQL version 14 or higher and have a configuration parameter *enable_memoize* on. Memoized plans allow caching results from parameterized scans inside nested loop joins. This does not change the index-based access utilized in this plan.

Partial Indexes

Partial indexes are among the best features of PostgreSQL. As implied by the name, a partial index is built on a subset of a table, defined by the WHERE clause of the CREATE INDEX operator.

For example, for flights scheduled in the future, the actual_departure column is null. To improve search by actual_departure, we can create an index for only flights with a non-null actual departure value:

```
CREATE INDEX flight_actual_departure_not_null
    ON flight(actual_departure)
    WHERE actual_departure IS NOT NULL
```

In this particular case, the difference in execution time won't be dramatic, because the flight table is not very large and, in the current distribution, only half of the flights have a null actual departure. However, if the values in a column are distributed unevenly, using a partial index can provide a great advantage.

For example, the column status in the flight table has only three possible values: "On schedule," "Delayed," and "Canceled." These values are unevenly distributed; there are significantly more flights with status "On schedule" than the other two. Creating an index on the column status would be impractical due to the very high selectivity of this column. However, it would be nice to be able to quickly filter out the canceled flights, especially because in contrast to real life, there are not that many canceled flights in the postgres_air schema.

We are going to create an index:

```
CREATE INDEX flight_canceled ON flight(flight_id)
WHERE status='Canceled';
```

This index will be used in all queries where we select canceled flights, regardless of any other filtering conditions, for example:

```
SELECT * FROM flight WHERE
    scheduled_departure between '2023-08-13' AND '2023-08-14'
    AND status='Canceled'
```

The execution plan for this query is shown in Figure 5-20.

	QUERY PLAN text	
1	Bitmap Heap Scan on flight (cost=60.11..64.12 rows=1 width=71)	
2	Recheck Cond: ((status = 'Canceled'::text) AND (scheduled_departure >= '2023-08-13 00:00:00-05'::timestamp with time zone) AND (scheduled_depa	
3	-> BitmapAnd (cost=60.11..60.11 rows=1 width=0)	
4	-> Bitmap Index Scan on flight_canceled (cost=0.00..9.00 rows=182 width=0)	
5	-> Bitmap Index Scan on flight_scheduled_departure (cost=0.00..50.85 rows=3443 width=0)	
6	Index Cond: ((scheduled_departure >= '2023-08-13 00:00:00-05'::timestamp with time zone) AND (scheduled_departure <= '2023-08-14 00:00.	

Figure 5-20. *The usage of a partial index*

Using the partial index decreases execution time from 0.72 seconds to 0.16 seconds.

Indexes and Join Order

As mentioned earlier, in short queries, the optimization goal is to avoid large intermediate results. That means ensuring that the most restrictive selection criteria are applied first. After that, for each join operation, we should ensure that the result continues to be small.

The size of join results may be small either because of restrictions on the joined tables (small number of records in join arguments) or because of a semi-join (one argument significantly restricts the result size).

Most of the time, the query planner chooses a correct join order, unless the wrong order is forced.

Let's start with creation of several more indexes:

```
CREATE INDEX account_login ON account(login);
CREATE INDEX account_login_lower_pattern ON account  (lower(login) text_
pattern_ops);
CREATE INDEX passenger_last_name ON passenger  (last_name);
CREATE INDEX boarding_pass_passenger_id ON boarding_pass  (passenger_id);
CREATE INDEX passenger_last_name_lower_pattern ON passenger  (lower(last_
name) text_pattern_ops);
CREATE INDEX passenger_booking_id ON passenger(booking_id);
CREATE INDEX booking_account_id ON booking(account_id);
CREATE INDEX booking_email_lower_pattern    ON booking
    (lower(email) text_pattern_ops);
```

Now, consider the example in Listing 5-13.

Listing 5-13. Order of joins example

```
SELECT
    b.account_id,
    a.login,
    p.last_name,
    p.first_name
FROM passenger p
JOIN booking b USING(booking_id)
JOIN account a ON a.account_id=b.account_id
WHERE lower(p.last_name) LIKE 'smith%'
    AND lower(login) LIKE 'smith%';
```

The execution plan for this query is shown in Figure 5-21. Note that although the first table listed is the table `passenger` and that the first selection criterion is applied to the same table, the execution starts with the table `account`.

	QUERY PLAN text
1	Nested Loop (cost=329.77..13041.92 rows=46 width=41)
2	-> Nested Loop (cost=329.34..12588.28 rows=574 width=37)
3	-> Bitmap Heap Scan on account a (cost=328.91..9077.97 rows=88 width=29)
4	Filter: ((lower(login) ~~ 'smith%'::text) AND (lower(login) ~~ 'smith%'::text))
5	-> Bitmap Index Scan on account_login_lower_pattern (cost=0.00..328.89 rows=8564 width=0)
6	Index Cond: ((lower(login) ~>=~ 'smith'::text) AND (lower(login) ~<~ 'smiti'::text) AND (lower(login) ~>=~ 'smith'::text) AN
7	-> Index Scan using booking_account_id on booking b (cost=0.43..39.80 rows=9 width=12)
8	Index Cond: (account_id = a.account_id)
9	-> Index Scan using passenger_booking_id on passenger p (cost=0.43..0.78 rows=1 width=16)
10	Index Cond: (booking_id = b.booking_id)
11	Filter: (lower(last_name) ~~ 'smith%'::text)

Figure 5-21. *Order of joins: execution starts from the smaller table, when selectivity is similar*

The reason is that the table `account` contains significantly fewer records than the `passenger` table, and although the selectivity of both filters is approximately the same, the corresponding index on the `account` table will yield fewer records. Note that in this case the pattern index on the `passenger` table is not used at all.

However, the execution plan changes significantly when the criteria look for passengers with an uncommon last name—that is, a last name with a very low selectivity. The execution plan in Figure 5-22 indicates that in this case, starting processing from the `passenger` table is more restrictive. In this case, the PostgreSQL query planner uses the pattern index on the `passenger` table and does not use the pattern index on the `account` table.

	QUERY PLAN text	🔒
1	Nested Loop (cost=1.29..9127.81 rows=1 width=41)	
2	-> Nested Loop (cost=0.87..8648.91 rows=1041 width=16)	
3	-> Index Scan using passenger_last_name_lower_pattern on passenger p (cost=0.43..8.46 rows=1041 width...	
4	Index Cond: ((lower(last_name) ~>=~ 'davey'::text) AND (lower(last_name) ~<~ 'davez'::text))	
5	Filter: (lower(last_name) ~~ 'davey%'::text)	
6	-> Index Scan using booking_pkey on booking b (cost=0.43..8.30 rows=1 width=12)	
7	Index Cond: (booking_id = p.booking_id)	
8	-> Index Scan using account_pkey on account a (cost=0.42..0.46 rows=1 width=29)	
9	Index Cond: (account_id = b.account_id)	
10	Filter: ((lower(login) ~~ 'smith%'::text) AND (lower(login) ~~ 'smith%'::text))	

Figure 5-22. *Different selectivity prompts a different join order*

Another thing worth noting while comparing these two plans is that since the first query yields significantly more rows, a bitmap index scan is used, while the second query uses the regular index scan due to the lower selectivity.

The SELECT statement in Listing 5-14 is similar, but instead of joining with the `passenger` table, the join is to the `frequent_flyer` table, which is approximately half of the size of the `account` table. Of course, to be able to search this table, two more indexes are required:

```
CREATE INDEX frequent_fl_last_name_lower_pattern ON frequent_
flyer  (lower(last_name) text_pattern_ops);

CREATE INDEX frequent_fl_last_name_lower ON frequent_
flyer  (lower(last_name));
```

In this case, execution will start from the table `frequent_flyer`, as shown in Figure 5-23.

Listing 5-14. Query selecting the number of bookings for each frequent flyer

```
SELECT
        a.account_id,
        a.login,
        f.last_name,
        f.first_name,
        count(*) AS num_bookings
FROM frequent_flyer f
JOIN account a USING(frequent_flyer_id)
JOIN booking b USING(account_id)
WHERE lower(f.last_name)='smith'
AND lower(login) LIKE 'smith%'
GROUP BY 1,2,3,4
```

	QUERY PLAN
	text
1	GroupAggregate (cost=4388.12..4400.94 rows=570 width=49)
2	Group Key: a.account_id, f.last_name, f.first_name
3	-> Sort (cost=4388.12..4389.54 rows=570 width=41)
4	Sort Key: a.account_id, f.last_name, f.first_name
5	-> Nested Loop (cost=1389.66..4362.03 rows=570 width=41)
6	-> Hash Join (cost=1389.23..4200.87 rows=26 width=41)
7	Hash Cond: (a.frequent_flyer_id = f.frequent_flyer_id)
8	-> Bitmap Heap Scan on account a (cost=87.45..2885.45 rows=5199 width=33)
9	Filter: (lower(login) ~~ 'smith%'::text)
10	-> Bitmap Index Scan on account_login_lower_pattern (cost=0.00..86.15 rows=2573 width=0)
11	Index Cond: ((lower(login) ~>=~ 'smith'::text) AND (lower(login) ~<~ 'smiti'::text))
12	-> Hash (cost=1293.75..1293.75 rows=642 width=16)
13	-> Bitmap Heap Scan on frequent_flyer f (cost=13.39..1293.75 rows=642 width=16)
14	Recheck Cond: (lower(last_name) = 'smith'::text)
15	-> Bitmap Index Scan on frequent_fl_last_name_lower (cost=0.00..13.23 rows=642 width=0)
16	Index Cond: (lower(last_name) = 'smith'::text)
17	-> Index Only Scan using booking_account_id on booking b (cost=0.43..5.35 rows=85 width=4)
18	Index Cond: (account_id = a.account_id)

Figure 5-23. *The execution plan for the query in Listing 5-14*

When Are Indexes Not Used

So far, this chapter has covered how indexes are used in queries. This section turns to situations where indexes are *not used*. Specifically, it discusses two situations: how to prevent PostgreSQL from using indexes in some circumstances and what to do when an index isn't being used and we think it ought to be.

Avoiding Index Usage

Why would it be desirable to avoid using an index? Often, database developers believe that using indexes improves the performance of any query. We can each recall situations where we were asked "to build some indexes to make this query run faster." However, an index is not always needed and in some cases may be counterproductive. Two examples from earlier in this chapter (Figures 5-1 and 5-6) showed execution plans with sequential reads that are nevertheless quite efficient.

The two main reasons we may want to avoid using indexes are as follows:

- A small table is completely read into main memory.

- We need a large proportion of the rows of a table to execute a query.

Is there a way to avoid using existing indexes? Most of the time, the optimizer is smart enough to figure out when it should or shouldn't use indexes. But on the rare occasions when it fails, we can modify selection criteria. Recall from the beginning of this chapter that column transformations can block the usage of indexes. At that time, it was framed as a negative impact of column transformation, but it can also be used to improve performance when the goal is to block index usage.

If a column is of a numeric type, it can be modified by adding zero to its value. For example, the condition `attr1+0=p_value` will block the usage of an index on column `attr1`. For any data type, the `coalesce()` function will always block the usage of indexes, so assuming `attr2` is not nullable, the condition can be modified to something like `coalesce(t1.attr2, '0')=coalesce(t2.attr2, '0')`.

Why Does PostgreSQL Ignore My Index?

Occasionally, there are extraordinarily frustrating cases, when the appropriate index exists, but for some reason, PostgreSQL is not using it. This is the moment when a database developer with experience with other systems that allow optimizer hints might start really missing them. However, most of the time, there is no reason for frustration. Having one of the best optimizers, PostgreSQL does the right thing in most cases. So, most likely, there is a good reason, and it is possible to find by examining the execution plan.

Let's consider an example. This example, as well as some examples in subsequent chapters, uses larger tables, which are not included in the postgres_air distribution due to their size. These tables are necessary to illustrate cases that occur in real life and that you might come across. Here, the table boarding_pass_large is being used, which has the same structure as the boarding_pass table, but contains three times as many rows— over 75,000,000 boarding passes. To create a larger table for experimentation, you can insert every row of the boarding_pass table three times.

In the postgres_air database, the current date is August 14, 2023. Let's select a sample of 100 passengers who checked in during the last week:

```
SELECT * FROM boarding_pass_large
WHERE update_ts::date BETWEEN '2023-08-07' AND '2023-08-14'
LIMIT 100
```

Predictably, the execution plan shown in Figure 5-24 shows a sequential scan.

	QUERY PLAN text	🔒
1	Limit (cost=0.00..606.19 rows=100 width=44)	
2	-> Seq Scan on boarding_pass_large (cost=0.00..2299878.44 rows=379401 width=44)	
3	Filter: (((update_ts)::date >= '2023-08-07'::date) AND ((update_ts)::date <= '2023-08-14'::date))	

Figure 5-24. *Sequential scan due to column transformation*

No problem, we've covered how to avoid this issue. Instead of converting the timestamp to date, we use an interval:

```
SELECT * FROM boarding_pass_large
WHERE update_ts BETWEEN '2023-08-07' AND '2023-08-15'
LIMIT 100
```

However, when we check the execution plan, we see that it still uses a sequential scan!

Why didn't removing the column transformation cause PostgreSQL to use the index? The answer is in Figure 5-25. It is the result of the combination of relatively high selectivity of this index on a large table and the presence of the LIMIT operator. The query planner estimates that the specified selection condition will select over 700,000 rows, which, recall, might require twice as many disk I/O operations. Since only 100 rows are required and since the order is not specified, it is faster to go ahead with a sequential scan of the table. There is a higher chance that the hundred records that satisfy this criterion will be found faster.

	QUERY PLAN text	
1	Limit (cost=0.00..266.18 rows=100 width=44)	
2	-> Seq Scan on boarding_pass_large (cost=0.00..1920477.08 rows=721490 width=44)	
3	Filter: ((update_ts >= '2023-08-07 00:00:00-05'::timestamp with time zone) AND (update_ts <= '2023-08-15 00:00:00-05'::timestamp with time z...	

Figure 5-25. *Sequential scan due to high index selectivity*

The situation would be different if those 100 records needed to be selected in a particular order. Unless the sort order is on the indexed attribute, PostgreSQL will need to select *all* records before it can decide which ones are first.

Let's change the SELECT statement to include ordering:

```
SELECT * FROM boarding_pass_large
WHERE update_ts BETWEEN '2023-08-07' AND '2023-08-15'
ORDER BY boarding_time
LIMIT 100
```

Now the execution plan (shown in Figure 5-26) looks dramatically different.

	QUERY PLAN text
1	Limit (cost=1904162.11..1904162.36 rows=100 width=44)
2	-> Sort (cost=1904162.11..1905965.84 rows=721490 width=44)
3	Sort Key: boarding_time
4	-> Bitmap Heap Scan on boarding_pass_large (cost=14983.84..1876587.28 rows=721490 width=44)
5	Recheck Cond: ((update_ts >= '2023-08-07 00:00:00-05'::timestamp with time zone) AND (update_ts <= '2023-08-15 00:00:00-05'::timestamp v
6	-> Bitmap Index Scan on boarding_pass_large_update_ts (cost=0.00..14803.47 rows=721490 width=0)
7	Index Cond: ((update_ts >= '2023-08-07 00:00:00-05'::timestamp with time zone) AND (update_ts <= '2023-08-15 00:00:00-05'::timestamp \

Figure 5-26. *Execution plan with sorting*

Comparing the execution time for these two queries, the one with a sequential scan ran for 140 milliseconds, and the one with forced index access ran for 620 milliseconds, so the sequential scan was indeed more efficient in this case.

Let PostgreSQL Do Its Job!

In this section, we will use several modifications of the queries from the previous sections to illustrate how PostgreSQL modifies execution plans based on data statistics.

We hope that by now, a convincing case has been made that the optimizer does its job right most of the time, and our goal in most cases is just to give it enough flexibility to make the right choice.

Let's get back to the query on a large table from the previous section:

```
SELECT * FROM boarding_pass_large
WHERE update_ts BETWEEN '2023-08-07' AND '2023-08-15'
LIMIT 100
```

The execution plan for this query is shown in Figure 5-25, and the PostgreSQL optimizer chose a sequential scan, because the interval of seven days was too large to get any benefits from index access. Now, let's reduce the time interval:

```
SELECT * FROM boarding_pass_large
WHERE update_ts BETWEEN '2023-08-12' AND '2023-08-15'
LIMIT 100
```

The execution plan for this query in Figure 5-27 shows that index-based access is used.

	QUERY PLAN text
1	Limit (cost=0.57..342.92 rows=100 width=44)
2	-> Index Scan using boarding_pass_large_update_ts on boarding_pass_large (cost=0.57..798572.71 rows=233262 width=44)
3	Index Cond: ((update_ts >= '2023-08-12 00:00:00-05'::timestamp with time zone) AND (update_ts <= '2023-08-15 00:00:00-05'::timesta

Figure 5-27. *A plan changes to index access when the time interval is smaller*

Continuing to check different intervals, we will see that eight days is the pivot point in this case. If the start of the interval is any date after August 7, the execution plan will show index usage.

Even more interestingly, if `LIMIT 100` is removed from the query, the execution plan will show an index scan. If we increase the interval by just one more day, the execution plan will divert to a bitmap scan, and if we increase it for one more day, it will flip to the sequential scan (see the corresponding execution plans in Figures 5-28, 5-29, and 5-30).

	QUERY PLAN text
1	Index Scan using boarding_pass_large_update_ts on boarding_pass_large (cost=0.57..1745769.79 rows=623844 width=44)
2	Index Cond: ((update_ts >= '2023-08-08 00:00:00-05'::timestamp with time zone) AND (update_ts <= '2023-08-15 00:00:00-05'::timestamp with t

Figure 5-28. *Execution plan using an index scan*

	QUERY PLAN text
1	Bitmap Heap Scan on boarding_pass_large (cost=14983.84..1876587.28 rows=721490 width=44)
2	Recheck Cond: ((update_ts >= '2023-08-07 00:00:00-05'::timestamp with time zone) AND (update_ts <= '2023-08-15 00:00:00-05'::timestamp with time z...
3	-> Bitmap Index Scan on boarding_pass_large_update_ts (cost=0.00..14803.47 rows=721490 width=0)
4	Index Cond: ((update_ts >= '2023-08-07 00:00:00-05'::timestamp with time zone) AND (update_ts <= '2023-08-15 00:00:00-05'::timestamp with time z...

Figure 5-29. *Execution plan using a bitmap scan*

	QUERY PLAN text
1	Seq Scan on boarding_pass_large (cost=0.00..1920477.08 rows=963658 width=44)
2	Filter: ((update_ts >= '2023-08-06 00:00:00-05'::timestamp with time zone) AND (update_ts <= '2023-08-15 00:00:00-05'::timestamp with

Figure 5-30. *Execution plan using a sequential scan*

Let's see another example—the query in Listing 5-13. We observed that depending on how selective the last name of the passenger is, the order of joins (and applying indexes) will change. In fact, experimenting with different last names, it is possible to identify the selectivity at which the execution plan flips (around 200 occurrences).

Finally, let's look at one relatively simple SQL statement. Three SELECT statements in Listing 5-15 are identical except the filtering values for each search criterion. In the first query, departure airport has high selectivity, and passenger name has low selectivity. In the second query, both values are highly selective, and in the last query, departure airport has low selectivity. The plans, shown in Figures 5-31, 5-32, and 5-33, differ in join algorithms, the order of joins, and the indexes that are used.

Listing 5-15. SELECT with three different sets of parameters

```
--#1

SELECT
     p.last_name,
     p.first_name
FROM passenger p
JOIN boarding_pass bp USING (passenger_id)
JOIN booking_Leg bl USING (booking_leg_id)
JOIN flight USING(flight_id)
WHERE departure_airport='LAX'
       AND lower(last_name)='clark'

--#2

SELECT
     p.last_name,
     p.first_name
FROM passenger p
JOIN boarding_pass bp USING (passenger_id)
JOIN booking_Leg bl USING (booking_leg_id)
JOIN flight USING(flight_id)
WHERE departure_airport='LAX'
       AND lower(last_name)='smith'

--#3

SELECT
    p.last_name,
    p.first_name
FROM passenger p
JOIN boarding_pass bp USING (passenger_id)
JOIN booking_Leg bl USING (booking_leg_id)
JOIN flight USING(flight_id)
WHERE departure_airport='FUK'
       AND lower(last_name)='smith'
```

	QUERY PLAN text
1	Hash Join (cost=9678.47..165905.98 rows=198 width=12)
2	Hash Cond: (bl.flight_id = flight.flight_id)
3	-> Nested Loop (cost=134.45..156334.18 rows=10582 width=16)
4	-> Nested Loop (cost=134.02..138080.14 rows=10582 width=20)
5	-> Bitmap Heap Scan on passenger p (cost=133.45..23039.81 rows=6825 width=16)
6	Recheck Cond: (lower(last_name) = 'clark'::text)
7	-> Bitmap Index Scan on passenger_last_name_lower_pattern (cost=0.00..131.75 rows=6825 width=0)
8	Index Cond: (lower(last_name) = 'clark'::text)
9	-> Index Scan using boarding_pass_passenger_id on boarding_pass bp (cost=0.56..16.82 rows=4 width=16)
10	Index Cond: (passenger_id = p.passenger_id)
11	-> Index Scan using booking_leg_pkey on booking_leg bl (cost=0.44..1.73 rows=1 width=8)
12	Index Cond: (booking_leg_id = bp.booking_leg_id)
13	-> Hash (cost=9384.33..9384.33 rows=12775 width=4)
14	-> Bitmap Heap Scan on flight (cost=243.43..9384.33 rows=12775 width=4)
15	Recheck Cond: (departure_airport = 'LAX'::bpchar)
16	-> Bitmap Index Scan on flight_departure_airport (cost=0.00..240.24 rows=12775 width=0)
17	Index Cond: (departure_airport = 'LAX'::bpchar)

Figure 5-31. *An execution plan for query #1*

	QUERY PLAN text
1	Hash Join (cost=9678.47..165905.98 rows=198 width=12)
2	Hash Cond: (bl.flight_id = flight.flight_id)
3	-> Nested Loop (cost=134.45..156334.18 rows=10582 width=16)
4	-> Nested Loop (cost=134.02..138080.14 rows=10582 width=20)
5	-> Bitmap Heap Scan on passenger p (cost=133.45..23039.81 rows=6825 width=16)
6	Recheck Cond: (lower(last_name) = ' smith'::text)
7	-> Bitmap Index Scan on passenger_last_name_lower_pattern (cost=0.00..131.75 rows=6825 width=0)
8	Index Cond: (lower(last_name) = ' smith'::text)
9	-> Index Scan using boarding_pass_passenger_id on boarding_pass bp (cost=0.56..16.82 rows=4 width=16)
10	Index Cond: (passenger_id = p.passenger_id)
11	-> Index Scan using booking_leg_pkey on booking_leg bl (cost=0.44..1.73 rows=1 width=8)
12	Index Cond: (booking_leg_id = bp.booking_leg_id)
13	-> Hash (cost=9384.33..9384.33 rows=12775 width=4)
14	-> Bitmap Heap Scan on flight (cost=243.43..9384.33 rows=12775 width=4)
15	Recheck Cond: (departure_airport = 'LAX'::bpchar)
16	-> Bitmap Index Scan on flight_departure_airport (cost=0.00..240.24 rows=12775 width=0)
17	Index Cond: (departure_airport = 'LAX'::bpchar)

Figure 5-32. *An execution plan for query #2*

	QUERY PLAN 🔒
	text
1	Nested Loop (cost=12.91..217066.10 rows=360 width=12)
2	-> Nested Loop (cost=12.47..191823.09 rows=13958 width=8)
3	-> Nested Loop (cost=11.91..34548.25 rows=9874 width=4)
4	-> Bitmap Heap Scan on flight (cost=11.35..1341.38 rows=377 width=4)
5	Recheck Cond: (departure_airport = 'FUK'::bpchar)
6	-> Bitmap Index Scan on flight_depart_arr_sched_dep_inc_sched_arr (cost=0.00..11.25 row...
7	Index Cond: (departure_airport = 'FUK'::bpchar)
8	-> Index Scan using booking_leg_flight_id on booking_leg bl (cost=0.56..87.17 rows=91 width=8)
9	Index Cond: (flight_id = flight.flight_id)
10	-> Index Scan using boarding_pass_booking_leg_id on boarding_pass bp (cost=0.56..15.70 rows=...
11	Index Cond: (booking_leg_id = bl.booking_leg_id)
12	-> Index Scan using passenger_pkey on passenger p (cost=0.43..1.81 rows=1 width=16)
13	Index Cond: (passenger_id = bp.passenger_id)
14	Filter: (lower(last_name) = 'smith'::text)

Figure 5-33. *An execution plan for query #3*

How to Build the Right Index(es)

At the start of this chapter, a minimal set of indexes was defined in the postgres_air schema. Almost every time we wanted to improve query performance, we suggested building yet another index. All of these indexes indeed helped improve execution time. What was never discussed was whether additional justification is needed to create a new index.

To Build or Not to Build

Twenty years ago, we were more cautious when deciding whether to add yet another index. Two major reasons against creating too many indexes are that indexes take up extra space in the database and that insert and update operations become slow when there are too many indexes to update along with the record itself. The prevailing guidance used to be to drop all indexes on a table before a bulk load and then to create them again. Some textbooks on databases still offer the same recommendation—not to drop the indexes, but to be mindful regarding the number of indexes on a table.

Since then, times have changed. With current hard- and software, the situation is different. Disk storage is cheaper, disks are faster, and, in general, fast response is more valuable than saving disk space. Twenty years ago, having a table in your database with the cumulative size of its indexes exceeding the size of the table itself was a red flag. These days, it's the norm for OLTP systems. But still, the question remains: When is enough enough?

Which Indexes Are Needed?

It is challenging to provide any general recommendations regarding which indexes are necessary. In OLTP systems, response time is usually critical, and any short query should be index-supported.

We recommend creating partial and covering indexes whenever it makes sense. Partial indexes are usually smaller than regular indexes and are more likely to fit in main memory. Covering indexes save trips to the table, thus allowing the engine to perform most processing in main memory.

Extra time needed for inserts and updates is usually less critical than fast response. However, you should always watch this time and evaluate the inventory of indexes if slowness is detected. The unique/primary key indexes and foreign keys that reference other unique/primary key fields are usual culprits of slowness, as well as triggers on insert/update. In each case, you will need to evaluate the importance of data integrity vs. the speed of updates.

There are a number of queries available online that calculate the total size of indexes on each table, and most monitoring tools will alert you about excessive growth.

Which Indexes Are Not Needed?

Even though we are usually not concerned with extra disk space needed for indexes, we do not want to create database objects that are useless. The PostgreSQL catalog view `pg_stat_all_indexes` shows the total number of index uses (scans, reads, and fetches) since the last statistics reset.

Note that some primary key indexes are *never* used for data retrieval; however, they are vital for data integrity and should not be removed.

Indexes and Short Query Scalability

In this section, we will discuss how to optimize short queries so that they will remain performant when data volumes increase.

In Chapter 1, we mentioned that optimization does not stop when a query goes to production. We should continue to monitor performance and proactively identify changes in performance dynamics.

With short queries, such performance monitoring is vital, since query behavior can change dramatically when data volumes grow, especially when the speed of growth is different for different tables.

When a query is index-supported, there is at least some assurance that it is scalable, because the number of accesses to index grows only logarithmically relative to table growth. But if the size of a table grows fast, the index might grow large enough not to fit in main memory, or it might be pushed out by indexes for competing queries. If this happens, execution time may increase sharply.

It is possible that in the beginning a query works fast without any indexes, and we might not know for sure which indexes will be needed in the future. It is also possible that a condition for a partial index was very restrictive and index access was very fast, but later, with more and more records satisfying the condition, the index became less efficient.

In short, although we strive to make sure short queries are scalable and will perform well even when data volumes grow, we can't assume that anything is optimized "forever." We should always keep an eye on data volume, value distributions, and other characteristics that can interfere with performance.

Summary

This chapter covered short queries and what techniques can be used to optimize them. The primary optimization goal for short queries is to apply the most restrictive search criteria first and to ensure that all intermediate results remain small. As such, the chapter discussed the role of indexes for short queries and showed how to determine what indexes are needed to create to support specific queries.

This chapter also showed various execution plans and how to read them to understand the order of joins and filtering, as well as discussing various types of indexes available in PostgreSQL and when they can be useful. More complex index types will be considered in depth in Chapter 14.

CHAPTER 6

Long Queries and Full Scans

Chapter 5 discussed short queries and explained how to identify short queries and optimization strategies and techniques applicable to them. It also covered the importance of indexes for short queries, the most commonly used index types, and their applications. Chapter 5 also provided an opportunity to practice reading execution plans and, hopefully, acquire confidence in the PostgreSQL optimizer.

This chapter concerns long queries. Some queries just can't run in a fraction of a second, no matter how well-written. This does not mean they cannot be optimized. Many practitioners hold that since analytical reports do not have strict response time requirements, it is not important how fast or slow they run. In extreme cases, report developers make no effort to make sure that reports are complete in a reasonable time, giving the excuse that the query only runs once a day or once a week or once a month.

This is a dangerous practice. If report performance is neglected, performance can easily degrade from minutes to hours or more. We have observed reports that run for six days before completion! And by the time the situation becomes that dire, it is not trivial to fix in a limited time frame. Often, when an analytical report is developed, source data volumes are really small, and everything performs well. It is the job of SQL developers to examine execution plans even if queries are running fine now and to be proactive to prevent future performance degradation.

Which Queries Are Considered Long?

Chapter 5 introduced the formal definition of a short query. It is logical to assume that all queries that are not short are long. This is true, but a definition based on negation might not be intuitive to apply in practice.

© Henrietta Dombrovskaya, Boris Novikov, Anna Bailliekova 2024
H. Dombrovskaya et al., *PostgreSQL Query Optimization*, https://doi.org/10.1007/979-8-8688-0069-6_6

The two examples of long queries from Chapter 5 (Listings 5-1 and 5-3) are copied here in Listings 6-1 and 6-2, respectively. The first of the two queries is a long query with massive output; the query returns every possible combination of arrival and departure airports. The second one produces only one line of output—showing the average length of flights and number of passengers for all flights in the postgres_air schema—but is still classified as a long query.

Listing 6-1. Long query with a large result set

```
SELECT
    d.airport_code AS departure_airport
    a.airport_code AS arrival_airport
FROM  airport a,
    airport d
WHERE a.airport_code <> d.airport_code
```

Listing 6-2. 3Long query with a one-row result set

```
SELECT
    avg(flight_length),
    avg (passengers)
FROM
    (SELECT
        flight_no,
        scheduled_arrival -scheduled_departure AS flight_length,
        count(passenger_id) passengers
    FROM flight f
      JOIN booking_leg bl ON bl.flight_id = f.flight_id
      JOIN passenger p ON p.booking_id=bl.booking_id
    GROUP BY 1,2) a
```

So what is a long query, anyway?

A query is considered *long* when query selectivity is high for at least one large table; that is, almost every row contributes to the output, even when the output size is small.

What kind of optimization goals should we have for long queries? A common misconception explicitly refuted in this chapter is that if a query is long, there is no way to significantly improve its performance. Moreover, each co-author has had the joy of improving the performance of a long query by an order of *several hundred times*. Such improvements are made possible when two optimization strategies are applied:

1.   Avoid multiple table scans.

2.   Reduce the size of the result at the earliest possible stage.

The remainder of this chapter explains these techniques in detail and will describe several methods to achieve this goal.

Long Queries and Full Scans

Chapter 5 stated that short queries require the presence of indexes on columns included in search criteria. For long queries, it is the converse: indexes are not needed, and if tables are indexed, we want to ensure that indexes are not used.

Why are full table scans desirable for long queries? As shown in Figure 3-3, when the number of rows needed is large enough, index access will require more I/O operations. What percentage or number of records is "large enough" varies and depends on many different factors. By now, it should not be a surprise that most of the time, PostgreSQL estimates this percentage correctly.

Chapter 5 said something very similar about short queries. But "how large is large enough" is more difficult to estimate than "how small is small enough."

The estimate of how many records is too many evolves as better hardware, faster disks, and more powerful CPUs become available. For this reason, this book tries to avoid giving specific number thresholds that will necessarily change. To build representative cases for this chapter, several tables were built with hundreds of millions of rows of data. These are too large to be included with the `postgres_air` distribution. However, it would be unsurprising if some of the examples in this chapter are no longer representative in a few years.

Long Queries and Hash Joins

In a majority of examples in this chapter, a hash join algorithm is used. This is exactly what we hope to see in the execution plan of a long query. Why is a hash join preferable in this case? In Chapter 3, we estimated the costs of both nested loop and hash join algorithms.

For nested loops, the cost of the join of tables R and S is

```
cost(nl,R,S)=size(R) * size(S)+size(R)*size(S)/size(JA)
```

For a hash join, it is

```
cost(hash,R,S)=size(R)+size(S)+size(R)*size(S)/size(JA)
```

where JA represents the number of distinct values of the join attribute. As mentioned in Chapter 3, a third term, which represents the size of the result set, should be added to the cost of both algorithms, but for the nested loop algorithm, this value is significantly less than the cost of the join itself. For long queries, the size of R and S is large (because they are not significantly restricted), making the cost of nested loops significantly higher than the cost of a hash join.

Suppose database statistics estimate the size of table R to be 1,000,000 rows and the size of table S 2,000,000 rows and the join attribute JA has 100,000 distinct values. According to the formulas in Chapter 3, the size of the join result will be

```
Z=size(R) * size(S) / size(JA) =20,000,000
```

Then, the number of operations of the nested loop algorithm will be

```
Z+size(R)* size(S)=2,000,020,000,000
```

and the number of operations needed for the hash join algorithm will be

```
Z+size(R)+ size(S)==23,000,000
```

which is almost 10,000 times smaller. The planner will estimate the cost of these algorithms based on similar calculations and, of course, will choose the hash join algorithm.

Hash joins work best when the first argument fits into main memory. The size of memory available can be tuned with server parameters.

In some cases, a merge join algorithm is used, for example, in Figure 6-10 later in this chapter. Chapter 3 noted that a merge join can be more efficient when at least one of the tables is presorted. In this case, since unique values are being selected, sorting is indeed performed.

Summarizing Chapter 5 and this chapter, most of the time, index access works well with the nested loop algorithm (and vice versa), and sequential scans work well with a hash join.

Since PostgreSQL does not have optimizer hints, is there any way to force a specific join algorithm? As already mentioned multiple times, the best thing we can do is not to restrict the optimizer in the manner we write SQL statements.

Long Queries and the Order of Joins

Join order for small queries was discussed in Chapter 5. For short queries, the desired join order is the one that would prompt the usage of indexes with lower selectivity first.

Since we do not expect indexes to be used in long queries, does the order of joins make a difference? Perhaps surprisingly, it does. Large tables can differ in size significantly. Also, in practice, when selecting "almost all records," the word "almost" can mean as little as 30% and as much as 100%. Even when indexes are not used, the order of joins matters, because it is important to keep interim datasets as small as possible.

The most restrictive joins (i.e., joins that reduce the result set size the most) should be executed first.

The optimizer will most often choose the correct order; however, it is the responsibility of the developer to verify that the optimizer has chosen correctly.

What Is a Semi-join?

Often, the most restrictive join in a query is a *semi-join*. Let's pause to offer a formal definition.

A semi-join between two tables R and S returns rows from table R for which there is at least one row from table S with matching values in the joining columns.

To clarify, a semi-join is not an extra SQL operation; it is not valid SQL to write a statement like SELECT a.* FROM a SEMI JOIN b. A semi-join is a special kind of join that satisfies two specific conditions: First, only columns from the first table appear in the result set. Second, rows from the first table are not duplicated where there is more than one match in the second table. Most often, a semi-join doesn't include the JOIN keyword at all. The first and most common way of specifying a semi-join is shown in Listing 6-3. This query finds all flight information for flights with at least one booking.

Listing 6-3. Defining a semi-join using the EXISTS keyword

```
SELECT * FROM flight f WHERE EXISTS
  (SELECT flight_id FROM booking_leg WHERE flight_id=f.flight_id)
```

This query uses an implicit join with table booking_leg to filter records from the table flight. In other words, instead of supplying values for filtering, we use column values from another table.

An equivalent query showing another way to specify a semi-join is shown in Listing 6-4.

Listing 6-4. Defining a semi-join using the IN keyword

```
SELECT * FROM flight WHERE flight_id IN
  (SELECT flight_id FROM booking_leg)
```

How can these queries contain joins when neither uses the JOIN keyword? The answer is in the execution plan, which is identical for both queries, shown in Figure 6-1.

	QUERY PLAN
	text
1	Nested Loop Semi Join (cost=0.56..438436.84 rows=197629 width=71)
2	-> Seq Scan on flight f (cost=0.00..23642.76 rows=683176 width=71)
3	-> Index Only Scan using booking_leg_flight_id on booking_leg (cost=0.56..3.32 rows=91 width=4)
4	Index Cond: (flight_id = f.flight_id)

Figure 6-1. *Execution plan for a semi-join*

You can see a SEMI JOIN in this plan, even though the keyword JOIN was not used in the query itself.

Although these two ways of writing queries with semi-joins are semantically identical, in PostgreSQL, only the first one guarantees the presence of SEMI JOIN in the execution plan. The plans are identical for both queries in Listings 6-3 and 6-4, but in other cases, the optimizer may choose to rewrite it as a regular join. This decision is based both on the cardinality of the relationship between two tables and filter selectivity.

Semi-joins and Join Order

Since a semi-join may significantly reduce the size of the result set and, by definition, will never increase its size, semi-joins are often the most restrictive join in the query, and as stated earlier, the most restrictive join should be executed first.

Semi-joins never increase the size of the result set; check whether it is beneficial to apply them first.

Of course, this is possible only when a semi-join condition applies to the columns of a single table. In cases when a semi-join condition references more than one table, those tables must be joined before the semi-join is applied.

Consider the example in Listing 6-5, which shows bookings departing from airports located in the United States.

Listing 6-5. Order of joins when a semi-join is present

```
SELECT departure_airport,
       booking_id,
       is_returning
  FROM booking_leg bl
    JOIN flight f USING (flight_id)
  WHERE departure_airport
        IN (SELECT
                   airport_code
              FROM airport
             WHERE iso_country='US')
```

Figure 6-2 shows the execution plan for this query.

	QUERY PLAN text	🔒
1	Hash Join (cost=18963.54..433030.38 rows=3645943 width=9)	
2	Hash Cond: (bl.flight_id = f.flight_id)	
3	-> Seq Scan on booking_leg bl (cost=0.00..310506.66 rows=17893566 ...	
4	-> Hash (cost=17223.52..17223.52 rows=139202 width=8)	
5	-> Hash Join (cost=20.41..17223.52 rows=139202 width=8)	
6	Hash Cond: (f.departure_airport = airport.airport_code)	
7	-> Seq Scan on flight f (cost=0.00..15398.78 rows=683178 width...	
8	-> Hash (cost=18.65..18.65 rows=141 width=4)	
9	-> Seq Scan on airport (cost=0.00..18.65 rows=141 width=4)	
10	Filter: (iso_country = 'US'::text)	

Figure 6-2. *Execution plan for the query from Listing 6-5*

This execution plan does not show a semi-join operation, but rather a hash join, since there are no duplicates to remove. However, it's still a logical semi-join and most restrictive, so it is executed first. It is also worth taking a brief diversion to note the sequential scan on the `airport` table. The sequential scan is used because there is no index on the `iso_country` field. Let's create this index and see whether it will speed things up.

If this index exists

```
CREATE INDEX airport_iso_country
ON airport(iso_country);
```

...the query planner will use it, as shown in Figure 6-3. However, the execution time in this case will be the same or worse than the time with a sequential scan, because the index is not selective enough. Let's drop this index for now.

	QUERY PLAN text	🔒
1	Hash Join (cost=18961.90..433028.74 rows=3645943 width=9)	
2	Hash Cond: (bl.flight_id = f.flight_id)	
3	-> Seq Scan on booking_leg bl (cost=0.00..310506.66 rows=17893566 width=9)	
4	-> Hash (cost=17221.87..17221.87 rows=139202 width=8)	
5	-> Hash Join (cost=18.77..17221.87 rows=139202 width=8)	
6	Hash Cond: (f.departure_airport = airport.airport_code)	
7	-> Seq Scan on flight f (cost=0.00..15398.78 rows=683178 width=8)	
8	-> Hash (cost=17.01..17.01 rows=141 width=4)	
9	-> Bitmap Heap Scan on airport (cost=5.24..17.01 rows=141 width=4)	
10	Recheck Cond: (iso_country = 'US'::text)	
11	-> Bitmap Index Scan on airport_iso_country (cost=0.00..5.21 rows=141 width...	
12	Index Cond: (iso_country = 'US'::text)	

Figure 6-3. *Execution plan with an index scan*

More on Join Order

Let's take a look at a more complex example in Listing 6-6, of a long query with more than one semi-join. This query, like the previous, finds bookings for flights departing from the United States, but is limited to bookings updated since July 1, 2020. Since we do not have an index on the update_ts column of the booking table, let's create it now and see whether it will be used:

```
CREATE INDEX booking_update_ts ON booking  (update_ts);
```

Listing 6-6. Two semi-joins in one long query

```
SELECT
    departure_airport,
    booking_id, '
    is_returning
FROM booking_leg bl
JOIN flight f USING (flight_id)
```

113

```
WHERE departure_airport IN
                (SELECT airport_code
                 FROM airport
                 WHERE iso_country='US')
        AND bl.booking_id IN
            (SELECT booking_id FROM booking
                    WHERE update_ts>'2023-07-01')
```

The execution plan in Figure 6-4 shows that a semi-join on `airport.iso_country` is executed first. Just as in the preceding code, although we use the keyword IN, the optimizer uses JOIN, not SEMI JOIN, because there is no need to eliminate duplicates.

	QUERY PLAN text	🔒
1	Hash Join (cost=208078.19..674465.64 rows=1181514 width=9)	
2	Hash Cond: (bl.booking_id = booking.booking_id)	
3	-> Hash Join (cost=18963.54..433030.38 rows=3645943 width=9)	
4	Hash Cond: (bl.flight_id = f.flight_id)	
5	-> Seq Scan on booking_leg bl (cost=0.00..310506.66 rows=17893566 width=9)	
6	-> Hash (cost=17223.52..17223.52 rows=139202 width=8)	
7	-> Hash Join (cost=20.41..17223.52 rows=139202 width=8)	
8	Hash Cond: (f.departure_airport = airport.airport_code)	
9	-> Seq Scan on flight f (cost=0.00..15398.78 rows=683178 width=8)	
10	-> Hash (cost=18.65..18.65 rows=141 width=4)	
11	-> Seq Scan on airport (cost=0.00..18.65 rows=141 width=4)	
12	Filter: (iso_country = 'US'::text)	
13	-> Hash (cost=159111.20..159111.20 rows=1828756 width=8)	
14	-> Seq Scan on booking (cost=0.00..159111.20 rows=1828756 width=8)	
15	Filter: (update_ts > '2023-07-01 00:00:00-05'::timestamp with time zone)	

Figure 6-4. Execution plan with two semi-joins

Three things in this execution plan are worth noting. First, although index-based access is used to obtain some interim results and we can see that the nested loop join algorithm is used in this case, the final join is hash based, because a significant portion of both datasets is used. Second, the semi-join uses a table sequential scan. And even though this way we are reading all the rows from the `airport` table, the result set size is smaller than it would be if we would join flights with booking legs and filter by the airport location afterward. That's the benefit of the optimizer choosing the most restrictive semi-join.

Lastly, although there is an index on the `update_ts` column of the `booking` table, this index is not used, because the condition `update_ts>'2023-07-01'` covers almost half the rows in this table.

However, if we change the filtering criteria in this query (shown in Listing 6-6) and reduce the interval to `update_ts>'2023-08-10'`, the execution plan will change drastically—see Figure 6-5. In this new execution plan, we can see that not only is the filter on `update_ts` more restrictive but also the optimizer judges that it may be beneficial to use the index access.

	QUERY PLAN text	🔒
1	Hash Join (cost=102683.56..461173.60 rows=35654 width=9)	
2	Hash Cond: (bl.flight_id = f.flight_id)	
3	-> Hash Join (cost=83720.02..441197.33 rows=174985 width=9)	
4	Hash Cond: (bl.booking_id = booking.booking_id)	
5	-> Seq Scan on booking_leg bl (cost=0.00..310506.66 rows=17893566 width=9)	
6	-> Hash (cost=83030.18..83030.18 rows=55187 width=8)	
7	-> Bitmap Heap Scan on booking (cost=1036.13..83030.18 rows=55187 width=8)	
8	Recheck Cond: (update_ts > '2023-08-10 00:00:00-05'::timestamp with time zone)	
9	-> Bitmap Index Scan on booking_update_ts (cost=0.00..1022.33 rows=55187 width...	
10	Index Cond: (update_ts > '2023-08-10 00:00:00-05'::timestamp with time zone)	
11	-> Hash (cost=17223.52..17223.52 rows=139202 width=8)	
12	-> Hash Join (cost=20.41..17223.52 rows=139202 width=8)	
13	Hash Cond: (f.departure_airport = airport.airport_code)	
14	-> Seq Scan on flight f (cost=0.00..15398.78 rows=683178 width=8)	
15	-> Hash (cost=18.65..18.65 rows=141 width=4)	

Figure 6-5. *Execution plan with two semi-joins with a different selectivity*

Is index access to the booking table indeed the best option in this case? We can compare by blocking index access applying a column transformation to the update_ts column, rewriting the filter the following way: coalesce(update_ts, '2023-08-11')> '2023-08-10'.

As seen in Figure 6-6, this forces a sequential scan. And, in fact, blocking the index and forcing the sequential scan performs better than index access on larger time intervals. As the time interval is reduced further, index access has the advantage. '20230807' appears to be a tipping point; for all dates starting from '2023-08-08', the index access will work better.

	QUERY PLAN text	
1	Hash Join (cost=208938.50..675530.96 rows=1215314 width=9)	
2	Hash Cond: (bl.booking_id = booking.booking_id)	
3	-> Hash Join (cost=18963.54..433030.38 rows=3645943 width=9)	
4	Hash Cond: (bl.flight_id = f.flight_id)	
5	-> Seq Scan on booking_leg bl (cost=0.00..310506.66 rows=17893566 width=9)	
6	-> Hash (cost=17223.52..17223.52 rows=139202 width=8)	
7	-> Hash Join (cost=20.41..17223.52 rows=139202 width=8)	
8	Hash Cond: (f.departure_airport = airport.airport_code)	
9	-> Seq Scan on flight f (cost=0.00..15398.78 rows=683178 width=8)	
10	-> Hash (cost=18.65..18.65 rows=141 width=4)	
11	-> Seq Scan on airport (cost=0.00..18.65 rows=141 width=4)	
12	Filter: (iso_country = 'US'::text)	
13	-> Hash (cost=159112.23..159112.23 rows=1881099 width=8)	
14	-> Seq Scan on booking (cost=0.00..159112.23 rows=1881099 width=8)	
15	Filter: (COALESCE(update_ts, '2023-08-11 00:00:00-05'::timestamp with time zone) > '2023-08-10 00:00:00-05'::timestamp with time z...	

Figure 6-6. *Forcing a full scan*

What Is an Anti-join?

Just like it sounds, an ANTI JOIN is the opposite of a SEMI JOIN. Formally

---

An anti-join between two tables R and S returns rows from table R for which there are no rows from table S with a matching value in the joining column.

As in the case of a semi-join, there is no ANTI JOIN operator. Instead, a query with an anti-join can be written in two different ways, shown in Listings 6-7 and 6-8. These queries return flights that have no bookings.

Listing 6-7. Defining an anti-join using the NOT EXISTS keyword

```
SELECT * FROM flight f WHERE NOT EXISTS
  (SELECT flight_id FROM booking_leg WHERE flight_id=f.flight_id)
```

Listing 6-8. Defining an anti-join using NOT IN

```
SELECT * FROM flight WHERE flight_id NOT IN
  (SELECT flight_id FROM booking_leg)
```

Just as with semi-joins, although both ways of writing a query with an anti-join are semantically equivalent, in PostgreSQL, only the NOT EXISTS version guarantees the anti-join in the execution plan. Figures 6-7 and 6-8 show the execution plan for Listings 6-7 and 6-8, respectively. In this particular case, both queries will be executed in approximately the same time, and the plan with an anti-join is only slightly faster. There are no generic guidelines for which syntax for an anti-join is better. Developers should try both ways to see which will perform better in their use case.

	Data Output	Explain	Messages	Notifications

	QUERY PLAN text	
1	Nested Loop Anti Join (cost=0.56..429448.81 rows=543600 width=71)	
2	-> Seq Scan on flight f (cost=0.00..23642.76 rows=683176 width=71)	
3	-> Index Only Scan using booking_leg_flight_id on booking_leg (cost=0.56..3.48 rows=128 width=4)	
4	Index Cond: (flight_id = f.flight_id)	

Figure 6-7. *Execution plan with an anti-join*

	QUERY PLAN text	
1	Seq Scan on flight (cost=0.00..232232347044.02 rows=341588 width=71)	
2	Filter: (NOT (SubPlan 1))	
3	SubPlan 1	
4	-> Materialize (cost=0.00..635290.62 rows=17828108 width=4)	
5	-> Seq Scan on booking_leg (cost=0.00..476508.08 rows=17828108 width=4)	

Figure 6-8. *Execution plan without an anti-join*

Semi- and Anti-joins Using the JOIN Operator

At this point, an astute reader might wonder why we can't use an explicit join and specify exactly what we need. Why use the EXISTS and IN operators? The answer is it's possible and, in some cases, it might indeed be a better solution than using semi-joins. But it takes care to construct a logically equivalent query.

The queries in Listings 6-3 and 6-4 are semantically equivalent, but Listing 6-9 is not. Recall that Listings 6-3 and 6-4 return information for flights that have at least one booking.

Listing 6-9. Join returning duplicates

```
SELECT f.*
FROM flight f
JOIN booking_leg bl USING (flight_id)
```

By contrast, Listing 6-9 will return as many rows for each flight as the number of bookings with the corresponding flight_id. To return only one record per flight, like the original query, it would need to be rewritten as shown in Listing 6-10.

Listing 6-10. Query with a join returning one row per flight

```
SELECT *
FROM flight f
JOIN (select distinct flight_id FROM booking_leg) bl USING (flight_id)
```

The execution plan for this query is shown in Figure 6-9, and it does not contain a semi-join.

	QUERY PLAN text	
1	Hash Join (cost=40189.02..828769.06 rows=139576 width=71)	
2	Hash Cond: (booking_leg.flight_id = f.flight_id)	
3	-> Unique (cost=0.56..777720.45 rows=139576 width=4)	
4	-> Index Only Scan using booking_leg_flight_id on booking_leg (cost=0.56..733150.18 rows=17828108 width=4)	
5	-> Hash (cost=23642.76..23642.76 rows=683176 width=71)	
6	-> Seq Scan on flight f (cost=0.00..23642.76 rows=683176 width=71)	

Figure 6-9. *Execution plan for the query in Listing 6-10*

It is not obvious from the execution plan whether this query will be faster or slower than the query with a semi-join. In practice, it runs more than twice as fast as the query from Listing 6-3.

If you only need the IDs of the flights that have a booking, it may be enough to run the query in Listing 6-11.

Listing 6-11. Query with a join returning only flight_id with one row per flight

```
SELECT flight_id
FROM flight f
JOIN (select distinct flight_id FROM booking_leg) bl USING (flight_id)
```

The execution plan for this query, shown in Figure 6-10, differs significantly from the one in Figure 6-9, and the execution is even faster.

| | QUERY PLAN | 🔒 |
	text	
1	Merge Join (cost=0.99..819305.18 rows=139576 width=4)	
2	Merge Cond: (f.flight_id = booking_leg.flight_id)	
3	-> Index Only Scan using flight_pkey on flight f (cost=0.42..36736.33 rows=683176 width=4)	
4	-> Unique (cost=0.56..777720.45 rows=139576 width=4)	
5	-> Index Only Scan using booking_leg_flight_id on booking_leg (cost=0.56..733150.18 rows=17828108 width=4)	

Figure 6-10. *Execution plan with a merge join*

What about anti-joins? An anti-join cannot create duplicates, which means that an OUTER JOIN with subsequent filtering of NULL values can be used. Thus, the query in Listing 6-7 is equivalent to the query in Listing 6-12.

Listing 6-12. Outer join with filtering of NULL values

```
SELECT f.flight_id
FROM flight f
LEFT OUTER JOIN booking_leg bl USING (flight_id)
WHERE bl.flight_id IS NULL
```

The execution plan for this query includes an anti-join—see Figure 6-11.

	QUERY PLAN text	🔒
1	Nested Loop Anti Join (cost=0.56..429448.81 rows=543600 width=4)	
2	-> Seq Scan on flight f (cost=0.00..23642.76 rows=683176 width=4)	
3	-> Index Only Scan using booking_leg_flight_id on booking_leg bl (cost=0.56..3.48 rows=128 width=4)	
4	Index Cond: (flight_id = f.flight_id)	

***Figure 6-11.** Execution plan for the query in Listing 6-12*

The optimizer recognizes this construct and rewrites it to an anti-join. This optimizer behavior is stable and can be relied upon.

When Is It Necessary to Specify Join Order?

So far, the optimizer has chosen the best join order without any intervention from the SQL developer, but this isn't always the case.

Long queries are more likely in OLAP systems. In other words, a long query is most likely an analytical report that most likely joins a number of tables. This number, as anyone who has worked with OLAP systems can attest, can be massive. When the number of tables involved in a query becomes too large, the optimizer no longer attempts to find the best possible join order. Although most system parameters are out of the scope of this book, there is one worth mentioning: `join_collapse_limit`.

This parameter caps the number of tables in a join that will be still processed by the cost-based optimizer. The default value of this parameter is 8. This means that if the number of tables in a join is eight or fewer, the optimizer will perform a selection of candidate plans, compare plans, and choose the best one. But if the number of tables is nine or more, it will simply execute the joins in the order the tables are listed in the SELECT statement.

Why not set this parameter to the highest possible value? There is no official upper limit to this parameter, so it can be the maximum integer, which is 2147483647. However, the higher you set this parameter, the more time will be spent choosing the best plan. The number of possible plans to consider for a query joining n tables is n! Thus, when n is 8, a maximum of 40,000 plans can be compared. If n is increased to 10, the number of plans to consider will increase to three million, and the number rises predictably from there—when this parameter is set to 20, the total number of plans is already too big to fit the integer. One of us once observed a data scientist locally changing this parameter to 30, to deal with a query with 30 joins. The results were excruciating—not only did the execution stall but even the EXPLAIN command couldn't return a result.

This is easy to experiment with; this parameter can be set locally on a session level, so run the command

```
SET join_collapse_limit = 10
```

and check the runtime of the EXPLAIN command.

In addition, recall that table statistics are not available for intermediate results, which may cause the optimizer to choose a suboptimal join order. If the SQL developer knows a better order of joins, it is possible to force the desired join order by setting join_collapse_limit to 1. In this case, the optimizer will generate a plan in which the joins will be executed in the order they appear in the SELECT statement.

Force a specific join order by setting the join_collapse_limit parameter to 1.

For example, if the command in Listing 6-13 is executed (i.e., an EXPLAIN on the query in Listing 6-6), the execution plan in Figure 6-12 shows that joins are executed exactly in the order they are listed, and the index on update_ts is not used (which in this case affects performance negatively).

Listing 6-13. Partially disabling cost-based optimization

```
SET join_collapse_limit=1;
EXPLAIN
  SELECT
      departure_airport,
      booking_id,
     is_returning
FROM booking_leg bl
JOIN flight f USING (flight_id)
WHERE departure_airport IN (
              SELECT
                    airport_code
              FROM airport
```

```
WHERE iso_country='US')
    AND bl.booking_id IN (
        SELECT
            booking_id
        FROM booking
        WHERE update_ts>'2023-08-08')
```

	QUERY PLAN text	
1	Hash Join (cost=164521.00..756238.45 rows=86548 width=9)	
2	Hash Cond: (bl.booking_id = booking.booking_id)	
3	-> Hash Join (cost=26627.92..608774.76 rows=3645943 width=9)	
4	Hash Cond: (f.departure_airport = airport.airport_code)	
5	-> Hash Join (cost=26607.50..561496.06 rows=17893566 width=9)	
6	Hash Cond: (bl.flight_id = f.flight_id)	
7	-> Seq Scan on booking_leg bl (cost=0.00..310506.66 rows=17893566 width=9)	
8	-> Hash (cost=15398.78..15398.78 rows=683178 width=8)	
9	-> Seq Scan on flight f (cost=0.00..15398.78 rows=683178 width=8)	
10	-> Hash (cost=18.65..18.65 rows=141 width=4)	
11	-> Seq Scan on airport (cost=0.00..18.65 rows=141 width=4)	
12	Filter: (iso_country = 'US'::text)	
13	-> Hash (cost=136218.57..136218.57 rows=133961 width=8)	
14	-> Bitmap Heap Scan on booking (cost=2510.63..136218.57 rows=133961 width=8)	
15	Recheck Cond: (update_ts > '2023-08-08 00:00:00-05'::timestamp with time zone)	
16	-> Bitmap Index Scan on booking_update_ts (cost=0.00..2477.14 rows=133961 width...	
17	Index Cond: (update_ts > '2023-08-08 00:00:00-05'::timestamp with time zone)	

Figure 6-12. *Execution plan with disabled cost-based optimization*

Another way to force a specific join order is using *common table expressions*, which will be discussed in Chapter 7.

Grouping: Filter First, Group Last

In Chapter 5, we mentioned that for short queries, grouping is not time-consuming. For long queries, the way we approach grouping may have a very significant impact on performance. Suboptimal decisions regarding the point at which grouping is performed often become a major source of overall query slowness.

Listing 6-14 shows a query that calculates the average price of every trip and the total number of passengers for each flight for all flights with any bookings.

Listing 6-14. Average ticket price and total number of passengers per flight

```
SELECT
      bl.flight_id,
      departure_airport,
      (avg(price))::numeric (7,2) AS avg_price,
      count(DISTINCT passenger_id) AS num_passengers
FROM booking b
JOIN booking_leg bl USING (booking_id)
JOIN flight f USING (flight_id)
JOIN passenger p USING (booking_id)
GROUP BY 1,2
```

To calculate these numbers for just one flight, a common anti-pattern is the query in Listing 6-15.

Listing 6-15. Average ticket price and total number of passengers on a specific flight

```
SELECT *
FROM
      (SELECT
            bl.flight_id,
            departure_airport,
            (avg(price))::numeric (7,2) AS avg_price,
            count(DISTINCT passenger_id) AS num_passengers
      FROM booking b
      JOIN booking_leg bl USING (booking_id)
```

```
       JOIN flight f USING (flight_id)
       JOIN passenger p USING (booking_id)
       GROUP BY 1,2) a
WHERE flight_id=222183
```

In this query, we select the data for one flight from an inline SELECT. Earlier versions of PostgreSQL could not process such constructs efficiently. The database engine would first execute the inner SELECT with grouping and only then select the line that corresponds to the specific flight. To make sure the query is executed efficiently, one would need to write it as shown in Listing 6-16.

Listing 6-16. Pushing a condition inside the GROUP BY

```
SELECT
       bl.flight_id,
       departure_airport,
       (avg(price))::numeric (7,2) AS avg_price,
        count(DISTINCT passenger_id) AS num_passengers
FROM booking b
JOIN booking_leg bl USING (booking_id)
JOIN flight f USING (flight_id)
JOIN passenger p USING (booking_id)
WHERE flight_id=222183
GROUP BY 1,2
```

But now, due to ongoing improvements to the optimizer, both queries will be executed using the execution plan in Figure 6-13. This plan uses index access, and the execution time for this query is about two seconds.

	Data Output Explain Messages Notifications
	QUERY PLAN
	text
1	GroupAggregate (cost=1201.39..1205.93 rows=89 width=30)
2	Group Key: bl.flight_id, f.departure_airport
3	-> Sort (cost=1201.39..1202.03 rows=256 width=18)
4	Sort Key: f.departure_airport
5	-> Nested Loop (cost=6.54..1191.15 rows=256 width=18)
6	-> Nested Loop (cost=6.11..1116.80 rows=89 width=26)
7	-> Index Scan using flight_pkey on flight f (cost=0.42..8.44 rows=1 width=8)
8	Index Cond: (flight_id = 222183)
9	-> Nested Loop (cost=5.68..1107.47 rows=89 width=22)
10	-> Bitmap Heap Scan on booking_leg bl (cost=5.25..355.42 rows=89 width=8)
11	Recheck Cond: (flight_id = 222183)
12	-> Bitmap Index Scan on booking_leg_flight_id (cost=0.00..5.23 rows=89 width=0)
13	Index Cond: (flight_id = 222183)
14	-> Index Scan using booking_pkey on booking b (cost=0.43..8.45 rows=1 width=14)
15	Index Cond: (booking_id = bl.booking_id)
16	-> Index Scan using passenger_booking_id on passenger p (cost=0.43..0.75 rows=9 width=8)
17	Index Cond: (booking_id = b.booking_id)

Figure 6-13. *Execution plan for one flight*

For all columns used in the GROUP BY clause, filtering should be pushed inside the grouping.

For PostgreSQL 12 and later, the optimizer takes care of this rewrite, but it may still be required in older versions.

Let's look at another example. Listing 6-17 calculates the same numbers (average price and number of customers) for all flights departing from ORD.

Listing 6-17. Select for multiple flights

```
SELECT
     flight_id,
      avg_price,
      num_passengers
FROM (SELECT
                  bl.flight_id,
      departure_airport,
      (avg(price))::numeric (7,2) AS avg_price,
      count(DISTINCT passenger_id) AS num_passengers
FROM booking b
JOIN booking_leg bl USING (booking_id)
JOIN flight f USING (flight_id)
JOIN passenger p USING (booking_id)
GROUP BY 1,2 )a  WHERE departure_airport='ORD'
```

The execution plan for this query is shown in Figure 6-14. This query takes about 1.5 minutes to execute. It is a large query, and most of the joins are executed using the hash join algorithm. The important part is that the condition on departure_airport is applied first before the grouping.

	QUERY PLAN
	text
1	Subquery Scan on a (cost=899526.09..935621.26 rows=962538 width=26)
2	-> GroupAggregate (cost=899526.09..925995.88 rows=962538 width=30)
3	Group Key: bl.flight_id, f.departure_airport
4	-> Sort (cost=899526.09..901932.43 rows=962538 width=18)
5	Sort Key: bl.flight_id
6	-> Nested Loop (cost=9545.27..784126.73 rows=962538 width=18)
7	Join Filter: (b.booking_id = p.booking_id)
8	-> Nested Loop (cost=9544.84..532480.61 rows=334023 width=26)
9	-> Hash Join (cost=9544.41..367021.97 rows=334023 width=12)
10	Hash Cond: (bl.flight_id = f.flight_id)
11	-> Seq Scan on booking_leg bl (cost=0.00..310506.66 rows=17893566 width=8)
12	-> Hash (cost=9384.99..9384.99 rows=12753 width=8)
13	-> Bitmap Heap Scan on flight f (cost=243.26..9384.99 rows=12753 width=8)
14	Recheck Cond: (departure_airport = 'ORD'::bpchar)
15	-> Bitmap Index Scan on flight_departure_airport (cost=0.00..240.07 rows=12753 width=0)
16	Index Cond: (departure_airport = 'ORD'::bpchar)
17	-> Index Scan using booking_pkey on booking b (cost=0.43..0.50 rows=1 width=14)
18	Index Cond: (booking_id = bl.booking_id)
19	-> Index Scan using passenger_booking_id on passenger p (cost=0.43..0.64 rows=9 width=8)
20	Index Cond: (booking_id = bl.booking_id)

Figure 6-14. *Execution plan for Listing 6-17*

However, more complex filtering conditions can't be pushed inside grouping. Listing 6-18 calculates the same statistics, but the list of flight_id is not passed directly but is selected from the booking_leg table.

Listing 6-18. Condition can't be pushed inside the grouping

```
SELECT
      flight_id,
      avg_price,
      num_passengers
FROM (SELECT
                  bl.flight_id,
                  departure_airport,
```

```
                    (avg(price))::numeric (7,2) AS avg_price,
                    count(DISTINCT passenger_id) AS num_passengers
      FROM booking b
      JOIN booking_leg bl USING (booking_id)
      JOIN flight f USING (flight_id)
      JOIN passenger p USING (booking_id)
      GROUP BY 1,2 )a
WHERE flight_id in
(SELECT
      flight_id
 FROM flight
WHERE scheduled_departure BETWEEN '07-03-2023' AND '07-05-2023');
```

The execution plan (Figure 6-15) shows that grouping is done first and filtering is applied to the result of grouping. This means that, first, the calculations are performed for all flights in the system and then the subset is selected. The total execution time for this query is ten minutes.

	QUERY PLAN text
1	Merge Join (cost=12639813.37..14715429.51 rows=586141 width=26)
2	Merge Cond: (bl.flight_id = flight.flight_id)
3	-> GroupAggregate (cost=12630373.17..14053302.95 rows=51742901 width=30)
4	Group Key: bl.flight_id, f.departure_airport
5	-> Sort (cost=12630373.17..12759730.42 rows=51742901 width=18)
6	Sort Key: bl.flight_id, f.departure_airport
7	-> Hash Join (cost=1080689.84..2817439.82 rows=51742901 width=18)
8	Hash Cond: (b.booking_id = bl.booking_id)
9	-> Hash Join (cost=243101.21..775846.44 rows=16318749 width=22)
10	Hash Cond: (p.booking_id = b.booking_id)
11	-> Seq Scan on passenger p (cost=0.00..334860.49 rows=16318749 width=8)
12	-> Hash (cost=145003.98..145003.98 rows=5643298 width=14)
13	-> Seq Scan on booking b (cost=0.00..145003.98 rows=5643298 width=14)
14	-> Hash (cost=526548.06..526548.06 rows=17893566 width=12)
15	-> Hash Join (cost=26607.50..526548.06 rows=17893566 width=12)
16	Hash Cond: (bl.flight_id = f.flight_id)
17	-> Seq Scan on booking_leg bl (cost=0.00..310506.66 rows=17893566 width=8)
18	-> Hash (cost=15398.78..15398.78 rows=683178 width=8)
19	-> Seq Scan on flight f (cost=0.00..15398.78 rows=683178 width=8)
20	-> Sort (cost=9440.20..9459.54 rows=7739 width=4)
21	Sort Key: flight.flight_id
22	-> Bitmap Heap Scan on flight (cost=115.75..8940.34 rows=7739 width=4)
23	Recheck Cond: ((scheduled_departure >= '2023-07-03 00:00:00-05'::timestamp with time zone) AND (scheduled_departure <= '2023-07-05 00:00:00-05'::timestamp w
24	-> Bitmap Index Scan on flight_scheduled_departure (cost=0.00..113.81 rows=7739 width=0)
25	Index Cond: ((scheduled_departure >= '2023-07-03 00:00:00-05'::timestamp with time zone) AND (scheduled_departure <= '2023-07-05 00:00:00-05'::timestamp w

Figure 6-15. *Execution plan for Listing 6-18*

The query in Listing 6-18 is an example of what we call *pessimization*—using practices that guarantee slowing down the execution of a query. It's easy to see why this query is written the way it is. First, a database developer figures out *how* to perform certain calculations or how to select specific values, and then they apply a filter to the result. Thus, they limit the optimizer to a certain order of operations, which in this case is not optimal.

Instead, the filtering can be done in the inner WHERE clause. When this change is made, there's no longer a need for an inline SELECT—see Listing 6-19.

Listing 6-19. Condition is pushed inside grouping

```
SELECT bl.flight_id,
       departure_airport,
       (avg(price))::numeric (7,2) AS avg_price,
       count(DISTINCT passenger_id) AS num_passengers
FROM booking b
```

```
JOIN booking_leg bl USING (booking_id)
JOIN flight f USING (flight_id)
JOIN passenger p USING (booking_id)
        WHERE scheduled_departure
        BETWEEN '07-03-2023' AND '07-05-2023'
GROUP BY 1,2
```

The execution time is about one minute, and the execution plan is shown in Figure 6-16. This can be expressed as the generalization of the technique explained in the previous example.

	QUERY PLAN text
1	GroupAggregate (cost=682651.29..698770.14 rows=586140 width=30)
2	Group Key: bl.flight_id, f.departure_airport
3	-> Sort (cost=682651.29..684116.64 rows=586140 width=18)
4	Sort Key: bl.flight_id, f.departure_airport
5	-> Nested Loop (cost=9037.94..614473.98 rows=586140 width=18)
6	Join Filter: (b.booking_id = p.booking_id)
7	-> Nested Loop (cost=9037.51..462442.83 rows=202697 width=26)
8	-> Hash Join (cost=9037.07..366514.63 rows=202697 width=12)
9	Hash Cond: (bl.flight_id = f.flight_id)
10	-> Seq Scan on booking_leg bl (cost=0.00..310506.66 rows=17893566 width=8)
11	-> Hash (cost=8940.34..8940.34 rows=7739 width=8)
12	-> Bitmap Heap Scan on flight f (cost=115.75..8940.34 rows=7739 width=8)
13	Recheck Cond: ((scheduled_departure >= '2023-07-03 00:00:00-05'::timestamp with time zone) AND (scheduled_departure <= '2023-07-05 00:00:00-05'::timestamp wi
14	-> Bitmap Index Scan on flight_scheduled_departure (cost=0.00..113.81 rows=7739 width=0)
15	Index Cond: ((scheduled_departure >= '2023-07-03 00:00:00-05'::timestamp with time zone) AND (scheduled_departure <= '2023-07-05 00:00:00-05'::timestamp w
16	-> Index Scan using booking_pkey on booking b (cost=0.43..0.47 rows=1 width=14)
17	Index Cond: (booking_id = bl.booking_id)
18	-> Index Scan using passenger_booking_id on passenger p (cost=0.43..0.64 rows=9 width=8)
19	Index Cond: (booking_id = bl.booking_id)

Figure 6-16. *Execution plan with filtering pushed inside grouping*

Filter rows are not needed for an aggregate prior to grouping.

Even the optimal execution of this query is not instantaneous, but it is the best we can achieve. Now is a good time to recall that optimization goals should be realistic. A long query on large data volumes can't be executed in a fraction of a second, even when executed optimally. The key is to use as few rows as necessary, but no fewer.

Grouping: Group First, Select Last

In some cases, the course of actions should be the opposite: GROUP BY should be executed as early as possible, followed by other operations. As you might have already guessed, this order of actions is desirable when grouping will reduce the size of the intermediate dataset.

The query in Listing 6-20 calculates the number of passengers departing from each city by month. In this case, it is not possible to reduce the number of rows needed, as all flights are used in the calculation.

Listing 6-20. Calculating number of passengers per city per month

```
SELECT
    city,
    date_trunc('month', scheduled_departure) AS month,
    count(*)  passengers
FROM airport   a
JOIN flight f ON airport_code = departure_airport
JOIN booking_leg l ON f.flight_id =l.flight_id
JOIN boarding_pass b ON b.booking_leg_id = l.booking_leg_id
GROUP BY 1,2
ORDER BY 3 DESC
```

The execution time for this query is 25 seconds, and the execution plan is in Figure 6-17.

	QUERY PLAN
◢	text
1	Sort (cost=11691560.21..11754793.94 rows=25293490 width=24)
2	Sort Key: (count(*)) DESC
3	-> GroupAggregate (cost=6456183.43..7025286.95 rows=25293490 width=24)
4	Group Key: a.city, (date_trunc('month'::text, f.scheduled_departure))
5	-> Sort (cost=6456183.43..6519417.15 rows=25293490 width=16)
6	Sort Key: a.city, (date_trunc('month'::text, f.scheduled_departure))
7	-> Hash Join (cost=804544.88..2049270.66 rows=25293490 width=16)
8	Hash Cond: (f.departure_airport = a.airport_code)
9	-> Hash Join (cost=804519.89..1919194.04 rows=25293490 width=12)
10	Hash Cond: (l.flight_id = f.flight_id)
11	-> Hash Join (cost=769001.43..1616337.75 rows=25293490 width=4)
12	Hash Cond: (b.booking_leg_id = l.booking_leg_id)
13	-> Seq Scan on boarding_pass b (cost=0.00..513692.90 rows=25293490 width=8)
14	-> Hash (cost=476508.08..476508.08 rows=17828108 width=8)
15	-> Seq Scan on booking_leg l (cost=0.00..476508.08 rows=17828108 width=8)
16	-> Hash (cost=23642.76..23642.76 rows=683176 width=16)
17	-> Seq Scan on flight f (cost=0.00..23642.76 rows=683176 width=16)
18	-> Hash (cost=16.66..16.66 rows=666 width=12)
19	-> Seq Scan on airport a (cost=0.00..16.66 rows=666 width=12)

Figure 6-17. *Execution plan with grouping done last*

The execution of this query is significantly improved with a nontrivial rewrite, as shown in Listing 6-21.

Listing 6-21. Query rewrite that forces grouping be done first

```
SELECT
    city,
    date_trunc('month', scheduled_departure),
    sum(passengers)  passengers
FROM airport  a
JOIN flight f ON airport_code = departure_airport
JOIN (
    SELECT flight_id, count(*) passengers
    FROM booking_leg l
    JOIN boarding_pass b USING (booking_leg_id)
    GROUP BY flight_id
    ) cnt
```

```
USING (flight_id)
GROUP BY 1,2
ORDER BY 3 DESC
```

What is happening here? First, the number of departing passengers is summed for each flight in the inline view cnt. After, the result is joined with the flight table to retrieve airport code and then joined with the airport table to find the city where each airport is located. After this, the flight totals are summed by city. This way, the execution time is 15 seconds. The execution plan is shown in Figure 6-18.

	QUERY PLAN text	
1	Sort (cost=3165092.63..3165617.34 rows=209882 width=49)	
2	Sort Key: (sum(cnt.passengers)) DESC	
3	-> GroupAggregate (cost=3134117.83..3139364.88 rows=209882 width=49)	
4	Group Key: a.city, (date_trunc('month'::text, f.scheduled_departure))	
5	-> Sort (cost=3134117.83..3134642.54 rows=209882 width=25)	
6	Sort Key: a.city, (date_trunc('month'::text, f.scheduled_departure))	
7	-> Hash Join (cost=2901723.58..3110542.59 rows=209882 width=25)	
8	Hash Cond: (f.departure_airport = a.airport_code)	
9	-> Hash Join (cost=2901698.01..3109438.00 rows=209882 width=20)	
10	Hash Cond: (cnt.flight_id = f.flight_id)	
11	-> Subquery Scan on cnt (cost=2874423.51..3076226.55 rows=209882 width=12)	
12	-> HashAggregate (cost=2874423.51..3074127.73 rows=209882 width=12)	
13	Group Key: l.flight_id	
14	Planned Partitions: 4	
15	-> Hash Join (cost=604073.24..1451664.58 rows=25293492 width=4)	
16	Hash Cond: (b.booking_leg_id = l.booking_leg_id)	
17	-> Seq Scan on boarding_pass b (cost=0.00..513692.92 rows=25293492 widt...	
18	-> Hash (cost=310506.66..310506.66 rows=17893566 width=8)	
19	-> Seq Scan on booking_leg l (cost=0.00..310506.66 rows=17893566 widt...	
20	-> Hash (cost=15398.78..15398.78 rows=683178 width=16)	
21	-> Seq Scan on flight f (cost=0.00..15398.78 rows=683178 width=16)	
22	-> Hash (cost=16.92..16.92 rows=692 width=13)	
23	-> Seq Scan on airport a (cost=0.00..16.92 rows=692 width=13)	

Figure 6-18. *Execution plan with grouping forced to be first*

133

Using SET Operations

We rarely use set theoretical operations (UNION, EXCEPT, etc.) in SQL queries. For large queries, however, these operations may prompt the optimizer to choose more efficient algorithms.

Use set operations to (sometimes) prompt an alternative execution plan and improve readability.

Often, we can

- Use EXCEPT instead of NOT EXISTS and NOT IN.

- Use INTERSECT instead of EXISTS and IN.

- Use UNION instead of complex selection criteria with OR.

Sometimes, there can be significant performance gains, and sometimes the execution time changes only slightly, but the code becomes cleaner and easier to maintain. Listing 6-22 shows a rewrite of the query in Listing 6-8, returning flights with no bookings.

Listing 6-22. Using EXCEPT instead of NOT IN

```
SELECT
      flight_id
FROM flight f
EXCEPT
SELECT
      flight_id
FROM booking_leg
```

Execution time is one minute and three seconds, which is almost twice as fast as an anti-join.

The execution plan with the EXCEPT operation is shown in Figure 6-19.

	QUERY PLAN Read-only column
1	SetOp Except (cost=3518478.09..3611034.51 rows=683176 width=8)
2	-> Sort (cost=3518478.09..3564756.30 rows=18511284 width=8)
3	Sort Key: "*SELECT* 1".flight_id
4	-> Append (cost=0.00..777820.10 rows=18511284 width=8)
5	-> Subquery Scan on "*SELECT* 1" (cost=0.00..30474.52 rows=683176 width=8)
6	-> Seq Scan on flight f (cost=0.00..23642.76 rows=683176 width=4)
7	-> Subquery Scan on "*SELECT* 2" (cost=0.00..654789.16 rows=17828108 width=8)
8	-> Seq Scan on booking_leg (cost=0.00..476508.08 rows=17828108 width=4)

Figure 6-19. *Execution plan with EXCEPT*

Listing 6-23 shows a rewrite of the query in Listing 6-4 using set operations, showing all flights with a booking.

Listing 6-23. Using INTERSECT instead of IN

```
SELECT
    flight_id
FROM flight f
INTERSECT
SELECT
    flight_id
FROM booking_leg
```

The execution time of this query is 49 seconds. This is less than the version of the query using the IN keyword and approximately equal to the runtime of the query with an index-only scan (see Listing 6-10). The execution plan is shown in Figure 6-20.

	QUERY PLAN
	text
1	HashSetOp Intersect (cost=0.00..824098.31 rows=139576 width=8)
2	-> Append (cost=0.00..777820.10 rows=18511284 width=8)
3	-> Subquery Scan on "*SELECT* 2" (cost=0.00..654789.16 rows=17828108 width=8)
4	-> Seq Scan on booking_leg (cost=0.00..476508.08 rows=17828108 width=4)
5	-> Subquery Scan on "*SELECT* 1" (cost=0.00..30474.52 rows=683176 width=8)
6	-> Seq Scan on flight f (cost=0.00..23642.76 rows=683176 width=4)

Figure 6-20. *Execution plan with INTERSECT*

We rarely need to rewrite complex selection criteria with OR into set theoretical UNION ALL, because most of the time the PostgreSQL optimizer does a decent job analyzing such criteria and making use of all suitable indexes. However, sometimes rewriting this way makes code more maintainable, especially when the query contains a large number of different selection criteria connected with OR. Listing 6-24 is a query that calculates the number of passengers on delayed flights from FRA using two different sets of selection criteria. The first group is passengers on flights delayed by more than an hour, with changes to the boarding pass more than 30 minutes after the scheduled departure. The second is passengers on flights delayed by more than a half hour but less than an hour.

Listing 6-24. Query with complex selection criteria with OR

```
SELECT
    CASE
            WHEN actual_departure>scheduled_departure + interval '1 hour'
                THEN 'Late group 1'
            ELSE 'Late group 2'
    END AS grouping,
    flight_id,
    count(*) AS num_passengers
FROM boarding_pass bp
JOIN booking_leg bl USING (booking_leg_id)
JOIN booking b USING (booking_id)
JOIN flight f USING (flight_id)
WHERE departure_airport='FRA'
        AND actual_departure>'2023-07-01'
```

136

```
    AND
      (
            (actual_departure>scheduled_departure + interval '30 minute'
              AND actual_departure<=scheduled_departure + interval '1 hour'
            )
          OR
          (actual_departure>scheduled_departure + interval '1 hour'
              AND bp.update_ts >scheduled_departure + interval '30 minute'
              )
        )
GROUP BY 1,2
```

The rewrite of this query using UNION ALL is shown in Listing 6-25. The execution time difference is not significant (about three seconds), but the code is more maintainable.

Listing 6-25. Rewrite of a complex condition with OR using UNION ALL

```
SELECT
    'Late group 1' AS grouping,
    flight_id,
    count(*) AS num_passengers
FROM boarding_pass bp
JOIN booking_leg bl USING (booking_leg_id)
JOIN booking b USING (booking_id)
JOIN flight f USING (flight_id)
WHERE departure_airport='FRA'
    AND actual_departure>scheduled_departure + interval '1 hour'
    AND bp.update_ts  > scheduled_departure + interval '30 minutes'
   AND actual_departure>'2023-07-01'
GROUP BY 1,2
UNION ALL
SELECT
    'Late group 2' AS grouping,
    flight_id,
    count(*) AS num_passengers
FROM boarding_pass bp
```

```
JOIN booking_leg bl USING(booking_leg_id)
JOIN booking b USING (booking_id)
JOIN flight f USING (flight_id)
WHERE departure_airport='FRA'
    AND  actual_departure>scheduled_departure + interval '30 minute'
    AND  actual_departure<=scheduled_departure + interval '1 hour'
    AND actual_departure>'2023-07-01'
GROUP BY 1,2
```

It's worth noting that with large queries you always need to take into consideration how much RAM you have available. For both hash joins and set theoretical operations, if the participating datasets can't fit into main memory, the execution speed increases significantly.

Avoiding Multiple Scans

Another source of slowness in long queries is the presence of multiple table scans. This common problem is the direct result of imperfect design. Designs can be fixed, at least theoretically. But since we often find ourselves in situations where we can't control the design, we are going to suggest ways to write performant queries even on an imperfect schema.

The situation that we are modeling in our `postgres_air` schema is not uncommon in the real world. The system is already up and running, and all of a sudden, we need to store some additional information for objects that are already present in the database.

For the past 30 years, the easiest solution in such cases is to use an entity-attribute-value (EAV) table, which can store arbitrary attributes—those needed now and any that will eventually be needed. In the `postgres_air` schema, this pattern is implemented in the table `custom_field`. For each passenger, a passport number, a passport expiration date, and the country that issued the passport are stored. The attributes are accordingly named `'passport_num'`, `'passport_exp_date'`, and `'passport_country'`.

This table is not included into the postgres_air distribution. To run the example locally, execute the following script from the postgres_air GitHub repository:

https://github.com/hettie-d/postgres_air/blob/main/tables/custom_field.sql

Now, imagine a request for a report that lists passenger names and their passport information. Listing 6-26 is a typical suggested solution: the table custom_field is scanned three times! In order to avoid spill to the disk, passengers are limited to the first five million, which allows us to show the true ratio of execution times. The execution plan in Figure 6-21 confirms three table scans, and the execution time for this query is five minutes.

Listing 6-26. Multiple scans of a large table

```
SELECT
    first_name,
    last_name,
    pn.custom_field_value AS passport_num,
    pe.custom_field_value AS passport_exp_date,
    pc.custom_field_value AS passport_country
FROM passenger p
JOIN custom_field pn ON pn.passenger_id=p.passenger_id
                                AND pn.custom_field_name='passport_num'
JOIN custom_field pe ON pe.passenger_id=p.passenger_id
                                AND pe.custom_field_name='passport_
                                exp_date'
JOIN custom_field pc ON pc.passenger_id=p.passenger_id
                                AND pc.custom_field_name='passport_
                                country'
WHERE p.passenger_id<5000000
```

	QUERY PLAN
	text
1	Hash Join (cost=3344203.17..4769951.67 rows=4306126 width=51)
2	Hash Cond: (pe.passenger_id = pn.passenger_id)
3	-> Seq Scan on custom_field pe (cost=0.00..1022564.75 rows=16454200 width=17)
4	Filter: (custom_field_name = 'passport_exp_date'::text)
5	-> Hash (cost=3244130.53..3244130.53 rows=4494451 width=50)
6	-> Hash Join (cost=1806471.88..3244130.53 rows=4494451 width=50)
7	Hash Cond: (pc.passenger_id = pn.passenger_id)
8	-> Seq Scan on custom_field pc (cost=0.00..1022564.75 rows=16273188 width=17)
9	Filter: (custom_field_name = 'passport_country'::text)
10	-> Hash (cost=1710124.97..1710124.97 rows=4743193 width=33)
11	-> Hash Join (cost=430701.56..1710124.97 rows=4743193 width=33)
12	Hash Cond: (pn.passenger_id = p.passenger_id)
13	-> Seq Scan on custom_field pn (cost=0.00..1022564.75 rows=16194911 width=17)
14	Filter: (custom_field_name = 'passport_num'::text)
15	-> Hash (cost=343266.86..343266.86 rows=5029896 width=16)
16	-> Seq Scan on passenger p (cost=0.00..343266.86 rows=5029896 width=16)
17	Filter: (passenger_id < 5000000)

Figure 6-21. *Execution plan with multiple scans*

Scanning this table three times is like sorting apples, oranges, and lemons from one black box into three buckets, doing so by first sorting out all the apples, returning all the oranges and lemons back into the box, then sorting the oranges, and then finally returning to the box for the lemons. A more effective way to do this job would be to place all three buckets before you and sort each fruit into the correct bucket when first removing it from the black box.

When retrieving multiple attributes from an entity-attribute-value table, join to the table only once and use FILTER in the aggregate function MAX() in SELECT list to return the appropriate values in each column.

To replicate this effect on the `custom_field` table, the query can be rewritten as shown in Listing 6-27.

Listing 6-27. One table scan to retrieve multiple attributes

```
SELECT
    last_name,
    first_name,
    coalesce(max (custom_field_value )
        FILTER (WHERE custom_field_name ='passport_num' ),'')
                                        AS passport_num,
    coalesce(max (custom_field_value )
        FILTER (WHERE custom_field_name ='passport_exp_date' ),'')
                                        AS passport_exp_date,
    coalesce(max (custom_field_value )
        FILTER (WHERE custom_field_name ='passport_country' ),'')
                                        AS passport_country
FROM passenger p
JOIN custom_field cf  USING (passenger_id)
WHERE cf.passenger_id<5000000
      AND p.passenger_id<5000000
GROUP by 1,2;
```

The execution plan for Listing 6-27 is shown in Figure 6-22.

	QUERY PLAN text
1	HashAggregate (cost=2215036.64..2303369.59 rows=1589943 width=108)
2	Group Key: p.last_name, p.first_name
3	Planned Partitions: 128
4	-> Hash Join (cost=462629.44..1739872.78 rows=4635745 width=38)
5	Hash Cond: (cf.passenger_id = p.passenger_id)
6	-> Seq Scan on custom_field cf (cost=0.00..1006402.40 rows=15119974 widt...
7	Filter: (passenger_id < 5000000)
8	-> Hash (cost=375657.36..375657.36 rows=5003286 width=16)
9	-> Seq Scan on passenger p (cost=0.00..375657.36 rows=5003286 width=...
10	Filter: (passenger_id < 5000000)

Figure 6-22. *One table scan*

This looks much better—only one table scan—except that when you try to execute it, it will run significantly longer. A closer look shows why: there may be many passengers with the same first and last names, so not only does it take longer but the result is also incorrect. Let's modify the query one more time—see Listing 6-28.

Listing 6-28. Correction for the query in Listing 6-27

```
SELECT
    last_name,
    first_name,
    p.passenger_id,
    coalesce(max (custom_field_value )
        FILTER (WHERE custom_field_name ='passport_num' ),'')
                                        AS passport_num,
    coalesce(max (custom_field_value )
        FILTER (WHERE custom_field_name ='passport_exp_date' ),'')
                                        AS passport_exp_date,
    coalesce(max (custom_field_value )
        FILTER (WHERE custom_field_name ='passport_country' ),'')
                                        AS passport_country
FROM passenger p
JOIN custom_field cf  USING (passenger_id)
WHERE cf.passenger_id<5000000
      AND p.passenger_id<5000000
GROUP by 3,1,2;
```

The execution plan in Figure 6-23 looks much better—the grouping column is now `passenger_id`.

	QUERY PLAN text	
1	HashAggregate (cost=2239664.04..2367509.19 rows=4635745 width=112)	
2	Group Key: p.passenger_id	
3	Planned Partitions: 256	
4	-> Hash Join (cost=462629.44..1739872.78 rows=4635745 width=42)	
5	Hash Cond: (cf.passenger_id = p.passenger_id)	
6	-> Seq Scan on custom_field cf (cost=0.00..1006402.40 rows=15119974 widt...	
7	Filter: (passenger_id < 5000000)	
8	-> Hash (cost=375657.36..375657.36 rows=5003286 width=16)	
9	-> Seq Scan on passenger p (cost=0.00..375657.36 rows=5003286 width=...	
10	Filter: (passenger_id < 5000000)	

Figure 6-23. *Execution plan for Listing 6-28*

There's one more optimization to make here; attributes from an EAV table are often joined to other tables, and we can reduce the size of the intermediate result set by "collapsing" and filtering this table to the needed values before executing other joins. This is a more specific case of the generalized technique of grouping before joining earlier.

Pull values from an EAV table into a subquery before joining to other tables.

Doing this for the passport example, we can modify the query one more time, as shown in Listing 6-29.

Listing 6-29. Moving grouping to the subquery

```
SELECT
     last_name,
     first_name,
     passport_num,
```

```
      passport_exp_date,
      passport_country
FROM  passenger p
JOIN (
SELECT
      cf.passenger_id,
      coalesce(max (custom_field_value )
            FILTER (WHERE custom_field_name ='passport_num' ),'')
                                          AS passport_num,
       coalesce(max (custom_field_value )
            FILTER (WHERE custom_field_name ='passport_exp_date' ),'')
                                          AS passport_exp_date,
        coalesce(max (custom_field_value )
            FILTER (WHERE custom_field_name ='passport_country' ),'')
                                          AS passport_country
FROM custom_field cf
WHERE cf.passenger_id<5000000
GROUP BY 1
   ) info  USING (passenger_id)
WHERE p.passenger_id<5000000
```

The execution plan is shown in Figure 6-24.

	QUERY PLAN text	🔒
1	Hash Join (cost=3995605.13..4895910.34 rows=3263588 width=108)	
2	Hash Cond: (info.passenger_id = p.passenger_id)	
3	-> Subquery Scan on info (cost=3532975.70..4048265.98 rows=10644540 width=100)	
4	-> GroupAggregate (cost=3532975.70..3941820.58 rows=10644540 width=100)	
5	Group Key: cf.passenger_id	
6	-> Sort (cost=3532975.70..3570775.63 rows=15119974 width=30)	
7	Sort Key: cf.passenger_id	
8	-> Seq Scan on custom_field cf (cost=0.00..1006402.40 rows=15119974 width=...	
9	Filter: (passenger_id < 5000000)	
10	-> Hash (cost=375657.36..375657.36 rows=5003286 width=16)	
11	-> Seq Scan on passenger p (cost=0.00..375657.36 rows=5003286 width=16)	
12	Filter: (passenger_id < 5000000)	

Figure 6-24. *Execution plan with grouping moved to the subquery*

Conclusion

This chapter formally defined long queries and explored optimization techniques for them.

The first important principle of this chapter is that indexes do not necessarily make queries run faster and can, in fact, make a long query run slower. A common misconception is that if no indexes can be built, there is nothing you can do to optimize a full table scan. Hopefully, this chapter has definitively demonstrated that there are multiple possibilities to optimize a full table scan.

As with short queries, long queries are optimized by reducing the size of intermediate results and doing the necessary work on as few rows as possible. In the case of short queries, this is accomplished by applying indexes on the most restrictive criteria. In the case of long queries, this is accomplished by being mindful of join order, applying semi- and anti-joins, and filtering before grouping, grouping before joining, and applying set operations.

CHAPTER 7

Long Queries: Additional Techniques

Chapter 6 discussed multiple ways of improving the performance of long queries. So far, every covered technique related to rewriting queries without creating any additional database objects. This chapter addresses additional ways of improving long query performance, including different ways to materialize intermediate results. Temporary tables, CTEs (common table expressions), views, and materialized views are discussed—when each tool can improve performance and how each can be abused and lead to performance degradation. Finally, this chapter covers partitioning and parallel execution.

Structuring Queries

Readers familiar with object-oriented programming (OOP) will be familiar with the concepts of decomposition (factoring) and encapsulation. OOP best practices dictate that code should be decomposed (or factored) into many smaller classes and objects responsible for a well-defined subset of system behavior, as well as encapsulated, restricting direct access to components and thus obscuring their implementation. These two principles make application code more readable and more manageable and make it easier to make changes.

Coming from this paradigm, when one is confronted with a single SELECT statement of 500+ lines, it's understandably tempting to apply these same principles, factoring the code into smaller pieces and encapsulating some of the logic.

However, SQL's declarative nature dictates a very different style of factoring SQL queries from what would be used with application code. In SQL, as in any language, code should be kept easy to understand and modify, but not at the expense of performance.

© Henrietta Dombrovskaya, Boris Novikov, Anna Bailliekova 2024
H. Dombrovskaya et al., *PostgreSQL Query Optimization*, https://doi.org/10.1007/979-8-8688-0069-6_7

We can approach factoring and encapsulation in a variety of ways in SQL, each with its own advantages and pitfalls. Some are used (with varying effectiveness) to improve performance and store intermediate results. Others are used to make code reusable. Others impact the way data is stored. This chapter covers several approaches, and others, such as functions, will be covered in depth in subsequent chapters.

In any case, any decomposition or encapsulation should correspond to a logical entity—for example, a report or a daily refresh.

Temporary Tables and CTEs

In Chapter 6, we mentioned that sometimes the attempts of SQL developers to speed up query execution may result in slowing execution. This often happens when they decide to use *temporary tables*.

Temporary Tables

To create a temporary table, one executes a regular `create table` statement, adding the keyword `temporary` or just `temp`:

```
CREATE TEMP TABLE interim_results
```

Temporary tables are visible to the current session only and are dropped when the session disconnects if not dropped explicitly before that. Otherwise, they are as good as regular tables, can be used in the queries with no limitations, and can even be indexed. Temporary tables are often used to store intermediate results of queries, so the `CREATE` statement often looks like

```
CREATE TEMP TABLE interim_results AS
SELECT ...
```

All of this looks very convenient, so what's wrong with this approach?

It all works great if you use a temporary table to store results of your query for some analysis and then discard it when done. But often, when a SQL developer starts to use temporary tables to store the results of each step, the code starts to look like this:

```
CREATE TEMP TABLE T1 AS SELECT <...> ;
CREATE TEMP TABLE T2 AS SELECT <...>
```

```
FROM T1
    INNER JOIN <...>
<...>
```

The chain of temporary tables can become quite long. Does it cause any problems? Yes, and there are many of them, including the following:

- *Indexes* – After selected data is stored in a temporary table, we can't use indexes that were created on the source table(s). We either need to continue without indexes or build new ones on temporary tables, which takes time.

- *Statistics* – Since we created a new table, the optimizer can't use statistical data on value distribution from the source table(s), so we need either to go without statistics or run the ANALYZE command on the temporary table.

- *Disk space* – Temporary tables are still tables that are stored on disk, so when they are overused, significant database size growth is possible.

- *Excessive I/O* – Also, since they are tables written to disk, it takes extra time to write to and read from disk.

The most important negative implication of excessive use of temporary tables is that this practice blocks the optimizer from doing rewrites.

By saving the results of each join in a temporary table, you prevent the optimizer from choosing the optimal join order; you "lock" in the order in which you created the temporary tables.

When we looked at the execution plan of the query in Listing 6-15, we observed that PostgreSQL was able to push the filtering condition inside grouping. What would happen if a temp table was created for intermediate results?

Listing 7-1. Inefficient usage of temp tables

```
CREATE TEMP TABLE flights_totals AS
SELECT
        bl.flight_id,
        departure_airport,
        (avg(price))::numeric (7,2) AS avg_price,
        count(DISTINCT passenger_id) AS num_passengers
```

```
FROM booking b
JOIN booking_leg bl USING (booking_id)
JOIN flight f USING (flight_id)
JOIN passenger p USING (booking_id)
GROUP BY 1,2;

SELECT
      flight_id,
      avg_price,
      num_passengers
FROM flights_totals
WHERE departure_airport='ORD';
```

Creating the temporary table took 50 seconds and produced over 500,000 rows, out of which we needed just 10,000. At the same time, the query in Listing 6-15 took just 0.1 seconds to execute.

Common Table Expressions (CTEs)

If temporary tables are dangerous, should a *CTE* (*common table expression*) be used instead? First, what are CTEs?

Common table expressions, or CTEs, can be thought of as defining temporary tables that exist just for one query. Each auxiliary statement in a WITH clause can be a SELECT, INSERT, UPDATE, or DELETE; and the WITH clause itself is attached to a primary statement that can also be a SELECT, INSERT, UPDATE, or DELETE.

Let's give a CTE a try. In Listing 7-2, the query from Listing 7-1 is modified to use a CTE instead of a temporary table.

Listing 7-2. Example of a query with a CTE

```
WITH flights_totals AS(
      SELECT
            bl.flight_id,
            departure_airport,
            (avg(price))::numeric (7,2) AS avg_price,
```

```
            count(DISTINCT passenger_id) AS num_passengers
    FROM booking b
    JOIN booking_leg bl USING (booking_id)
    JOIN flight f USING (flight_id)
    JOIN passenger p USING (booking_id)
    GROUP BY 1,2)
SELECT
    flight_id,
    avg_price,
    num_passengers
FROM flights_totals
WHERE departure_airport='ORD'
```

What you will see in the execution plan depends on whether you are running a PostgreSQL version below 12 or 12 and above. For all versions below 12, a CTE was processed exactly like a temporary table. The results were materialized in main memory with possible disk failover. That means that there was no advantage to using a CTE instead of a temporary table.

To be fair, a CTE's intended purpose was different. The idea behind a CTE was that if you needed to use some (possibly complex) subselect more than once, you could define it as a CTE and reference it in a query multiple times. In this case, PostgreSQL will compute results just once and reuse them as many times as needed.

Because of this intended usage, the optimizer planned CTE execution separately from the rest of the query and did not push any join conditions inside the CTE, providing a so-called *optimization fence*. This is especially important if WITH is used in INSERT/DELETE/UPDATE statements where there may be side effects or in recursive CTE calls. In addition, having the optimization fence means that the tables involved in the CTE are not counted against join_collapse_limit. This allows us to effectively use PostgreSQL optimizer capabilities with queries that join a large number of tables.

For the query in Listing 7-2, in PostgreSQL versions before 12, the CTE flight_ totals would be calculated for all flights, and only after that a subset of flights would be selected.

PostgreSQL 12 brought a drastic change to CTE optimization. For SELECT statements with no recursion, if a CTE is used in a query only once, it will be inlined into the outer query (removing the optimization fence). If it is called more than once, the old behavior will be preserved.

What is more important, the behavior described earlier is a default, but it can be overwritten by using the keywords MATERIALIZED and NOT MATERIALIZED. (See Listing 7-3.) The first one forces the old behavior, and the second one forces inlining, regardless of all other considerations.

Listing 7-3. Usage of the MATERIALIZED keyword

```
WITH flights_totals AS MATERIALIZED (
        SELECT
                bl.flight_id,
                departure_airport,
                (avg(price))::numeric (7,2) AS avg_price,
            count(DISTINCT passenger_id) AS num_passengers
    FROM booking b
    JOIN booking_leg bl USING (booking_id)
    JOIN flight f USING (flight_id)
    JOIN passenger p USING (booking_id)
    GROUP BY 1,2)
SELECT
    flight_id,
    avg_price,
    num_passengers
FROM flights_totals
WHERE departure_airport='ORD'
```

Figure 7-1 presents the execution plan for Listing 7-2, the way it works in PostgreSQL 12. If the keyword MATERIALIZED is added, as shown in Listing 7-3, the old behavior will be forced, as shown in Figure 7-2.

	QUERY PLAN
◢	text
1	Subquery Scan on flights_totals (cost=899526.09..935621.26 rows=962538 width=26)
2	-> GroupAggregate (cost=899526.09..925995.88 rows=962538 width=30)
3	Group Key: bl.flight_id, f.departure_airport
4	-> Sort (cost=899526.09..901932.43 rows=962538 width=18)
5	Sort Key: bl.flight_id
6	-> Nested Loop (cost=9545.27..784126.73 rows=962538 width=18)
7	Join Filter: (b.booking_id = p.booking_id)
8	-> Nested Loop (cost=9544.84..532480.61 rows=334023 width=26)
9	-> Hash Join (cost=9544.41..367021.97 rows=334023 width=12)
10	Hash Cond: (bl.flight_id = f.flight_id)
11	-> Seq Scan on booking_leg bl (cost=0.00..310506.66 rows=17893566 width=8)
12	-> Hash (cost=9384.99..9384.99 rows=12753 width=8)
13	-> Bitmap Heap Scan on flight f (cost=243.26..9384.99 rows=12753 width=8)
14	Recheck Cond: (departure_airport = 'ORD'::bpchar)
15	-> Bitmap Index Scan on flight_departure_airport (cost=0.00..240.07 rows=12753 width=0)
16	Index Cond: (departure_airport = 'ORD'::bpchar)
17	-> Index Scan using booking_pkey on booking b (cost=0.43..0.50 rows=1 width=14)
18	Index Cond: (booking_id = bl.booking_id)
19	-> Index Scan using passenger_booking_id on passenger p (cost=0.43..0.64 rows=9 width=8)
20	Index Cond: (booking_id = bl.booking_id)

Figure 7-1. *Execution plan for a CTE with inlining*

	QUERY PLAN text
1	CTE Scan on flights_totals (cost=14081839.16..15242007.67 rows=257815 width=26)
2	Filter: (departure_airport = 'ORD'::bpchar)
3	CTE flights_totals
4	-> GroupAggregate (cost=12663855.42..14081839.16 rows=51563045 width=30)
5	Group Key: bl.flight_id, f.departure_airport
6	-> Sort (cost=12663855.42..12792763.04 rows=51563045 width=18)
7	Sort Key: bl.flight_id, f.departure_airport
8	-> Hash Join (cost=1151589.89..2886328.12 rows=51563045 width=18)
9	Hash Cond: (b.booking_id = bl.booking_id)
10	-> Hash Join (cost=314001.30..846710.40 rows=16313907 width=22)
11	Hash Cond: (p.booking_id = b.booking_id)
12	-> Seq Scan on passenger p (cost=0.00..334787.07 rows=16313907 width=8)
13	-> Hash (cost=215591.02..215591.02 rows=5661302 width=14)
14	-> Seq Scan on booking b (cost=0.00..215591.02 rows=5661302 width=14)
15	-> Hash (cost=526548.02..526548.02 rows=17893566 width=12)
16	-> Hash Join (cost=26607.46..526548.02 rows=17893566 width=12)
17	Hash Cond: (bl.flight_id = f.flight_id)
18	-> Seq Scan on booking_leg bl (cost=0.00..310506.66 rows=17893566 width=8)
19	-> Hash (cost=15398.76..15398.76 rows=683176 width=8)
20	-> Seq Scan on flight f (cost=0.00..15398.76 rows=683176 width=8)

Figure 7-2. *Forced materialization of a CTE*

Prior to these recent changes, we would discourage SQL developers from using multiple embedded CTEs, when a SQL statement would look like this:

```
WITH z AS (
    WITH y AS (
        WITH x AS (SELECT ...)
            SELECT ... FROM a JOIN x ...)
            SELECT ... FROM b
            JOIN y...)
```

```
SELECT ... FROM c
    JOIN z
```

...

However, with the changes introduced in PostgreSQL 12, such queries are much more manageable. We would still encourage SQL developers to be mindful not to force a suboptimal execution plan, but using a chain of CTEs is much better than using a sequence of temporary tables; in the latter case, the optimizer is helpless.

To conclude, it's important to mention that there are situations where storing intermediate results is beneficial. However, almost always there are better ways than using temporary tables. We will discuss other options later in this chapter.

Views: To Use or Not to Use

Views are the most controversial database object. They seem to be easy to understand, and the advantages of creating a view seem so obvious. Why might they cause problems?

Although we are sure that most readers have had a chance to create at least a couple of views for some project, let's give a formal definition. The simplest definition is

---

A `view` is a database object that stores a query that defines a virtual table.

A view is a virtual table in the sense that syntactically, views may be used in a SELECT statement in the same way as a table. However, they differ significantly from tables in that no data is stored; only the query that defines the view is stored in the database.

Let's take another look at the query in Listing 6-14. This query calculates the totals for all flights in the postgres_air schema, but we want to use this query logic to select the totals for specific flights and/or departure airports. Listing 7-4 creates a view that encapsulates this logic.

Listing 7-4. Create a view

```
CREATE VIEW flight_stats AS
SELECT
    bl.flight_id,
```

```
      departure_airport,
      (avg(price))::numeric (7,2) AS avg_price,
      count(DISTINCT passenger_id) AS num_passengers
FROM booking b
JOIN booking_leg bl USING (booking_id)
JOIN flight f USING (flight_id)
JOIN passenger p USING (booking_id)
GROUP BY 1,2
```

Now it is easy to select flight statistics for any particular flight:

```
SELECT *
 FROM flight_stats
 WHERE flight_id=222183
```

This query plan looks identical to the plan in Figure 6-13. The reason is that in the first step of query processing, the query parser transforms views into inline subqueries. In this case, this works to our advantage, since the filtering condition is pushed inside the grouping. But if a nonconstant search criterion is used, the results might be disappointing. In Listing 7-5, flight statistics from the view `flight_stats` are limited by the flight's departure date.

Listing 7-5. Query using the view

```
SELECT *
FROM flight_stats fs
JOIN (SELECT
                flight_id
          FROM flight f
          WHERE actual_departure between '2023-08-01' and '2023-08-14'
            ) fl
          ON fl.flight_id=fs.flight_id
```

The execution plan for this query is shown in Figure 7-3.

	QUERY PLAN text
1	Hash Join (cost=12641030.68..14717215.42 rows=3663700 width=34)
2	Hash Cond: (bl.flight_id = f.flight_id)
3	-> GroupAggregate (cost=12630373.17..14053302.95 rows=51742901 width=30)
4	Group Key: bl.flight_id, f_1.departure_airport
5	-> Sort (cost=12630373.17..12759730.42 rows=51742901 width=18)
6	Sort Key: bl.flight_id, f_1.departure_airport
7	-> Hash Join (cost=1080689.84..2817439.82 rows=51742901 width=18)
8	Hash Cond: (b.booking_id = bl.booking_id)
9	-> Hash Join (cost=243101.21..775846.44 rows=16318749 width=22)
10	Hash Cond: (p.booking_id = b.booking_id)
11	-> Seq Scan on passenger p (cost=0.00..334860.49 rows=16318749 width=8)
12	-> Hash (cost=145003.98..145003.98 rows=5643298 width=14)
13	-> Seq Scan on booking b (cost=0.00..145003.98 rows=5643298 width=14)
14	-> Hash (cost=526548.06..526548.06 rows=17893566 width=12)
15	-> Hash Join (cost=26607.50..526548.06 rows=17893566 width=12)
16	Hash Cond: (bl.flight_id = f_1.flight_id)
17	-> Seq Scan on booking_leg bl (cost=0.00..310506.66 rows=17893566 width=8)
18	-> Hash (cost=15398.78..15398.78 rows=683178 width=8)
19	-> Seq Scan on flight f_1 (cost=0.00..15398.78 rows=683178 width=8)
20	-> Hash (cost=10052.84..10052.84 rows=48373 width=4)
21	-> Bitmap Heap Scan on flight f (cost=760.25..10052.84 rows=48373 width=4)
22	Recheck Cond: ((actual_departure >= '2023-08-01 00:00:00-05'::timestamp with time zone) AND (actual_departure <= '2023-08-14 00:00:00-05'::timestar
23	-> Bitmap Index Scan on flight_actual_departure (cost=0.00..748.15 rows=48373 width=0)
24	Index Cond: ((actual_departure >= '2023-08-01 00:00:00-05'::timestamp with time zone) AND (actual_departure <= '2023-08-14 00:00:00-05'::timesta

Figure 7-3. *Execution plan in which the condition can't be pushed*

Looking at this execution plan, we observe that first, the statistics for all flights are calculated, and only after that are the results joined with selected flights. The execution time of this query is ten minutes.

Without using the view, we follow the pattern explained in Chapter 6, filtering the flights before grouping, as shown in Listing 7-6.

Listing 7-6. Rewriting the query without the view

```
SELECT
    bl.flight_id,
    departure_airport,
    (avg(price))::numeric (7,2) AS avg_price,
    count(DISTINCT passenger_id) AS num_passengers
FROM booking b
JOIN booking_leg bl USING (booking_id)
```

```
JOIN flight f USING (flight_id)
JOIN passenger p USING (booking_id)
WHERE actual_departure between '2023-08-01' AND '2023-08-14'
GROUP BY 1,2
```

The execution plan for this query is shown in Figure 7-4 and shows that the restrictions on the flight table are applied first. The execution time for this query is three minutes.

	QUERY PLAN
	text
1	GroupAggregate (cost=1773339.64..1874091.39 rows=3663700 width=30)
2	Group Key: bl.flight_id, f.departure_airport
3	-> Sort (cost=1773339.64..1782498.89 rows=3663700 width=18)
4	Sort Key: bl.flight_id, f.departure_airport
5	-> Hash Join (cost=654792.33..1223638.13 rows=3663700 width=18)
6	Hash Cond: (p.booking_id = b.booking_id)
7	-> Seq Scan on passenger p (cost=0.00..334860.49 rows=16318749 width=8)
8	-> Hash (cost=630294.22..630294.22 rows=1266969 width=26)
9	-> Hash Join (cost=390159.18..630294.22 rows=1266969 width=26)
10	Hash Cond: (b.booking_id = bl.booking_id)
11	-> Seq Scan on booking b (cost=0.00..145003.98 rows=5643298 width=14)
12	-> Hash (cost=368135.07..368135.07 rows=1266969 width=12)
13	-> Hash Join (cost=10657.51..368135.07 rows=1266969 width=12)
14	Hash Cond: (bl.flight_id = f.flight_id)
15	-> Seq Scan on booking_leg bl (cost=0.00..310506.66 rows=17893566 width=8)
16	-> Hash (cost=10052.84..10052.84 rows=48373 width=8)
17	-> Bitmap Heap Scan on flight f (cost=760.25..10052.84 rows=48373 width=8)
18	Recheck Cond: ((actual_departure >= '2023-08-01 00:00:00-05'::timestamp with time zone) AND (actual_departure <= '2023-08-14 00:00:00-05'
19	-> Bitmap Index Scan on flight_actual_departure (cost=0.00..748.15 rows=48373 width=0)
20	Index Cond: ((actual_departure >= '2023-08-01 00:00:00-05'::timestamp with time zone) AND (actual_departure <= '2023-08-14 00:00:00-05

Figure 7-4. *Execution plan for Listing 7-6*

It is misleading when database textbooks, including those teaching PostgreSQL basics, state that views can be used "like tables." In practice, views that were originally created solely to encapsulate a stand-alone query are often used in other queries, joined to other tables and views, including joining multiple times to tables already included in the view, without knowing what's going on behind the scenes.

On the one hand, people usually create a view precisely for the purpose of encapsulation, so that others can use it without needing to figure out selection logic. On the other hand, this opacity is the cause of poor query performance. This effect becomes especially pronounced when some columns in a view are the results of transformation. Consider the view flight_departure in Listing 7-7.

Listing 7-7. View with column transformation

```
CREATE VIEW flight_departure as
SELECT
      bl.flight_id,
      departure_airport,
      coalesce(actual_departure, scheduled_departure)::date
      AS  departure_date,
      count(DISTINCT passenger_id) AS num_passengers
 FROM booking b
 JOIN booking_leg bl USING (booking_id)
 JOIN flight f USING (flight_id)
 JOIN passenger p USING (booking_id)
GROUP BY 1,2,3
```

Executing the query

```
SELECT
      flight_id,
      num_passengers
FROM flight_departure
WHERE flight_id =22183
```

...the filter on the flight will be pushed inside the view, and the query will be executed in 63 ms. A user who isn't aware that flight_departure is a view might think that all columns have comparable performance and might be surprised to see the result when running the following query:

```
SELECT
      flight_id,
      num_passengers
 FROM flight_departure
 WHERE departure_date= '2023-08-01'
```

This query takes 2.5 sec or forty times longer to execute. The difference is because the departure_date column is a transformation, and as discussed in Chapter 5, no indexes can be utilized to apply this filter. The execution plan for this query is shown in Figure 7-5. Notice that although indexes on scheduled_departure and actual_departure are not used, PostgreSQL still correctly identifies the order of joins and searches the flight table first and then uses index access for tables booking and passenger.

	QUERY PLAN text	
1	Subquery Scan on flight_departure (cost=512344.83..521400.17 rows=258724 width=12)	
2	-> GroupAggregate (cost=512344.83..518812.93 rows=258724 width=20)	
3	Group Key: bl.flight_id, f.departure_airport, ((COALESCE(f.actual_departure, f.scheduled_departure))::da...	
4	-> Sort (cost=512344.83..512991.64 rows=258724 width=16)	
5	Sort Key: bl.flight_id, f.departure_airport	
6	-> Nested Loop (cost=18858.24..484660.18 rows=258724 width=16)	
7	Join Filter: (b.booking_id = p.booking_id)	
8	-> Nested Loop (cost=18857.80..416906.41 rows=89471 width=36)	
9	-> Hash Join (cost=18857.37..376334.93 rows=89471 width=28)	
10	Hash Cond: (bl.flight_id = f.flight_id)	
11	-> Seq Scan on booking_leg bl (cost=0.00..310506.66 rows=17893566 width=8)	
12	-> Hash (cost=18814.67..18814.67 rows=3416 width=24)	
13	-> Seq Scan on flight f (cost=0.00..18814.67 rows=3416 width=24)	
14	Filter: ((COALESCE(actual_departure, scheduled_departure))::date = '2023-08-01'::d...	
15	-> Index Only Scan using booking_pkey on booking b (cost=0.43..0.45 rows=1 width=8)	
16	Index Cond: (booking_id = bl.booking_id)	
17	-> Index Scan using passenger_booking_id on passenger p (cost=0.43..0.64 rows=9 width=8)	
18	Index Cond: (booking_id = bl.booking_id)	

Figure 7-5. *Execution plan when some indexes can't be utilized*

An even worse case of performance degradation is shown in Listing 7-8. Unfortunately, this is a real-life case. When a person using a view does not know what query was used to create it, they might use it to select data that is much easier to obtain from the underlying tables.

Listing 7-8. Selection of only one column from the view

```
SELECT
       flight_id
FROM flight_departure
WHERE departure_airport='ORD'
```

This query doesn't concern itself with the number of passengers on a flight; it merely selects flights departing from ORD for which any tickets were sold. And yet, the execution plan for Listing 7-8 is quite complex—see Figure 7-6.

	QUERY PLAN
	text
1	Subquery Scan on flight_departure (cost=886771.95..918054.44 rows=962538 width=4)
2	-> GroupAggregate (cost=886771.95..908429.06 rows=962538 width=20)
3	Group Key: bl.flight_id, f.departure_airport, ((COALESCE(f.actual_departure, f.scheduled_departure))::date)
4	-> Sort (cost=886771.95..889178.30 rows=962538 width=12)
5	Sort Key: bl.flight_id, ((COALESCE(f.actual_departure, f.scheduled_departure))::date)
6	-> Nested Loop (cost=9545.27..774662.60 rows=962538 width=12)
7	Join Filter: (b.booking_id = p.booking_id)
8	-> Nested Loop (cost=9544.84..520610.13 rows=334023 width=36)
9	-> Hash Join (cost=9544.41..367021.97 rows=334023 width=28)
10	Hash Cond: (bl.flight_id = f.flight_id)
11	-> Seq Scan on booking_leg bl (cost=0.00..310506.66 rows=17893566 width=8)
12	-> Hash (cost=9384.99..9384.99 rows=12753 width=24)
13	-> Bitmap Heap Scan on flight f (cost=243.26..9384.99 rows=12753 width=24)
14	Recheck Cond: (departure_airport = 'ORD'::bpchar)
15	-> Bitmap Index Scan on flight_departure_airport (cost=0.00..240.07 rows=12753 width=0)
16	Index Cond: (departure_airport = 'ORD'::bpchar)
17	-> Index Only Scan using booking_pkey on booking b (cost=0.43..0.46 rows=1 width=8)
18	Index Cond: (booking_id = bl.booking_id)
19	-> Index Only Scan using passenger_booking_id on passenger p (cost=0.43..0.64 rows=9 width=4)
20	Index Cond: (booking_id = bl.booking_id)

Figure 7-6. *Execution plan for the query in Listing 7-8*

This query runs for 3.1 seconds. However, a query that selects the same information without using the view

```
SELECT
     flight_id
FROM flight
WHERE departure_airport='ORD'
     AND flight_id IN (SELECT flight_id FROM booking_leg)
```

...will use available indexes and will run for just 120 ms.

Why Use Views?

Now that we've seen so many examples of the negative effects of using views, is there anything to say in their defense? Are there any situations in which views can improve query performance?

Internally in PostgreSQL, any creation of a view includes creation of *rules,* implicitly, in most cases. The `select` rules may restrict access to underlying tables. Rules, triggers, and automatic updates make views in PostgreSQL extremely sophisticated and provide functionality very similar to tables.

However, they do not provide any performance benefit. The best, and perhaps only justified, use of views is as a security layer or to define a reporting entity, to ensure that all joins and business logic are defined correctly.

Materialized Views

Most modern database systems allow users to create materialized views, but their implementations and precise behavior vary.

Let's begin with a definition.

A *materialized view* is a database object that combines both a query definition and a table to store the results of the query at the time it is run.

A materialized view is different from a view, because query results are stored, not just the view definition. This means that a materialized view reflects the data at the time it was last refreshed, not current data. It is different from a table, because you can't modify data in a materialized view directly, but you can only refresh it using a predefined query.

Creating and Using Materialized Views

Let's walk through an example to help illustrate the definition of a materialized view. Listing 7-9 creates a materialized view.

Listing 7-9. Create a materialized view

```
CREATE MATERIALIZED VIEW flight_departure_mv AS
SELECT
      bl.flight_id,
      departure_airport,
      coalesce(actual_departure, scheduled_departure)::date departure_date,
      count(DISTINCT passenger_id) AS num_passengers
FROM booking b
JOIN booking_leg bl USING (booking_id)
JOIN flight f USING (flight_id)
JOIN passenger p USING (booking_id)
GROUP BY 1,2,3
```

What happens when this command is run? First, in this particular case, it will take a very long time to execute. But when it finishes, there will be a new object in the database, which stores the results of this execution of the query in the database. In addition, the query itself will be stored along with the data. In contrast to views, when materialized views are referenced in queries, they behave exactly like tables. The optimizer won't substitute them with their defining queries, and they will be accessed as tables. Indexes can also be created on materialized views, although they cannot have primary and foreign keys:

```
CREATE UNIQUE INDEX flight_departure_flight_id
ON flight_departure_mv(flight_id);
--
CREATE INDEX flight_departure_dep_date
ON flight_departure_mv(departure_date);
--
CREATE INDEX flight_departure_dep_airport
ON flight_departure_mv(departure_airport);
```

Executing this query

```
SELECT
      flight_id,
      num_passengers
 FROM flight_departure_mv
 WHERE departure_date= '2023-08-01'
```

...will take only 60 ms, and the execution plan will show an index scan.

Refreshing Materialized Views

A REFRESH command populates the materialized view with the results of the base query at the time the refresh is executed. The syntax for the REFRESH command follows:

```
REFRESH MATERIALIZED VIEW flight_departure_mv
```

Materialized views in PostgreSQL are less mature than in some other DBMS, like Oracle. Materialized views cannot be updated incrementally, and the refresh schedule can't be specified in the materialized view definition. Each time the REFRESH command is executed, the underlying table is truncated, and the results of the SELECT statement are inserted. If an error occurs during refresh, the refresh process is rolled back, and the materialized view remains unchanged.

During refresh, the materialized view is locked, and its contents are unavailable to other processes. To make the prior version of a materialized view available during refresh, the CONCURRENTLY keyword is added:

```
REFRESH MATERIALIZED VIEW CONCURRENTLY flight_departure_mv
```

A materialized view can only be refreshed concurrently if it has a unique index. The concurrent refresh will take longer than regular refresh, but access to the materialized view won't be blocked.

Should I Create a Materialized View?

It is difficult to provide specific, universal conditions in which creating a materialized view is beneficial, but there follow some guidelines for decision-making. Since materialized view refreshes take time and selecting from a materialized view is going to be much faster than from a view, consider the following:

- How often does the data in the base tables change?

- How critical is it to have the most recent data?

- How often do we need to select this data (or rather how many reads per one refresh are expected)?

- How many different queries will use this data?

What should the thresholds for "often" and "many" be? It's subjective, but let's look at some examples to illustrate. Listing 7-10 defines a materialized view very similar to the view in Listing 7-9, except that it selects flights that departed yesterday.

Listing 7-10. Materialized view for yesterday's flights

```
CREATE MATERIALIZED VIEW flight_departure_prev_day AS
SELECT
        bl.flight_id,
      departure_airport,
      coalesce(actual_departure, scheduled_departure)::date
      departure_date,
      count(DISTINCT passenger_id) AS num_passengers
FROM booking b
JOIN booking_leg bl USING (booking_id)
JOIN flight f USING (flight_id)
JOIN passenger p USING (booking_id)
WHERE (actual_departure BETWEEN CURRENT_DATE -1
                                        AND  CURRENT_DATE
            )
        OR (
            actual_departure IS NULL
            AND scheduled_departure BETWEEN CURRENT_DATE -1
                                                AND CURRENT_DATE
            )
GROUP BY 1,2,3
```

Information about flights that departed yesterday is not going to change, so it is safe to assume that the view will not need to be refreshed until the next day. On the other hand, this materialized view can be used in several different queries that will all perform faster if query results are materialized.

Let's consider another potential candidate for materializing, Listing 6-29. Suppose a materialized view with the subquery is created, as in Listing 7-11.

Listing 7-11. Create a materialized view from the subquery

```
CREATE MATERIALIZED VIEW passenger_passport AS
SELECT
    cf.passenger_id,
    coalesce(max (custom_field_value )
        FILTER (WHERE custom_field_name ='passport_num' ),'')    AS
        passport_num,
    coalesce(max (custom_field_value )
        FILTER (WHERE custom_field_name ='passport_exp_date' ),'') AS
        passport_exp_date,
    coalesce(max (custom_field_value )
        FILTER (WHERE custom_field_name ='passport_country' ),'') AS
        passport_country
FROM custom_field cf
GROUP BY 1;
```

This materialized view is going to be very helpful. First, it has been shown already that this query takes a long time to execute, so time will be saved by pre-calculating the results. Second, passport information does not change (this information is associated with booking, and the same person will be assigned a different `passenger_id` in a different booking). It looks like a great candidate for a materialized view, if not for a few potential issues.

First, passengers are not required to submit their passport information during booking. This means that although once it is entered, this information will remain the same, for any particular flight, passport information may continue to be entered until the gate is closed. Hence, this materialized view will need to be constantly refreshed, and each refresh takes about ten minutes.

Second, this materialized view will keep growing. Unlike the previous example, when each day's refresh will cover data solely from the previous day, data about passengers' passports will grow, and it will take longer and longer to refresh a materialized view. Such situations are frequently overlooked in the early stage of a project, when there is little data in any table and materialized views refresh quickly. Since PostgreSQL does not allow an incremental materialized view refresh, a possible solution could be to create another table, with the same structure as the materialized view in Listing 7-11, and periodically upend new rows when new passport information becomes available.

However, if the latter solution is adopted, it's unclear why the `custom_field` table is needed in the first place, if data is needed in the format specified by the `passenger_passport` materialized view. This will be a topic in the next chapter, which discusses the impact of design on performance.

Do Materialized Views Need to Be Optimized?

Although the query of a materialized view is executed less frequently than the materialized view itself is used, we still need to pay attention to its execution time. Even when a materialized view is a short query (e.g., when it contains data for the previous day, as in Listing 7-9), it may end up doing full scans of large tables, if proper indexes are not in place or an execution plan is suboptimal.

As mentioned earlier, we don't accept the excuse that something doesn't need to be optimized because it runs infrequently, whether once a month, once a week, or once a day. No one is happy with reports that run for six hours, no matter how infrequently. In addition, these periodic reports are often all scheduled at the same time—usually 8 AM on a Monday—starting the week with more stress than anyone needs. The stress will be even more pronounced if some *dependencies* between materialized views are present. In this case, materialized views should be refreshed in a specific order, increasing the total wait time till the final report can be refreshed.

It's worth mentioning one more problem that can be caused by slow-refreshing materialized views. If we start to take a database backup after refresh of a materialized view started and finish it before the refresh ends, this materialized view will be stored in the backup in an inconsistent state, and if you restore from this backup (e.g., in your development environment), you won't be able either drop or recreate it. With everything being said, we believe it's evident that materialized views should be optimized in a manner like any other SQL query. The techniques discussed in Chapters 5 and 6 can and should be applied to materialized views.

Dependencies

When views and materialized views are created, a side effect is the creation of *dependencies*. Both views and materialized views have queries associated with them, and when any attribute involved in those queries is altered, the dependent views and materialized views need to be recreated.

Actually, PostgreSQL doesn't even permit an alter or drop on a table or materialized views if they have dependent views and materialized views. Making a change requires adding the CASCADE keyword to the ALTER or DROP command.

If views and materialized views are built on top of other views, altering or removing one column in one base table may result in recreating several dozen dependent database objects. Creating a view does not take substantial time, but rebuilding multiple dependent materialized views does, and all this time the materialized views will be unavailable, even if they allow concurrent refreshes.

Subsequent chapters discuss functions and stored procedures, which can eliminate such dependencies.

Partitioning

So far, this chapter has discussed different ways of splitting queries into smaller parts.

Partition is a different sort of division—dividing the data. A partitioned table consists of several partitions, each of which is defined as a table. The partitioned table itself is a virtual table and does not store any rows. Instead, each table row is stored in one of the partitions according to rules specified when the partitioned table is created.

Partition support is relatively new in PostgreSQL, and beginning with PG 10, improvements are made in every release, making partitioned tables easier to use. Currently, PostgreSQL supports the following partitioning methods: range, list, and hash partitioning.

The most common case is range partitioning, meaning that each partition contains rows that have values of an attribute in the range assigned to the partition. Ranges assigned to different partitions cannot intersect, and a row that does not fit into any partition cannot be inserted.

As an example, let's create a partitioned version of the boarding_pass table. The sequence of commands is shown in Listing 7-12.

Listing 7-12. Create a partitioned table

```
---create table
---
CREATE TABLE boarding_pass_part (
    boarding_pass_id SERIAL,
```

```sql
    passenger_id BIGINT NOT NULL,
    booking_leg_id BIGINT NOT NULL,
    seat TEXT,
    boarding_time TIMESTAMPTZ,
    precheck BOOLEAN,
    update_ts TIMESTAMPTZ
)
PARTITION BY RANGE (boarding_time);
--create partitions
--
CREATE TABLE boarding_pass_may
PARTITION OF boarding_pass_part
FOR VALUES
FROM ('2023-05-01'::timestamptz)
TO ('2023-06-01'::timestamptz) ;
--
CREATE TABLE boarding_pass_june
PARTITION OF boarding_pass_part
FOR VALUES
FROM ('2023-06-01'::timestamptz)
TO ('2023-07-01'::timestamptz);
--
CREATE TABLE boarding_pass_july
PARTITION OF boarding_pass_part
FOR VALUES
FROM ('2023-07-01'::timestamptz)
TO ('2023-08-01'::timestamptz);
--
CREATE TABLE boarding_pass_aug
PARTITION OF boarding_pass_part
FOR VALUES
FROM ('2023-08-01'::timestamptz)
TO ('2023-09-01'::timestamptz);
--
INSERT INTO boarding_pass_part SELECT * from boarding_pass;
```

Does Partitioning Improve Performance?

There is a common belief that partitioning of a large table improves query performance. This is not always the case. Moreover, partitioning can often decrease performance, and you may need to rewrite your old queries to make sure that performance won't be negatively affected.

The way partitioning *can* improve performance is that if a query contains conditions on the partitioning key, the search is limited to these partitions only. This makes partitioning especially useful for long queries where full scans are the best option: partitioning can significantly reduce the time for table scans. For index access the difference is negligible: partitioning removes only one level from the B-tree.

How should a partitioning key for a table be selected? The way the Postgres optimizer works, two conditions should be met: 1) the partitioning key should be used in (almost) all queries that run on this table, or at least in critical queries, 2) these values should be known prior to the SQL statement execution. The latter means that this value can't be passed as a parameter or as a result of a subselect.

Let's look at an example from Chapter 6, Listing 6-21. If this query is limited to boarding time between July 15 and July 31

```
SELECT
    city,
    date_trunc('month', scheduled_departure),
    sum(passengers)  passengers
FROM airport  a
JOIN flight f ON airport_code = departure_airport
JOIN (
    SELECT
            flight_id,
            count(*) passengers
    FROM    booking_leg l
    JOIN boarding_pass b USING (booking_leg_id)
    WHERE boarding_time > '07-15-23'
    and boarding_time <'07-31-23'
GROUP BY flight_id
) cnt
```

```
USING (flight_id)
GROUP BY 1,2
ORDER BY 3 DESC
```

...this will be still a long query, which will perform a full table scan of the boarding_
pass table. The execution plan is identical to the one in Figure 6-18.

However, executing the similar query using the partitioned table boarding_pass_
part (see Listing 7-13), this query will take advantage of partitions.

Listing 7-13. Querying a partitioned table

```
SELECT
    city,
    date_trunc('month', scheduled_departure),
    sum(passengers)  passengers
FROM airport   a
JOIN flight f ON airport_code = departure_airport
JOIN (
    SELECT
            flight_id,
            count(*) passengers
    FROM    booking_leg l
    JOIN boarding_pass_part b USING (booking_leg_id)
    WHERE boarding_time > '07-15-23'
    and boarding_time <'07-31-23'
GROUP BY flight_id
) cnt
USING (flight_id)
GROUP BY 1,2
ORDER BY 3 DESC
```

The execution plan in Figure 7-7 proves that instead of scanning the whole table,
the optimizer chooses to scan only one partition, since the query is filtered on boarding
time. And while query runtime on a non-partitioned table is approximately the same
regardless of filtering by boarding time, for a partitioned table, the execution time is
more than twice as fast, because all the rows are located in one partition.

	QUERY PLAN text
1	Sort (cost=1526392.02..1526916.72 rows=209882 width=49)
2	Sort Key: (sum(cnt.passengers)) DESC
3	-> GroupAggregate (cost=1495417.22..1500664.27 rows=209882 width=49)
4	Group Key: a.city, (date_trunc('month'::text, f.scheduled_departure))
5	-> Sort (cost=1495417.22..1495941.92 rows=209882 width=25)
6	Sort Key: a.city, (date_trunc('month'::text, f.scheduled_departure))
7	-> Hash Join (cost=1412529.77..1471841.97 rows=209882 width=25)
8	Hash Cond: (f.departure_airport = a.airport_code)
9	-> Hash Join (cost=1412504.20..1470737.38 rows=209882 width=20)
10	Hash Cond: (cnt.flight_id = f.flight_id)
11	-> Subquery Scan on cnt (cost=1385229.70..1437525.94 rows=209882 width=12)
12	-> HashAggregate (cost=1385229.70..1435427.12 rows=209882 width=12)
13	Group Key: l.flight_id
14	Planned Partitions: 4
15	-> Hash Join (cost=604073.24..1038919.77 rows=6156621 width=4)
16	Hash Cond: (b.booking_leg_id = l.booking_leg_id)
17	-> Seq Scan on boarding_pass_july b (cost=0.00..300688.40 rows=6156621 width=8)
18	Filter: ((boarding_time > '2023-07-15 00:00:00-05'::timestamp with time zone) AND (boarding_time < '202:
19	-> Hash (cost=310506.66..310506.66 rows=17893566 width=8)
20	-> Seq Scan on booking_leg l (cost=0.00..310506.66 rows=17893566 width=8)
21	-> Hash (cost=15398.78..15398.78 rows=683178 width=16)
22	-> Seq Scan on flight f (cost=0.00..15398.78 rows=683178 width=16)
23	-> Hash (cost=16.92..16.92 rows=692 width=13)
24	-> Seq Scan on airport a (cost=0.00..16.92 rows=692 width=13)

Figure 7-7. *Execution plan with a partitioned table*

Partitions may have their own indexes that obviously are smaller than an index on the whole partitioned table. This option might be beneficial for short queries. However, this might significantly improve performance only if almost all queries extract data from the same partition. The cost of search in a B-tree is proportional to its depth. An index on a partition, most likely, will eliminate only one level of the B-tree, while the choice of needed partition also requires some amount of resources. These resources are likely comparable with the amount needed for an extra index level. Of course, a query may refer to a partition instead of the whole partitioned table, hiding the cost of choosing the partition to the application issuing the query.

Therefore, the benefits of partitioning for short queries should not be overestimated.

Why Create a Partitioned Table?

After reading the previous section, readers may wonder whether there is any justification to create partitioned tables. In fact, there are many, and we cover them in this section.

Partitions can be added to a partitioned table or dropped. The DROP command is executed significantly faster than bulk DELETE and does not require subsequent vacuuming. A typical use case is a table partitioned on date ranges (e.g., partition per month), a new partition is added, and the oldest one is dropped at the end of every month.

In addition, it is possible to ATTACH and DETACH partitions. This way, you can add an existing table as a partition to a partition table and detach partitions without deleting data. For example, you can keep the last three months of data in a partitioned table, add a new partition in the beginning of each month, detach the oldest partition, and then attach it to the archiving table.

Partitioning may be used to distribute large amounts of data across several database servers: a partition can be a foreign table.

The primary reason for partitioning, however, is the maintenance. When a table reaches terabyte size, it becomes challenging to copy such table or to run pg_dump on it. Most importantly, it becomes difficult to run *autovacuum* on this table. We will cover autovacuum and its importance for maintaining a healthy PostgreSQL database; for now, we just want to mention that autovacuum is extremely unlikely to complete on a 1 TB table.

Parallelism

Starting in version 10, PostgreSQL has capability to enable parallel query execution. Two configuration parameters, max_parallel_workers and max_parallel_workers_per_gather, define how many parallel processes are available and how many can be spanned in one session.

We still recall the excitement of the community when this feature was introduced. Indeed, parallelism was and often is billed as a silver bullet to solve all performance problems, and we feel compelled to warn you about not setting expectations too high regarding parallelism—this is true in any RDBMS, not just PostgreSQL.

Parallel execution can be viewed as yet another way to split up the query: the amount of work needed to execute a query is divided between processing units (processors or cores).

Any parallel algorithm has a certain part that must be executed on a single unit. Also, additional overheads appear as a cost of synchronizations between parallel processes. For these reasons, parallel processing is mostly beneficial when bulk data is processed. Specifically, parallel execution is beneficial for massive scans and hash joins. Both scans and hash joins are typical for long queries, for which the speed-up is usually most significant.

In contrast, the speed-up for short queries is usually negligible. Parallel execution of different queries may improve throughput, but this is not related to parallel execution of a single query.

Sometimes the optimizer may replace index-based access (that would be used within sequential execution) with a parallel table scan. This may be caused by imprecise cost estimation. In such cases, parallel execution may be slower than sequential execution.

All execution plans in this book were created with parallelism turned off.

In addition, whatever scalability benefits are provided by parallel execution cannot fix poor design or compensate for inefficient code for a simple mathematical reason: scalability benefits from parallelism are at best linear, while the cost of nested loops is quadratic.

Summary

This chapter covered different ways to break queries into smaller functional parts and the advantages and disadvantages of each approach. It covered the potential pitfalls of one often-used optimization tool—temporary tables—and showed how common table expressions can be used as an alternative that doesn't stymie the query optimizer. It also discussed views and materialized views and their impact on performance. Finally, it briefly addressed partitioning and parallel execution.

CHAPTER 8

Optimizing Data Modification

Up to this point, our focus has been on optimizing *queries*, which means that only data retrieval has been covered. We haven't touched on anything related to data manipulation, that is, updating, removing, or adding records. This is the subject of this chapter, which discusses how data manipulation affects performance and how performance for these operations can be improved.

What Is DML?

Any database system has two languages: DDL (data definition language), used to create tables and other database objects, and DML (data manipulation language), which is used to query and modify data in the database. In PostgreSQL, both DDL and DML are parts of SQL, but some commands are related to DDL (ALTER TABLE, CREATE MATERIALIZED VIEW, DROP INDEX, etc.), while others are related to DML (INSERT, UPDATE, DELETE). It is also common to refer to these commands as DDL and DML, respectively, so a reference to "running DDL" means executing data definition commands and "running DML" means executing INSERT, UPDATE, or DELETE.

Two Ways to Optimize Data Modification

The execution of any DML statement consists of two parts: selecting the records to be modified and the data modification itself. In the case of INSERT, the first part may be omitted when constants are being inserted. However, if an INSERT-SELECT construct is used, the records that are needed for the insert must be found first.

© Henrietta Dombrovskaya, Boris Novikov, Anna Bailliekova 2024
H. Dombrovskaya et al., *PostgreSQL Query Optimization*, https://doi.org/10.1007/979-8-8688-0069-6_8

For this reason, optimizing a DML statement consists of two parts: optimizing selection and optimizing data modification.

If the search part is the problem, then it is the SELECT part of the command that should be optimized. This is well covered in prior chapters. This chapter concerns itself with the second part—optimizing writing data.

In the overwhelming majority of cases, even OLTP systems execute significantly fewer DML statements than SELECT statements. This is the primary reason that people seldom talk about optimizing DML. However, long-running DML may cause problems not only because the updated data isn't available in the system in a timely manner but also because it can create *blocking locks,* which slow down the execution of other statements.

How Does DML Work?

To discuss the optimizations applicable to data modification SQL commands, we need to understand how they are executed.

Low-Level Input/Output

At the end of the day, any SQL operation, no matter how complex, comes down to a couple low-level operations: reading and writing individual database blocks. The reason is simple: data contained in the database can only be processed when blocks are fetched to main memory, and all modifications are first done in main memory and then written to disk.

A fundamental difference between reads and writes is that reads from disk must be completed before data can be processed; thus, a SELECT statement cannot be completed before all needed blocks are fetched into memory. In contrast, the changes inside a block are completed before the write starts; thus, a SQL operation can be completed without any delays. There is no need to wait until the modified data are actually written to the disk. This is somewhat counterintuitive: usually one would expect that an update requires more resources than a read.

Of course, writes do require much more resources than reads: the database must modify indexes and register updates in the WAL (write-ahead log). Still, this happens in main memory as far as single DML statements are concerned. WAL records are forced to disk asynchronously: by default, PostgreSQL guarantees that they are written at commit.

This sounds great: any INSERT, UPDATE, or DELETE appears to run much faster than a SELECT. If so, why are optimizations still needed?

There are two major reasons: First, writes are still needed and hence consume some amount of hardware resources, mostly I/O bandwidth. The cost of writes is tied to the cost of transferring pages and is not necessarily visible on any individual operation, but it still slows down processing and can even affect the performance of SELECT statements. An additional workload is produced in the background (e.g., modified blocks being written to disk) and during maintenance. Typically, this maintenance performs data restructuring, for example, the VACUUM operation in PostgreSQL. Some restructuring tasks block access to the modified object for the entire duration of the restructuring operation.

Second, modifications may interfere with other modifications and even with retrieval. As long as data is not modified, the order of processing is immaterial. Data can be accessed from different SELECT statements simultaneously. In contrast, modifications cannot be simultaneous, and the order of operations is crucial. In order to ensure correctness, some operations must be delayed or even declined. Correctness is the responsibility of the concurrency control (a.k.a. transaction processing) subsystem. Transaction processing is not the focus of this book; however, discussion of modifications cannot avoid some considerations related to the transactional behavior of the DBMS.

The Impact of Concurrency Control

To ensure the correct order of operations, transaction dispatchers usually rely on locking. If a transaction requires a lock and another transaction already has a conflicting lock, the execution is delayed until the conflicting lock is released. This is called lock waiting. Lock waiting is the primary cause of delays in modification operations.

Another function of concurrency control is to ensure that updates are not lost. Any updates performed by a committed transaction must be reliably stored on a hard drive before commit. The mechanism for this is the write-ahead log (WAL). All data modifications must be registered in WAL records on the hard drive before a transaction can commit. The WAL is written sequentially, and on slow rotating drives, sequential reads and writes are two orders of magnitude faster than random reads and writes. This difference is negligible on SSDs. Although there is no need to wait until all changes are written from the cache to the database, commits still must wait until the WAL is flushed.

As result, committing too frequently can significantly slow down processing. An extreme case is running each DML statement in a separate transaction. This actually happens if an application does not use transaction control statements and therefore the database wraps each statement into a separate transaction. On the other hand, transactions that are too long may cause slowness due to locking.

The preceding considerations apply to any high-performance database. Let's look at techniques specific to PostgreSQL.

One of the distinguishing features of PostgreSQL is MVCC: multi-version concurrency control. PostgreSQL never performs "updates in place," that is, never "updates" a record. Instead, a new version of an item (e.g., a table row) is created and stored in a free space in the same or a newly allocated block, while the previous version is still accessible.

Figure 8-1 shows the structure of a block from Figure 3-1 after a deletion (or update) of the second row. The space previously occupied by this row cannot be used for another row; and, in fact, the data is still accessible.

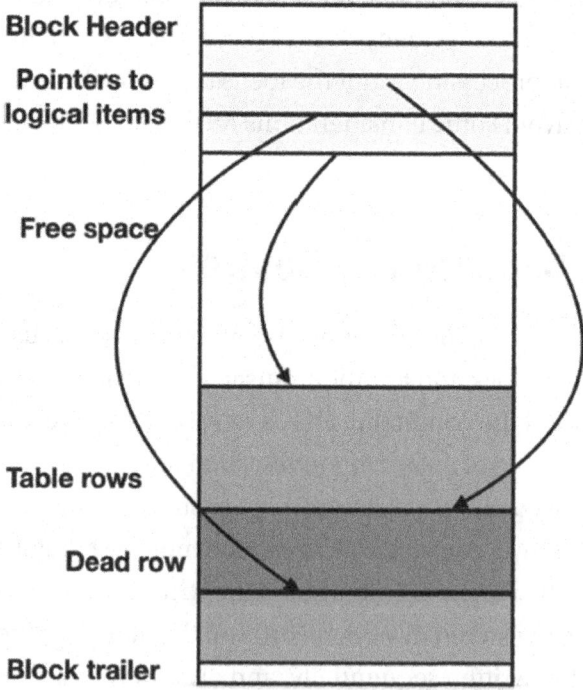

Figure 8-1. *Block layout after deletion of a row*

This feature may have both positive and negative impacts on performance.

The obsolete versions are not kept forever. A VACUUM operation removes them and consolidates the free space in a block when old versions are no longer needed for currently running transactions.

PostgreSQL uses the snapshot isolation (SI) concurrency control protocol to prevent undesirable interference between transactions. Note that database textbooks usually explain locking as it is used in a two-phase locking concurrency control protocol, which significantly differs from the way locks are used in PostgreSQL. Any intuition gained from textbooks or experiences with other systems might be misleading.

Under SI, a transaction always reads the latest committed version of a row. If another transaction has updated this row but did not commit before the start of the read operation, the read operation will return an obsolete version. This is an advantage as the older version is available and locking is not needed to read it. That is, the multi-version concurrency control improves throughput as there is no need to delay read operations.

According to SI, concurrent writes of the same data are not allowed: if two concurrent (i.e., running at the same time) transactions attempt to modify the same data, one of the two transactions must be aborted. In general, there are two strategies to enforce this rule. One is called *first update wins*, and the other is called *first commit wins*. It is easier to enforce the first strategy: we know that an update was executed right away, and the second transaction can be aborted without any wait. However, PostgreSQL utilizes the second strategy.

To enforce this rule, PostgreSQL uses write locks for any modification operation. Before a transaction can make any data changes, it has to acquire a lock for updates. If a lock cannot be obtained because some other transaction is modifying the same data, the operation is delayed until the termination of the transaction that holds the conflicting lock. If the lock is released because the holding transaction is aborted, the lock is granted to the waiting transaction, and a data modification operation can be completed. Otherwise, if the transaction commits successfully, the subsequent behavior depends on the transaction isolation level. For READ COMMITTED, which is the default in PostgreSQL, the waiting transaction will read the modified data, acquire a write lock, and complete the modification. This behavior is possible because on this isolation level, a read operation can read a version committed before the start of the SELECT statement, rather than the start of the transaction. If the isolation level is REPEATABLE READ, the waiting transaction will be aborted. This implementation results in waits but avoids unneeded aborts.

We do not discuss the SERIALIZABLE level because it is used vanishingly rarely.

Now, let's take a look at some important special cases.

Data Modification and Indexes

In Chapter 5, when we talked about creating new indexes, we mentioned that adding indexes to a table can potentially slow DML operations. How much slower depends on storage and system characteristics (e.g., disk speed, processors, and memory), but according to multiple PostgreSQL experts' observations, adding an extra index results in only a 1% increase in INSERT/UPDATE time.

You can perform some experiments using the postgres_air schema. For example, start with a table that has many indexes, such as the flight table.

First, create a copy of the table flight with no indexes:

```
CREATE TABLE flight_no_index AS
SELECT * FROM flight LIMIT 0;
```

Then, insert rows from the table flight into the table flight_no_index:

```
INSERT INTO flight_no_index
SELECT * FROM flight LIMIT 100
```

Note the execution time. Then, truncate the new table, and start building the same indexes built in Chapter 5 for the table flight on table flight_no_index. Repeat the insert. There is no difference in execution time for a small number of rows (around a couple hundred rows), but some slowness is observed when inserting 100,000 rows. For typical operations performed in the OLTP environment, however, there will be no material difference.

Naturally, creating indexes takes time, and it is worth mentioning that the CREATE INDEX operation in PostgreSQL locks the table for all DML operations (reads are still allowed). CREATE INDEX CONCURRENTLY takes longer to complete but allows DML to be executed.

As we mentioned earlier, PostgreSQL inserts new versions of updated rows. This has certain negative impacts on performance: in general, new versions are inserted into different locations, and therefore all indexes on the table must be modified. To reduce this negative effect, PostgreSQL uses a technique that sometimes is referred to as HOT (heap-only tuples); an attempt is made to insert the new version into the same block. If the block has sufficient free space and the update does not involve modifying any indexed columns, then there is no need to modify any indexes. In reality, things are a little bit more complicated, but we are not going to get into internals at this point.

DML and Vacuum

As mentioned earlier, PostgreSQL never removes old versions of rows immediately. The DELETE statement marks deleted rows as removed, while UPDATE inserts a new version of a row and marks the previous version as outdated. As soon as these rows are not needed for active transactions, they become dead. As the number of dead rows grows, it effectively reduces the number of active rows in a block and thus slows down subsequent heap scans.

The space occupied by dead rows (i.e., deleted tuples) remains unused until it is reclaimed by a VACUUM operation. This situation is called *table bloat*. Most of the time, even with a relatively high rate of updates, routine vacuuming initiated by the autovacuum daemon addresses the dead tuples promptly, so that they do not cause any significant delays.

The recommendations on tuning AUTOVACUUM system parameters can be found in PostgreSQL documentation and on many consulting companies' websites. While choosing the optimal values for these parameters, you will need to find a right balance between reducing I/O spikes, making sure vacuum can be completed relatively fast, and still having the job done (i.e., keeping bloat at bay).

Mass UPDATE/DELETE

What happens if a mass UPDATE/DELETE is performed, that is, an operation that affects a large fraction of the table? If you run this type of workload, you might notice that SELECTs from the affected table become significantly slower. The visibility map forces recheck to go to the heap blocks; in addition, the number of active tuples on a page decreases. This will result in more blocks needing to be read into memory for each select operation.

While there are multiple ways to tune autovacuum on a very busy system, if the level of updates/deletes is too high, it might be impossible to reduce table and index bloat, even with perfectly tuned autovacuum parameters. You might need to evaluate the whole system architecture to see whether the volume of data modification is justified. This includes checking whether applications perform several consecutive updates on the same set of records or whether it would make sense to partition a table and replace mass updates with DROP/DETACH partition and subsequently CREATE/ATTACH partition.

Frequent Updates

Now, let's consider a different case: a table experiences frequent updates (although each of these updates affects a single row or a very small number of rows).

Depending on the nature of these updates, sometimes it might be possible to reduce both the overhead of index updates and the table bloat by setting the table's `fillfactor`. This storage parameter sets the percentage of free space in table blocks, and it can be defined in the `WITH` clause of the `CREATE TABLE` statement. By default, the value of this parameter is 100, which tells PostgreSQL to fit as many rows as possible and minimize the size of free space in every block. Thus, usually free space can appear only after updates or deletions followed by vacuuming.

However, if the size of table rows is small enough to store multiple records in one block and updates do not affect indexed attributes, we can specify smaller values of `fillfactor`. PostgreSQL allows values as low as 10, leaving 90% of block space for updated versions of rows. Of course, small values of the `fillfactor` parameter result in an increased number of blocks needed to store table data and hence increase the number of reads needed for a heap scan of the table. This significantly slows down long queries but might be less significant for short queries, especially when only one row is selected from a block. Setting the `fillfactor` to lower than 100% increases the likelihood of HOT updates described earlier in this section.

Referential Integrity and Triggers

The presence of multiple foreign keys in a table can potentially slow DML. This is not to suggest that referential integrity checks are bad. On the contrary, the ability to maintain referential integrity is one of the most powerful features of relational systems. The reason they might slow data manipulation operations is that for each `INSERT/UPDATE` operation on a table with integrity constraints, the database engine has to check whether the new values of the constrained columns are present in the respective parent tables, thus executing additional implicit SELECT statements. These checks may take virtually no time, for example, if the parent table is a small lookup containing just a handful of rows. However, if the parent table size is comparable with the size of the child table, the overhead may be more noticeable. As in most other cases, the actual delay time depends on system parameters and hardware characteristics.

The execution times with and without constraints can be compared by creating a copy of the flight table:

```
CREATE TABLE flight_no_constr AS
SELECT * FROM flight LIMIT 0;
```

Then, once again, start adding the same constraints as the flight table has to the flight_no_constr table, and once again, try to perform inserts. You may notice that adding an integrity check on the aircraft_code attribute does not impact the time to insert, but adding constraints on departure_airport and arrival_airport would noticeably slow down inserts.

Note that operations on the parent table are also affected: when a record in the parent table is updated or deleted, the database engine must check that there are no records in each of the child tables that reference the updated or deleted value.

Triggers can potentially slow down data modification operations as well, for the same reason as referential integrity constraints: each trigger invocation may result in executing multiple additional SQL commands. The extent to which each trigger slows down execution depends on its complexity.

It's worth noting that referential integrity constraints in PostgreSQL are implemented using system triggers, so all observations regarding integrity constraints are applicable to triggers. However, the potential performance impact of triggers does not mean that triggers should not be used. On the contrary, if there are some actions or checks that should be performed for any DML operation on the table, it is beneficial to implement them using database triggers instead of programming these checks in the application. The latter approach will be less efficient and would not cover the cases when the data in the table is modified directly in the database instead of accessing it through the application.

Summary

In this chapter, we briefly discussed the implication of data manipulation operations on system performance. Typically, DML commands are executed at least an order of magnitude less frequently than SELECT statements. However, if data modification inefficiencies are not addressed in a timely manner, they may result in blocking locks and affect the performance throughout the application.

CHAPTER 9

Design Matters

In the Introduction, we noted that optimization begins during requirements gathering and design. To be precise, it starts with system design, including the database design, but it is impossible to come up with the right design unless we invest time in gathering information about the objects that should be present in the database. In this chapter, we will discuss a variety of design options and will show how design decisions can impact performance.

Design Matters

Chapter 1 explained two different solutions for storing information about phone numbers, shown in Figures 1-1 and 1-2. Let's return to this example.

Listing 9-1 shows the table definitions used in the `postgres_air` schema. The `account` table contains information about user accounts, and the `phone` table contains information about all phone numbers associated with accounts. This relationship is supported by a foreign key constraint.

Listing 9-2 shows an alternative design, where all phones are stored together with account information.

Listing 9-1. Two-table design

```
/* account table */
CREATE TABLE account(
        account_id integer,
        login text,
        first_name text,
         last_name text,
         frequent_flyer_id integer,
         update_ts timestamp with time zone,
```

© Henrietta Dombrovskaya, Boris Novikov, Anna Bailliekova 2024
H. Dombrovskaya et al., *PostgreSQL Query Optimization*, https://doi.org/10.1007/979-8-8688-0069-6_9

```
        CONSTRAINT account_pkey PRIMARY KEY (account_id),
        CONSTRAINT frequent_flyer_id_fk FOREIGN KEY (frequent_flyer_id)
        REFERENCES frequent_flyer (frequent_flyer_id)
);
/*phone table */
CREATE TABLE phone(
        phone_id integer,
        account_id integer,
        phone text,
        phone_type text,
        primary_phone boolean,
        update_ts timestamp with time zone,
        CONSTRAINT phone_pkey PRIMARY KEY (phone_id),
        CONSTRAINT phone_account_id_fk FOREIGN KEY (account_id)
        REFERENCES account (account_id)
);
```

Listing 9-2. One-table design

```
/* account table */
CREATE TABLE account(
        account_id integer,
        login text,
        first_name text,
        last_name text,
        frequent_flyer_id integer,
        home_phone text,
        work_phone text,
        cell_phone text,
        primary_phone text,
        update_ts timestamp with time zone,
        CONSTRAINT account_pkey PRIMARY KEY (account_id),
        CONSTRAINT frequent_flyer_id_fk FOREIGN KEY (frequent_flyer_id)
        REFERENCES frequent_flyer (frequent_flyer_id)
);
```

There are multiple reasons the two-table design was chosen for the `postgres_air` schema; as discussed in Chapter 1, many people do not have landlines at home or a dedicated work phone. Many people have more than one cell phone or a virtual number, like Google Voice. All these scenarios can be supported with the two-table solution and can't fit into the one-table solution, unless we start to add columns to accommodate each of these cases. Indicating a primary phone in the one-table solution would require repeating one of the numbers in the `primary_phone` column, creating room for inconsistency. From a performance perspective, the two-table solution is also more beneficial.

In the two-table solution, searching for an account by phone number is a straightforward SELECT statement:

```
SELECT
       DISTINCT account_id
FROM phone
WHERE phone='8471234567'
```

This query will be executed using an index-only scan.

In the one-table design, a similar query would look like this:

```
SELECT
       account_id
FROM account
WHERE home_phone= '8471234567'
         OR work_phone= '8471234567'
         OR cell_phone= '8471234567'
```

To avoid a full scan, three different indexes must be built.

Does this mean that the one-table design is worse than the two-table design? It depends on how the data is accessed. If the schema is supporting a system used by travel agents, the most likely use case is needing to pull a customer account based on the phone number. When an agent asks a customer for their phone number, the customer is unlikely to specify the type of the phone.

On the other hand, consider a report on customer accounts that have been updated in the last 24 hours. This report should include home phone, work phone, and cell phone in separate columns regardless of if any are empty and should include accounts that have had any modification in the last 24 hours—including updates to phone numbers. In this case, the one-table solution, shown in Listing 9-3, is much simpler and more efficient.

Listing 9-3. Usage of one-table design

```
SELECT *
FROM account
WHERE update_ts BETWEEN now()- interval '1 day' AND now();
```

Producing the same result in the two-table design is more involved—see Listing 9-4.

Listing 9-4. Same query with a two-table design

```
SELECT
      a.account_id,
      login,
      first_name,
      last_name,
      frequent_flyer_id,
      home_phone
      work_phone,
      cell_phone,
      primary_phone
FROM account a
JOIN (
      SELECT
             account_id,
             max(phone) FILTER (WHERE phone_type='home')
                   AS home_phone,
             max(phone) FILTER (WHERE phone_type='work')
                   AS work_phone,
             max(phone) FILTER (WHERE phone_type='mobile')
                   AS cell_phone,
             max(phone) FILTER (WHERE primary_phone IS true)
                   AS primary_phone
      FROM phone
      WHERE account_id IN (
             SELECT
                   account_id
```

```
        FROM phone
        WHERE update_ts BETWEEN now()- interval '1 day' AND now()
        UNION
        SELECT
              account_id
        FROM account
        WHERE update_ts BETWEEN now()- interval '1 day' AND now()
        )
   GROUP BY 1)  p
USING (account_id);
```

These two examples are illustrative for another reason—the query for which the two-table solution is preferred is more likely to occur in an OLTP system, and the query that is better served by the one-table solution is more likely in an OLAP system. ETL tools can be used to transform data from OLTP systems to a format that is better suited to business intelligence needs.

A similar situation was shown in Chapter 6, where a nonoptimal database design prompted a nonoptimal query (see Listing 6-26). Even the optimized version of the query remained relatively slow. These examples illustrate impact of database design on performance and that sometimes the negative consequences of poor design can't be remedied by improving the query or building additional indexes.

Subsequent sections of this chapter address the most common design choices that may negatively affect performance.

Why Use a Relational Model?

While all the previous examples are relational, as PostgreSQL is built on a relational model, we're aware that many people think of relational databases as outdated or out of fashion. Public talks with titles like "What comes after relational databases?" are given at a regular cadence.

This section isn't a defense of relational databases. Relational databases don't need defending, and, so far, no would-be successor has had gained even close to a comparable level of adoption. Rather, the goal is to explain the limitations of other models.

Types of Databases

So what alternatives exist to relational models? There are a wide variety of database systems and data stores currently in use, using a wide variety of data models and storage techniques. These include traditional relational systems with row-based or column-based storage, scalable distributed systems, stream processing systems, and much more.

We've seen more than one non-relational database system work its way through the Gartner hype cycle, from the peak of overinflated expectations to the trough of disillusionment. It is worth noting, however, that the core of the relational model is a query language based on Boolean logic, rather than any specific way of storing data. This is likely the reason many systems created as alternatives to the traditional RDBMS ended up with variations of SQL as a high-level query language and hence the associated Boolean logic.

While relational databases do not appear close to being dethroned, there are technologies developed and validated within new systems that have proven useful and been widely adopted. Three popular approaches are entity-attribute-value models, key-value stores, and hierarchical systems, the last often referred to as document stores.

Entity-Attribute-Value Model

In the entity-attribute-value (EAV) model, values are scalar (often text, to accommodate multiple data types). To review from Chapter 6, this model features a table with three columns, the first for an identifier for an entity, the second an identifier for an attribute of that entity, and the third the value of that attribute for that entity. This is done in the name of "flexibility," which in reality means imprecise or unknown requirements. Unsurprisingly, this flexibility comes at the expense of performance. Chapter 6 introduced the `custom_field` table, noted that this design was not optimal, and showed how it could negatively affect performance. Even after applying optimization techniques to avoid multiple table scans, execution was relatively slow.

In addition to performance impacts, this design curtails data quality management. In the case introduced in Chapter 6, three custom fields contain data of three different types: `passport_num` is a number, `passport_exp_date` is a date, and `passport_country` is a text field, which should contain a valid country name. However, in the `custom_field` table, they all are stored in the text field `custom_field_value`, which does not allow strong type checks or referential integrity constraints.

Key-Value Model

The key-value model stores complex objects within a single field, so the structure is not exposed to the database. Individual attributes of the object then are much more complex to extract, effectively kneecapping the database engine in doing tasks beyond returning a single object via a primary key. In the most extreme case, a design may package all fields other than the primary key into a single JSON object.

Since PostgreSQL introduced JSON support in version 9.2, this approach has become very popular with database and application developers. JSONB was introduced in version 9.4, and more enhancements have followed in every subsequent version. With this support, table columns defined as JSON are commonplace. For example, the `passenger` table from the `postgres_air` schema could be defined as shown in Listing 9-5.

Listing 9-5. Table with JSON

```
CREATE TABLE passenger_json (
     passenger_id INT,
     passenger_info JSON);
```

An example of the `passenger_info` JSON is shown in Listing 9-6.

Listing 9-6. Example of a JSON value

```
{"booking_ref" : "8HNB12",
"passenger_no": "1",
"first_name" : "MARIAM",
"last_name" : "WARREN",
"update_ts" : "2023-04-17T19:45:55.022782-05:00",
}
```

Yes, the suggested design looks universal and does not require any DDL changes no matter how many new data elements are added in the future. However, the same issues affect this design as the EAV model. This approach makes it impossible to perform type checks on scalar values, and referential integrity constraints can't be defined. Additionally, what is often overlooked is a substantial increase in the data volume required to store JSON. Indeed, the names of the keys are repeated in each record. Depending on the type and size of values stored, the data volume may increase several times over.

Tools and approaches for working with JSON fields are discussed later in this chapter.

Hierarchical Model

Hierarchical structures are easy to understand and use. In fact, hierarchical structures were first implemented in databases in the 1960s due to their ease of use, as well as their relatively small memory requirements. Of course, at that time, neither XML nor JSON was available. These structures work great as long as everything fits into a single hierarchy. However, using hierarchies becomes both complex and inefficient as soon as data fits into more than one hierarchy.

Let's illustrate with examples from the postgres_air schema, shown in Figure 9-1. For an airport, the list of departing flights is one hierarchy, and the list of arriving flights is another. Boarding passes may fit into the same hierarchy as departing flights. At the same time, they can be a part of a completely different hierarchy that starts from bookings. Note that passengers and booking legs can't fit into the same hierarchy without duplication.

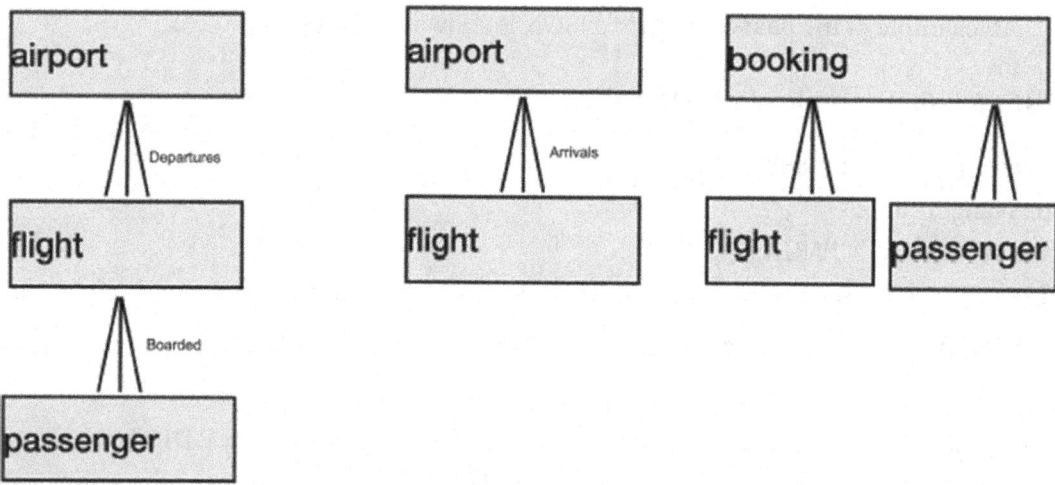

Figure 9-1. *Examples of hierarchies in the postgres_air schema*

The early hierarchical databases (IMS/360) provided several hierarchical views of data to the client application but supported more complex data structures internally.

Combining the Best of Different Worlds

PostgreSQL is not just a relational system. It is object-relational, meaning that column data types are not necessarily scalar. In fact, columns can store structured types including arrays, composite types, or objects represented as JSON or XML documents.

Using these features responsibly provides all the potential benefits of several alternative approaches in combination with more traditional relational features.

"Responsibly" is the operative word here. For example, PostgreSQL allows the multiple-hierarchy approach mentioned in the previous section. We can build hierarchical representations for a client application on top of an internal relational structure in the database. Such an approach combines the best of both worlds: data is extracted efficiently via the power of relational query, and the application can consume complex objects in a friendly data exchange format. More details on this approach are provided in Chapter 14.

Although distributed systems aren't covered in this book, it's worth mentioning that PostgreSQL has a massive set of extensions (additional libraries not included into basic distribution) that support distributed querying including DBMSs other than PostgreSQL. These extensions are called *foreign data wrappers (FDWs)*, and they provide almost transparent ways of accessing data that can reside in more than 60 types of DBMSs, both relational and non-relational.

Flexibility vs. Efficiency and Correctness

A frequent argument for a flexible design is that "the data structure/schema definition may change." Then, the argument goes adding a column is a DDL (data definition) change and adding a row (in the key-value model) is just adding a row.

True, real-life systems evolve, and to adequately reflect these changes, existing data structures must be modified. This may entail adding or removing some attributes or changing data types or changing the cardinality of relationships. However, the inevitability of making changes does not necessitate the use of alternative models, such as document stores or key-value systems. The cost of making changes to the database schema must always be weighed against the potential performance and data integrity pitfalls of these flexible solutions.

The previous section mentioned the difficulty of creating any integrity constraints in a non-relational design. For some reason, there is a widespread belief that NoSQL databases are "faster" than relational databases. This statement may be true in a very limited number of scenarios, but in most cases, the situation is the opposite. There may be performance gains from horizontal distribution, but they are counterbalanced by the cost of needing to take additional steps to verify data integrity. Additional potential performance problems emerge because of the difficulties of creating indexes in EAV and key-value models.

For example, in the case of the `custom_field` table, `passport_exp_date` should be a date, and it is often compared with other dates, for example, with the date of the flight to make sure that the passport doesn't expire prior to the date of departure. However, this date is stored in a text field, which means that it must be converted to a date to perform a type-specific compare. Moreover, this conversion can only be applied to rows that contain date-type values.

PostgreSQL has partial indexes, so it's possible to create an index on only those rows that contain a passport expiration date. However, they cannot be indexed as a date that could be efficiently used as search criteria, because indexes cannot be built with mutable functions like so:

```
CREATE INDEX custom_field_exp_date_to_date
ON custom_field(to_date(custom_field_value, 'MM-DD-YYYY'))
WHERE custom_field_name='passport_exp_date'
```

This is because all date/time conversion functions are `mutable`, because they depend on the current session settings. In order to be able to use a conversion function in an index, one would need to write a custom conversion function. Chapter 11 covers creating user-defined functions. This function will have to include exception handling, which means that a value erroneously added in the wrong format won't be indexed. In addition, the search itself will be significantly slower than having a `date` field in the first place.

What about the case of packaging all the attributes in a JSON column? Similar problems with indexing occur. It is possible to create an index on JSON; for example, for the table `passenger_json` in Listing 9-5, it is possible to create an index on `booking_ref` as shown in Listing 9-7.

Listing 9-7. Indexing a JSON column

```
CREATE INDEX passenger_j_booking_ref
ON passenger_json ((passenger_info ->> 'booking_ref'));
```

It will work slower than an index on the original passenger table, but it will work better than a sequential scan. However, for any value that is intended to be numeric or contain a date, the same conversion as the previous example will follow.

This is not to say there is no justification for any of these non-relational solutions.

For example, a table describing some regulations in the EU had about 500 columns and a single row added every time the regulations changed, approximately one row every five years. Replacement of this table with a variation of key-value (augmented with a couple of additional columns characterizing the value) made both database and application developers happy. There was no issue of efficiency because of the size of the data.

When considering JSON columns, our recommendation is to use them only in cases when the data only needs to be used as one whole object, such as when storing external documents (e.g., an externally sourced credit report). Even in these cases, if some attributes that will be used in search criteria can be isolated, it is advisable to parse them into additional, stand-alone columns as well as storing them as components of a larger object.

Must We Normalize?

There is hardly a term in relational theory more misused than "normalization." It is commonplace for any number of DBAs, database developers, system architects, and others to declare that a system should be "normalized," but few could provide a description of the outcome they are seeking, let alone a definition for normalization.

This isn't just snobbery; it's not necessary for everyone working in the field of data management to memorize the definitions of every normal form. Relational normalization algorithms aren't often used in practice. In this sense, normalization is "dead" theory, the way that Latin is a dead language. However, scholars still find use in studying Latin, and analogously, some knowledge of normalization is essential for good database design.

Informally, a database schema is normalized if all column values depend only on the table primary key, and data is decomposed into multiple tables to avoid repetition.

One of the ways to create a normalized schema is to start by building an ER model: if entities are properly defined, the database schema produced from the ER model will be normalized. We can say that ER design implicitly includes discovery of dependencies. If it is not normalized, typically this indicates that some entities are missing.

Is it really important to normalize a database schema? Does it help performance? As is often the case, it depends.

The primary purpose of normalization is *not* to improve performance. Normalization creates a clean logical structure and helps ensure data integrity, especially when it is supported by referential integrity constraints. Normalization is needed for the same reasons that the relational model is needed: not necessarily to store the data, but to ensure data integrity and to be able to use relational querying language. The mapping between logical and storage structures is not necessarily one-to-one. Ideally, a clean logical structure should be provided for the application based on a storage structure optimized for performance.

On the other hand, there are many real-world entities that are denormalized and where normalization does not provide any benefits. The best-known example is the postal address. The US postal address consists of the following components: street address, city, zip code, and state.

It is not normalized, as anyone who has ever sent a package at an automated USPS kiosk knows. The automated check won't allow you to enter a zip code that does not match the previously entered address. However, we doubt that anyone would decide to normalize addresses when they are stored in a database table.

An often-heard argument in support of denormalized data structure is that "joins take time" and that denormalization is needed if we need queries to execute faster. Short queries, as discussed in Chapter 5, when constructed properly, require negligible additional time for joins, and this should not be traded for data accuracy.

However, there are cases when performance can indeed be improved through normalization, for example, when we need to select distinct values of some attribute with high selectivity or, in general, any subset of columns that are repetitive in a non-normalized table. In the postgres_air schema, the status of flights in the flight table is specified explicitly, which means that to find the list of possible flight statuses, one can execute the following query:

```
SELECT DISTINCT status
FROM flight
```

Use and Misuse of Surrogate Keys

Surrogate keys are unique values generated by the system in order to identify objects stored in the database. In PostgreSQL, surrogate values may be obtained as values selected from a sequence. When a row is inserted, a column specified with pseudo-type `serial` receives the next value from a sequence associated with the table automatically.

Surrogate keys are widely used. Some companies have internal standards that require use of surrogate keys for every table. However, surrogates have both advantages and disadvantages.

The advantage of surrogates is that the values assigned to different objects are guaranteed to be unique. However, the value of a surrogate is not related to other attributes of the object and is useless when a stored object needs to be matched to a real-world object.

Uniqueness of surrogates may hide certain errors. A real-world object may be represented in the database multiple times with different surrogate keys. For example, if a single purchase is registered in a system twice, a customer's card will be charged twice for a single product, and the issue is difficult to resolve without manual intervention. That being said, although our recommendation is to use some real-world unique attribute for a primary key, it is not always possible. In a database that stores all purchases in the supermarket, there is no way to distinguish between two bottles of Coke subsequently scanned by the same customer at the self-checkout. These two cases must be distinguishable in the source system: the purchase of two Coke bottles in one transaction, as opposed to a duplication of the same transaction to purchase a single Coke. Similarly, hospital systems may have multiple medical record numbers (MRNs) associated with one patient; it's critical to have a surrogate key in this case so all the patient's clinical data is stored together.

Sometimes, the presence of a surrogate key in the table is wrongly associated with normalization. A requirement to use surrogate keys is commonly explained as a way to make the database schema normalized. And, indeed, if there is a unique identifier assigned to each row, everything will be normalized. But since the unique identifiers would bear no relation to real-world objects, the result may be one real-world object mapped to multiple occurrences in the database. For example, we've seen a system in which each time a customer would enter their address, the system would assign a unique identifier for the city, if the city was not in the database yet. This way, the system ended up with six different versions of "Chicago." Needless to say, this has nothing to do with normalization and may jeopardize both data accuracy and performance.

The use of surrogate keys may also result in extra joins. The `flight` table refers to the `airport` table using three-character codes that are widely used in the real world. Airport codes can be extracted from the flight table in this design:

```
SELECT
      departure_airport,
      arrival_airport,
      scheduled_departure
FROM flight;
```

However, if a surrogate key was used for the airport table, returning airport codes would necessitate two trips to the airport table:

```
SELECT
      d.airport_code,
      a.airport_code,
      f.scheduled_departure
FROM flight f
JOIN airport d ON d.airport_id = f.departure_airport_id
JOIN airport a ON a.airport_id = f.arrival_airport_id
```

Let's take a closer look at the use of surrogate keys in the `postgres_air` schema.

The definition of the `airport` table in the `postgres_air` schema is shown in Listing 9-8. The primary key of that table is `airport_code`. This column contains three-character codes that are used to identify airports in all flight booking systems worldwide, and these codes never change. Hence, they are reliable as unique identifiers, and surrogate keys are not needed.

Listing 9-8. The airport table

```
CREATE TABLE airport(
        airport_code char(3)NOT NULL,
        airport_name text NOT NULL,
        city text COLLATE NOT NULL,
        airport_tz text NOT NULL,
         continent text,
         iso_country text,
         iso_region text,
```

```
    intnl boolean NOT NULL,
    update_ts timestamptz,
    CONSTRAINT airport_pkey PRIMARY KEY (airport_code)
);
```

Similarly, aircrafts are identified with three-character codes, and we use these codes as a primary key for the `aircraft` table—see Listing 9-9.

Listing 9-9. The aircraft table

```
CREATE TABLE aircraft (
    model text,
    range numeric NOT NULL,
    class integer NOT NULL,
    velocity numeric NOT NULL,
    code text NOT NULL,
    CONSTRAINT aircraft_pkey PRIMARY KEY (code)
);
```

For the booking table (see Listing 9-10), the surrogate primary key `booking_id` is used, even though bookings have a six-character booking reference that uniquely identifies the booking and is never changed. The booking reference is also a surrogate key, although it is not derived from a database sequence. We could use the booking reference as a primary key. Thus, the column `booking_id` is redundant, though it provides some future-proofing if there is an anticipated need for bookings to come from more than one booking application. This also makes the table definition similar to definitions found in many industrial systems.

Listing 9-10. The booking table

```
CREATE TABLE booking (
        booking_id bigint NOT NULL,
        booking_ref text NOT NULL,
        booking_name text,
        account_id integer,
        email text NOT NULL,
        phone text NOT NULL,
        update_ts timestamptz,
```

```
        price numeric(7,2),
        CONSTRAINT booking_pkey PRIMARY KEY (booking_id),
        CONSTRAINT booking_booking_ref_key UNIQUE (booking_ref),
        CONSTRAINT booking_account_id_fk FOREIGN KEY (account_id)
        REFERENCES account (account_id)
);
```

The booking_leg table (Listing 9-11) links bookings to flights. Therefore, a natural key for this table would consist of flight_id and booking_id, that is, of two foreign keys referencing tables flight and booking. This pair of columns would be an excellent primary key. The decision to create an additional surrogate key booking_leg_id was driven by the idea to avoid references to the compound key from the dependent table (the booking_leg table is referenced from the boarding_pass table, which is the largest table in the database).

Listing 9-11. The booking_leg table

```
CREATE TABLE booking_leg (
        booking_leg_id SERIAL,
        booking_id integer NOT NULL,
        booking_ref text NOT NULL,
      flight_id integer NOT NULL,
      leg_num integer,
      is_returning boolean,
      update_ts timestamp with time zone,
     CONSTRAINT booking_leg_pkey PRIMARY KEY (booking_leg_id),
     CONSTRAINT booking_id_fk FOREIGN KEY (booking_id)
     REFERENCES booking (booking_id),
     CONSTRAINT flight_id_fk FOREIGN KEY (flight_id)
     REFERENCES flight (flight_id)
);
```

A surrogate key is needed for the passenger table (see Listing 9-12) because the same person may be a passenger on multiple bookings and a passenger is not necessarily registered as a client in the booking system (a flight may be booked by someone else on behalf of the passenger).

Listing 9-12. The passenger table

```
CREATE TABLE passenger(
        passenger_id serial,
        booking_id integer NOT NULL,
        booking_ref text,
        passenger_no integer,
        first_name text NOT NULL,
        last_name text NOT NULL,
        account_id integer,
        update_ts timestamptz,
        CONSTRAINT passenger_pkey PRIMARY KEY (passenger_id),
        CONSTRAINT pass_account_id_fk FOREIGN KEY (account_id)
        REFERENCES account (account_id),
        CONSTRAINT pass_booking_id_fk FOREIGN KEY (booking_id)
        REFERENCES booking (booking_id),
 CONSTRAINT pass_frequent_flyer_id_fk FOREIGN KEY (account_id)
 REFERENCES account (account_id)
);
```

There is no obvious way to identify accounts; therefore, a surrogate key must be used for the account table, shown in Listing 9-13.

Listing 9-13. The account table

```
CREATE TABLE account(
        account_id SERIAL,
        login text NOT NULL,
        first_name textNOT NULL,
        last_name text NOT NULL,
        frequent_flyer_id integer,
        update_ts timestamp with time zone,
        CONSTRAINT account_pkey PRIMARY KEY (account_id),
        CONSTRAINT frequent_flyer_id_fk FOREIGN KEY(frequent_flyer_id)
        REFERENCES frequent_flyer (frequent_flyer_id)
);
```

Loyalty program customers might be identified by card number. However, the separate surrogate key frequent_flyer_id facilitates replacements for a lost or stolen card, without needing to map or migrate data from one customer record to another or losing the data for a loyal customer.

In contrast, the surrogate flight_id in the flight table is needed. The natural identification of a flight consists of flight_num and scheduled_departure. The flight number is the same on different days, while departure time may vary on different days and can be changed slightly (e.g., 5–10 minutes later) when the flight is already partially booked. The flight_id represents a particular occurrence of the flight with a specific flight number as shown in Listing 9-14.

Listing 9-14. The flight table

```
CREATE TABLE flight (
        flight_id serial,
        flight_no text NOT NULL,
        scheduled_departure timestamptz NOT NULL,
        scheduled_arrival timestamptz NOT NULL,
        departure_airport char(3) NOT NULL,
        arrival_airport char(3) NOT NULL,
        status text NOT NULL,
        aircraft_code char(3) NOT NULL,
        actual_departure timestamptz,
        actual_arrival timestamptz,
        update_ts timestamptz,
        CONSTRAINT flight_pkey PRIMARY KEY (flight_id),
        CONSTRAINT aircraft_code_fk FOREIGN KEY (aircraft_code)
        REFERENCES aircraft (code),
        CONSTRAINT arrival_airport_fk FOREIGN KEY (departure_airport)
        REFERENCES airport (airport_code),
        CONSTRAINT departure_airport_fk FOREIGN KEY (departure_airport)
        REFERENCES airport (airport_code)
);
```

The table boarding_pass (Listing 9-15) has a surrogate key, but it is not referenced from any other table and is therefore useless. The natural key of this table consists of two columns: flight_id and passenger_id.

Listing 9-15. Boarding pass

```
CREATE TABLE boarding_pass (
        pass_id integer NOT NULL,
        passenger_id bigint,
        booking_leg_id bigint,
        seat text,
        boarding_time timestamptz,
        precheck boolean,
        update_ts timestamptz,
        CONSTRAINT boarding_pass_pkey PRIMARY KEY (pass_id),
        CONSTRAINT booking_leg_id_fk FOREIGN KEY (booking_leg_id)
        REFERENCES booking_leg (booking_leg_id),
        CONSTRAINT passenger_id_fk FOREIGN KEY (passenger_id)
         REFERENCES passenger (passenger_id)
);
```

Summary

This chapter discussed the impact of design decisions on performance. Discussion covered both choices within a relational model relating to normalization and surrogate keys, as well as popular non-relational models. The limitations of these models were explored, along with examples of alternative approaches.

CHAPTER 10

What About Configuration Parameters?

The Introduction to this book mentioned that most of the time, when people talk about "database tuning," they assume that all performance problems can be fixed by figuring out optimal PostgreSQL configuration parameters.

Although some parameter tuning can indeed improve database performance, we are usually talking about 10%, 20%, and, in rare cases, up to 50% performance improvement, if parameters were previously set poorly. Those might sound like impressive numbers, but individual query optimization routinely makes queries run several times faster, in some cases, ten or more times faster, and restructuring applications (as we will see in Chapter 11) can improve overall system performance by hundreds of times.

This chapter discusses the most important PostgreSQL configuration parameters. We will demonstrate their impact on database performance and compare this impact with the techniques covered in previous chapters.

PostgreSQL Configuration Parameters Overview

There are over 300 PostgreSQL configuration parameters, and even an experienced DBA may not remember all of them. If you are an application developer or a database developer, you might not even know that PostgreSQL configuration parameters exist, let alone what they are and what they mean. There is a good reason for such ignorance since, in real life, ordinary users don't have any say in how these parameters are set. Indeed, configuration parameters are set for the whole PostgreSQL instance, which may have multiple databases, so any individual user will get the same settings as every other user. To be completely transparent, in some cases, ordinary users **can** specify some parameters just for themselves, but let's hold our horses for now.

© Henrietta Dombrovskaya, Boris Novikov, Anna Bailliekova 2024
H. Dombrovskaya et al., *PostgreSQL Query Optimization*, https://doi.org/10.1007/979-8-8688-0069-6_10

Let's take a look at some configuration parameters that can make the most impact on the query performance.

Memory Allocation

There are a lot of myths related to PostgreSQL memory allocation parameters. Many recommendations and formulas, which can be found on the Internet, were issued many years and many PostgreSQL versions ago, and many of them have never been revisited since. As a result, many of these recommendations are either wrong or can be used only as a first approximation and tuned later.

shared_buffers

The data stored in a PostgreSQL database must be read from a hard drive to main memory before anyone can use it. The memory area allocated for this purpose is called shared memory buffers. This parameter sets the number of shared memory buffers used by the database server. The limit of 64 GB goes back to older versions of Linux and nowadays is mythical. This is one of the few memory-related parameters that PostgreSQL uses at its face value, meaning that it sets the hard limit for shared buffers. Also, resetting this parameter requires an instance restart. The only actual limitation to this value is that after subtracting it from total RAM, there should be enough memory left for work_mem (discussed later).

Recommendation: Start with 25% of RAM and increase it until cache_hit_ratio is close to 90%.

effective_cache_size

This parameter is advisory. It does not reserve any memory, and PostgreSQL uses it for query planning purposes only. It indicates how much memory the operating system has available for caching data (so it includes memory cache, disk cache, filesystem cache, etc.). The way the query planner uses it is not straightforward, but the higher it is defined, the higher the chance of using indexes rather than a sequential scan.

Recommendation: 75% RAM is usually recommended but not required (and this number is not related to the shared_buffers value).

Connections and Sessions

The next set of parameters is related to individual user sessions.

max_connections

This parameter sets the maximum number of concurrent connections to the PostgreSQL instance, which can be handled simultaneously. This is a hard limit; if the maximum number of connections is reached, the system will become non-responsive. No users except for a superuser will be allowed to connect. This situation will persist until the superuser kills some connections. Changing this parameter requires a system restart. You might wonder why this limit is necessary, and if it can't be changed on the fly, why not set it as high as possible so that we never run into these problems?

Too many connections are undesirable in any database because each connection takes up additional resources, even when idle. The most important resource is the memory allocated for each session—we will address the details in the next section. On the application side, this problem is addressed by setting up an application connection pool so that application users do not initiate new database connections but instead use one of the already opened connections from the available pool. If we set the value of max_connections really high, the system may become slow and non-responsive because there won't be enough resources for all connections. In addition, there are some internal limitations in the PostgreSQL kernel itself, which makes it undesirable to have more than several hundred connections at any given moment.

Now that we have described many of the problems that occur when there are too many connections, we should note that these horror stories are not guaranteed and are at least in part exaggerated. If there are enough hardware resources available on the host, even several thousand max_connections may work perfectly well.

Recommendation: Start from several hundred, observe system behavior, and adjust accordingly.

work_mem

The work_mem setting controls the amount of memory that can be used per query operation node and is generally used for sorting data and hash tables. This is also a hard limit, meaning that this is the maximum size of memory PostgreSQL will allocate to any query node.

Any hash operation that requires more than this amount of memory will resort to swapping to disk and will therefore take longer to complete.

A well-known formula suggests dividing 25% of the total system memory by max_connections. Therefore, a decrease in max_connections will allow for a higher value of work_mem. Note that in this case, like in many others, it is assumed that the host has only one database, so be mindful when assigning the value for this parameter. Remember that PostgreSQL won't perform any calculations to check whether your settings make sense. Everyone might be happy until the next session cannot obtain enough RAM from the operating system and throws an out-of-memory error.

Fortunately, work_mem is one of the PostgreSQL parameters that can be set dynamically within a session or even for a duration of a transaction. So a possible solution could be to set the work_mem dynamically from the application. Suppose it is known that a particular query will be sorting a large dataset. In that case, it can be advantageous to increase the work_mem of that individual query (being careful not to over-allocate).

For example, if the session requires 200 GB for work_mem, you can run the following command:

```
set work_mem = '200GB';
```

This would set the session's work_mem to a new value and allow subsequent queries within that session to utilize more memory for sorting or hashing. To return to the standard value, run the following:

```
reset work_mem;
  maintenance_work_mem
```

This parameter determines the maximum amount of memory used for maintenance operations like VACUUM, CREATE INDEX, ALTER TABLE, ADD FOREIGN KEY, and data-loading operations (e.g., COPY). These operations may increase the I/O on database servers while they are running, so allocating more memory to them may lead to these operations finishing more quickly. There is a formula to calculate this value as well, but we will discuss this parameter in connection with the PostgreSQL VACUUM process.

Tuning Parameters for Better Performance

The statements like the one we made in the beginning of this chapter (comparing performance gains from parameter tuning to performance gains from query tuning) are notably difficult to illustrate. To follow along with the examples in this chapter, you will need to restore an additional clean copy of the postgres_air database. Alternatively, you can temporarily remove the indexes that we created in previous chapters and restore them after we are done with our experiments. Let's start with the query presented in Listing 10-1.

Listing 10-1. Query to optimize

```
SELECT
      f.flight_no,
      f.actual_departure,
       count(passenger_id) passengers
FROM flight f
JOIN booking_leg bl ON bl.flight_id = f.flight_id
JOIN passenger p ON p.booking_id=bl.booking_id
WHERE f.departure_airport = 'JFK'
      AND f.arrival_airport = 'ORD'
      AND f.actual_departure BETWEEN '2023-08-08' and '2023-08-12'
GROUP BY f.flight_id, f.actual_departure;
```

First, we will run it with default memory allocation parameters:

```
shared_buffers=128MB
work_mem=4MB
```

To observe the changes to buffer use, in this chapter, we use the EXPLAIN command with additional parameters—EXPLAIN (ANALYZE, BUFFERS, TIMING). The execution plan for this query is shown in Figure 10-1.

QUERY PLAN
text

```
-> Gather Merge  (cost=268857.90..268862.65 rows=10 width=24) (actual time=1070.505..1071.270 rows=11 loops=1)
   Workers Planned: 2
   Workers Launched: 2
   Buffers: shared hit=923 read=171410
   -> Partial GroupAggregate  (cost=267857.88..267861.48 rows=5 width=24) (actual time=1064.207..1064.214 rows=4 loops=3)
      Group Key: f.flight_id
      Buffers: shared hit=923 read=171410
      -> Sort  (cost=267857.88..267859.06 rows=473 width=20) (actual time=1064.200..1064.204 rows=54 loops=3)
         Sort Key: f.flight_id
         Sort Method: quicksort  Memory: 28kB
         Buffers: shared hit=923 read=171410
         Worker 0:  Sort Method: quicksort  Memory: 29kB
         Worker 1:  Sort Method: quicksort  Memory: 28kB
         -> Hash Join  (cost=2683.38..267836.86 rows=473 width=20) (actual time=397.967..1064.161 rows=54 loops=3)
            Hash Cond: (p.booking_id = bl.booking_id)
            Buffers: shared hit=909 read=171410
            -> Parallel Seq Scan on passenger p  (cost=0.00..239655.37 rows=6798237 width=8) (actual time=0.329..834.198 rows=5437898 loops=3)
               Buffers: shared hit=288 read=171385
            -> Hash  (cost=2681.74..2681.74 rows=131 width=20) (actual time=3.591..3.593 rows=69 loops=3)
               Buckets: 1024  Batches: 1  Memory Usage: 12kB
               Buffers: shared hit=599 read=25
               -> Nested Loop  (cost=268.50..2681.74 rows=131 width=20) (actual time=3.269..3.564 rows=69 loops=3)
                  Buffers: shared hit=599 read=25
                  -> Bitmap Heap Scan on flight f  (cost=263.41..979.10 rows=5 width=16) (actual time=3.246..3.453 rows=4 loops=3)
                     Recheck Cond: ((departure_airport = 'JFK'::bpchar) AND (arrival_airport = 'ORD'::bpchar))
                     Filter: ((actual_departure >= '2023-08-08 00:00:00-05'::timestamp with time zone) AND (actual_departure <= '2023-08-12 00:00:00-05'::timestamp with time
                     Rows Removed by Filter: 178
                     Heap Blocks: exact=152
                     Buffers: shared hit=510 read=25
                     -> BitmapAnd  (cost=263.41..263.41 rows=203 width=0) (actual time=3.174..3.175 rows=0 loops=3)
                        Buffers: shared hit=54 read=25
                        -> Bitmap Index Scan on flight_departure_airport  (cost=0.00..112.77 rows=10179 width=0) (actual time=1.490..1.490 rows=10530 loops=3)
                           Index Cond: (departure_airport = 'JFK'::bpchar)
                           Buffers: shared hit=24 read=11
                        -> Bitmap Index Scan on flight_arrival_airport  (cost=0.00..150.39 rows=13595 width=0) (actual time=1.420..1.420 rows=12922 loops=3)
                           Index Cond: (arrival_airport = 'ORD'::bpchar)
                           Buffers: shared hit=30 read=14
                  -> Bitmap Heap Scan on booking_leg bl  (cost=5.10..339.68 rows=85 width=8) (actual time=0.011..0.018 rows=17 loops=12)
                     Recheck Cond: (flight_id = f.flight_id)
                     Heap Blocks: exact=17
                     Buffers: shared hit=89
                     -> Bitmap Index Scan on leg_flight  (cost=0.00..5.08 rows=85 width=0) (actual time=0.006..0.006 rows=17 loops=12)
                        Index Cond: (flight_id = f.flight_id)
                        Buffers: shared hit=38
Planning:
  Buffers: shared hit=63 read=2
Planning Time: 2.154 ms
Execution Time: 1071.430 ms
```

Figure 10-1. *Execution plan with default memory allocations*

Looking at this query plan, we see that the optimizer uses two indexes on table *flight* and then scans all the blocks checking for the actual departure. Notice, also, that the number of shared buffers is insufficient (to achieve consistent results, run the same query or EXPLAIN ANALYZE more than once) and that PostgreSQL chooses to run two parallel workers to speed up the process. The total execution time is a just over one second.

Since we are not modeling the effect of multiple simultaneously running queries, the parameters that might make a material impact on the query execution time are shared_buffers (this change requires restart) and work_mem (can be modified in session). Let's first try to increase the size of work_mem, then change the shared_buffers parameter to 1 GB, restart the database, and repeat the work_mem changes.

Gradually increasing work_mem to up to 1 GB, we won't notice any significant changes in the execution plan and execution time. The limiting factor appears to be insufficient shared_buffers. We do not see any disk usage, which means that there is enough work_mem from the start. Figure 10-2 shows the execution plan with 128 MB shared_buffers and 500 MB work_mem. Execution time is fluctuating around 1 sec.

Figure 10-2. *Execution plan with increased work_mem and default shared_buffers*

Now, let's increase shared_buffers to 1 GB and restart our Postgres instance. Before we start measuring the execution time, we run this query a couple of times making sure that whatever can fit into the shared buffers is there.

Unfortunately, the execution time decrease is insignificant. The execution plan will stay the same, with slightly fewer reads due to the increase in shared_buffers (see Figure 10-3 for a portion of the execution plan).

```
Buffers: shared hit=1236 read=171097
-> Gather Merge  (cost=268846.01..268850.76 rows=10 width=24) (actual time=707.388..708.271 rows=11 loops=1)
    Workers Planned: 2
    Workers Launched: 2
    Buffers: shared hit=1236 read=171097
    -> Partial GroupAggregate  (cost=267845.99..267849.59 rows=5 width=24) (actual time=702.716..702.723 rows=4 loops=3)
        Group Key: f.flight_id
        Buffers: shared hit=1236 read=171097
        -> Sort  (cost=267845.99..267847.17 rows=473 width=20) (actual time=702.711..702.714 rows=54 loops=3)
```

Figure 10-3. *A part of the execution plan with increased shared_buffers, which shows less reads than in Figure 10-2*

If we keep increasing the work_mem to 200 MB, 500 MB, and 1 GB, we will notice a slow decrease in the execution time, finally getting as low as 750 ms. However, we need to be mindful that this increase in work_mem won't be possible on a production server for multiple sessions simultaneously. Anyway, this query does not seem to be too complicated. Are there other ways to improve its performance?

Are There Better Ways?

In all the execution plans produced during our experiments, there is one major deficiency: Postgres has to read the heap (table rows) in order to find records where the actual departure is between August 8 and August 12. That indicates that an index on this attribute might help. Let's go ahead and create the missing index:

```
CREATE INDEX flight_actual_departure
ON flight (actual_departure);
```

Immediately, there is a difference in the execution plan (see Figure 10-4).

```
                            Buckets: 1024  Batches: 1  Memory Usage: 12kB
                    Buffers: shared hit=284
                -> Nested Loop  (cost=524.84..2242.12 rows=131 width=20) (actual time=4.853..4.956 rows=69 loops=3)
                    Buffers: shared hit=284
                    -> Bitmap Heap Scan on flight f  (cost=519.74..539.48 rows=5 width=16) (actual time=4.821..4.831 rows=4 loops=3)
                        Recheck Cond: ((departure_airport = 'JFK'::bpchar) AND (arrival_airport = 'ORD'::bpchar) AND (actual_departure >= '2023-08-08 00:00:00-05'::timestamp with time zone) AND (ac
                        Heap Blocks: exact=4
                        Buffers: shared hit=195
                        -> BitmapAnd  (cost=519.74..519.74 rows=5 width=0) (actual time=4.792..4.793 rows=0 loops=3)
                            Buffers: shared hit=183
                            -> Bitmap Index Scan on flight_departure_airport  (cost=0.00..112.77 rows=10179 width=0) (actual time=1.451..1.451 rows=10530 loops=3)
                                Index Cond: (departure_airport = 'JFK'::bpchar)
                                Buffers: shared hit=35
                            -> Bitmap Index Scan on flight_arrival_airport  (cost=0.00..150.39 rows=13595 width=0) (actual time=1.351..1.351 rows=12922 loops=3)
                                Index Cond: (arrival_airport = 'ORD'::bpchar)
                                Buffers: shared hit=44
                            -> Bitmap Index Scan on flight_actual_departure  (cost=0.00..256.09 rows=16366 width=0) (actual time=1.579..1.579 rows=15873 loops=3)
                                Index Cond: ((actual_departure >= '2023-08-08 00:00:00-05'::timestamp with time zone) AND (actual_departure <= '2023-08-12 00:00:00-05'::timestamp with time zone))
                                Buffers: shared hit=104
                    -> Bitmap Heap Scan on booking_leg bl  (cost=5.10..339.68 rows=85 width=8) (actual time=0.012..0.022 rows=17 loops=12)
                        Recheck Cond: (flight_id = f.flight_id)
                        Heap Blocks: exact=17
                        Buffers: shared hit=89
                        -> Bitmap Index Scan on leg_flight  (cost=0.00..5.08 rows=85 width=0) (actual time=0.007..0.007 rows=17 loops=12)
                            Index Cond: (flight_id = f.flight_id)
                            Buffers: shared hit=38
Planning:
  Buffers: shared hit=34
Planning Time: 0.430 ms
Execution Time: 540.307 ms
```

Figure 10-4. *Execution plan with an index on the actual_departure column*

In addition, the execution time finally decreased, and we are down to a 0.5 sec execution time. However, the difference is still not as dramatic as we would like it to be. Notice in examining the new execution plan that PostgreSQL performs a full scan on the passenger table (see Figure 10-5).

```
        -> Hash Join  (cost=2243.76..267385.35 rows=473 width=20) (actual time=490.297..2186.655 rows=54 loops=3)
            Hash Cond: (p.booking_id = bl.booking_id)
            Buffers: shared hit=498 read=171481
            -> Parallel Seq Scan on passenger p  (cost=0.00..239646.72 rows=6797372 width=8) (actual time=0.521..1941.157 rows=5437898 loops=3)
                Buffers: shared hit=192 read=171481
            -> Hash  (cost=2242.12..2242.12 rows=131 width=20) (actual time=4.722..4.725 rows=69 loops=3)
                Buckets: 1024  Batches: 1  Memory Usage: 12kB
                Buffers: shared hit=284
```

Figure 10-5. *A part of the execution plan with a full table scan*

Noticing the join condition and foreign key constraint on the booking_id field, we might hypothesize that an index on booking_id might help. And, in fact, when a new index is created

```
CREATE INDEX IF NOT EXISTS passenger_booking_id
    ON postgres_air.passenger
    (booking_id);
```

...the execution plan changes dramatically—see Figure 10-6. Now, the total execution time is just 10 ms, **fifty times** less than with the best possible parameter tuning.

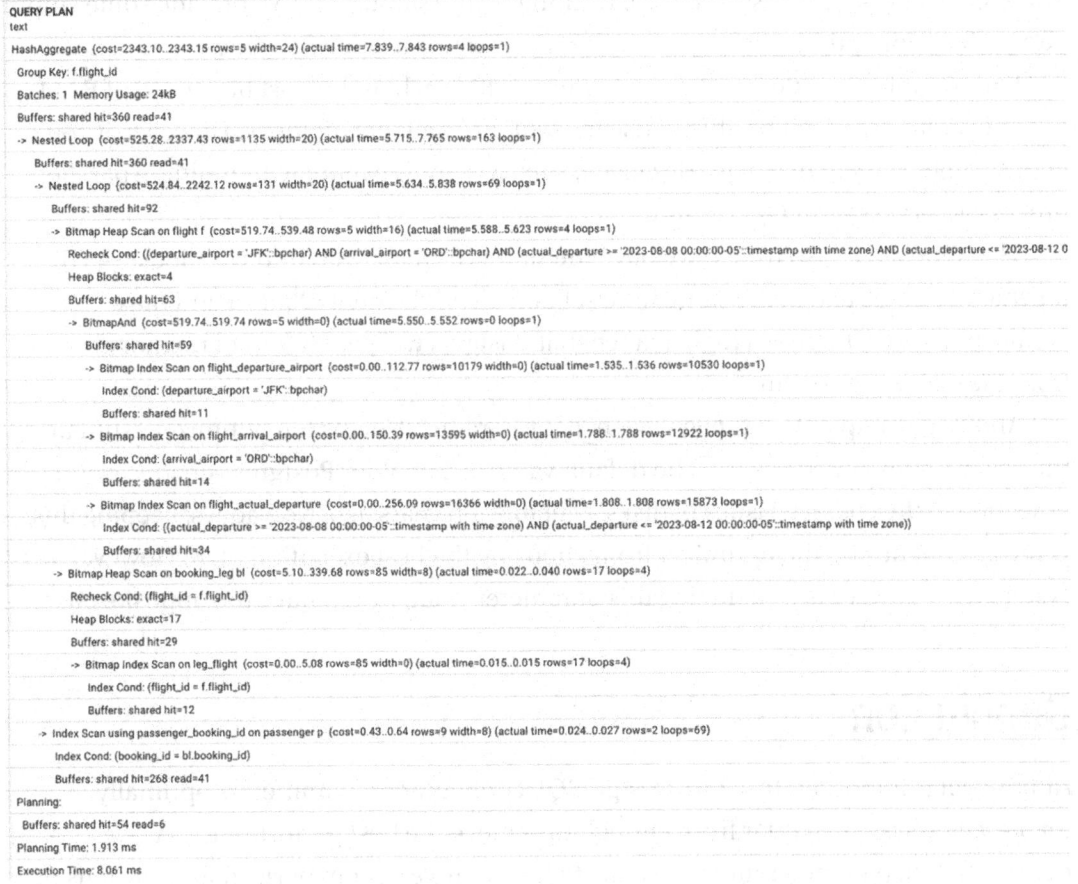

Figure 10-6. Execution plan with two indexes

More importantly, if we roll back the system parameters to the default settings and reduce the shared_buffers to 128 MB, nothing will change in either the execution plan or the execution time. No wonder—looking closely at the new execution plan in Figure 10-6, now that there are no massive table scans, the increased shared buffers are not needed anymore!

Other Limitations of Parameter Tuning

When we think about the meaning of the Postgres configuration parameters, it's important to remember that, in essence, all we are doing is communicating to the query planner what hardware resources it has available. Postgres is agnostic to the size of the RAM of the host on which it is running, the type of storage, how many cores are available, and what other systems are running on the same host. We provide some "input parameters" for optimization by setting up parameters to specific values.

For example, if we define shared_buffers=128MB when the host has 16 GB of RAM, the query planner won't be able to use most of the available memory. However, it could choose other ways to make queries faster, such as running them with multiple parallel processes, as we saw in Figure 10-3.

The opposite is also true. If we have the same 16 GB of RAM and we allocate 4 GB for shared buffers and at the same time set default work_mem=200MB and max_connections=700, there is a high chance that Postgres will get an "out of memory" error from the operating system.

Another example: The `random_page_cost` parameter helps the optimizer estimate the cost of index-based access. The default value of 4 in older Postgres versions was a reflection of the characteristics of disks available ten years ago. Nowadays, keeping this value at 4 might stop the optimizer from choosing the best execution plan. However, if a system uses slower disks, reducing this parameter value would have the opposite effect.

Conclusion

Although it is important to set up PostgreSQL configuration parameters optimally for a specific system, it is far from enough to achieve the best performance. As we demonstrated, parameter tuning usually helps improve system performance by tens of percents, in some cases even more. At the same time, the creation of missing indexes can make queries run dozens of times faster and, at the same time, reduce resource usage.

CHAPTER 11

Application Development and Performance

Midway through this book, having covered multiple techniques along the way, it's time to step back and address the additional performance aspects that were foreshadowed in Chapter 1. We wrote then that the approach of this book is broader than just optimizing individual queries.

Database queries are parts of applications, and this chapter concerns optimizing processes rather than individual queries. Although this is not typically considered "database optimization" in its traditional sense, not addressing process deficiencies could easily cancel out any performance gains gleaned from optimizing individual queries. And since both application and database developers tend to ignore this area of potential improvement, we are going to claim it.

Response Time Matters

Chapter 1 enumerated reasons for poor performance, as well as covering why query optimization is necessary. What wasn't covered was *why* an application needs to be performant.

Hopefully, halfway through this book, you have not yet forgotten why you started reading it in the first place. Perhaps, the need to improve overall system performance or the performance of a specific part of the system became inescapably urgent. However, surprising as it may sound, it is still not uncommon to hear the opinion that slow response time is not such a big deal.

We reject this categorically: it *is* a big deal, and you do not need to go any further than your marketing department for confirmation. With today's consumer expectations, the saying *time is money* could not be more apt.

Multiple marketing research studies[1] have demonstrated that fast response time on a website or from a mobile app is critical to attract and maintain incoming traffic. In most cases, acceptable response time is below 1.5 seconds. If response time increases to over 3 seconds, 50% of visitors abandon a site, and more than three quarters of them never come back.

Specific examples include the numbers reported by Google that demonstrate that slowing search by 0.4 seconds results in a loss of eight million searches per day. Another example is Amazon finding that slowing page load time by one second results in $1.6 billion of lost sales in a year. In cases like these, what problem must be addressed to improve the situation?

World Wide Wait

If you've ever talked to an application developer who works on a database application or if you are an application developer yourself, the following might sound familiar: "the application works perfectly fine until it hits the database!"

That statement, which we interpret as "an application often has performance issues when it interacts with a database," is often instead understood as "databases are slow," which is quite frustrating to hear. A DBMS is, after all, specialized software designed to provide *faster* data access, not to slow things down.

And in fact, if you ask the DBA overseeing database health on the same project, they might reply that the database is performing perfectly. If that's the case, why do users experience the "World Wide Wait"— interminable loading screens and slow response times?

Often, even if each individual database query executed by the application returns results in less than 0.1 seconds, the application page response time can be ten seconds or more. From the DBA's perspective, the system is performant, but the end user experience is poor. The problem, then, is not in the execution speed of each query but in the patterns of interactions between the application and the database.

---

[1] www.fastcompany.com/1825005/how-one-second-could-cost-amazon-16-billion-sales/; https://builtvisible.com/improving-site-speed-talk-about-the-business-benefit/

Performance Metrics

Chapter 1 discussed optimization goals, mentioning that many performance metrics, such as customer satisfaction, are "external" to the database and can't be used by the optimizer. In fact, these metrics are external not only to the database but to the entire application.

The time needed to perform a given business function is difficult to measure and, consequently, difficult to improve. Chasing easily measured optimization goals can produce poor incentives. For example, an application developer can force a user to click ten buttons instead of one, and sometimes this will reduce the response time for each of the ten buttons. This might improve some benchmark results, but it would hardly improve user experience and satisfaction.

However, these are precisely the metrics the end user is interested in. They do not care about any individual query; they care about overall experience. They want an application to respond quickly, and they do not want to stare at "wait" and "loading" screens.

Impedance Mismatch

So what is the underlying cause of poor overall performance?

In very general terms, the cause is the incompatibility of database models and programming language models, often termed *impedance mismatch*. In electrical engineering, impedance is a generalization of the resistance to alternating current in a circuit when voltage is applied. The impedance phase angle for any component is the phase shift between the voltage across that component and current through that component; if this angle is close to 90 degrees, the delivered power is close to 0 even if both voltage and current are high.

Similarly, the expressiveness and efficiency of database query languages does not match the strengths of imperative programming languages. Even though both can have great strength, they might deliver less power than expected.

Both imperative programming languages and declarative query languages work extremely well to accomplish the tasks they were designed for. The problems start when we try to make them work together. The cause of poor performance is an incompatibility of database models and programming language models.

Applications and databases are designed to operate with

- Objects of different sizes (granularity)—single objects vs. bulk (sets of) objects

- Access patterns (navigation vs. search by attribute values)

- Different means of identification—address vs. a set of attribute values

In the remaining sections of this chapter, we discuss the consequences of this incompatibility in more detail.

A Road Paved with Good Intentions

The preceding might sound like we are blaming application developers for every performance problem and for their unwillingness to "think like a database." But assigning blame is not a productive way to solve problems, including poor application performance. A more productive approach would be to try to understand how good intentions can lead to such excruciating results.

Let's start by examining some common application development patterns.

Application Development Patterns

The most common modern software engineering architecture pattern is a layered architecture. Typically, there are four layers:

- End user interface

- Business logic

- Persistence

- Database

Each layer may only communicate with adjacent layers, and encapsulation and independence are encouraged both within each level and especially across levels. In this model, the business object "customer" is totally ignorant of the database table "Customer" and, in fact, could be connected to any arbitrary database so long as the persistence layer defined a mapping between the data in the database and the objects in the business layer.

There are a few important reasons for this, chief among them facilitating fast development, maintainability, ease of application updates, and making components reusable. It seems facially obvious that a change in the end user interfaces shouldn't de facto cause a change in the database schema. This strict separation also facilitates rapid work in parallel: developers can work on different parts of the application, and rest assured that the other parts of the application outside their narrow domains do not depend on the internal structure or implementation of the objects the developer is touching. And it of course seems useful that multiple applications can be built on the same foundation of business logic—that the internal logic of the application does not have to be duplicated for each new built environment.

So far, so good—-so what is the problem? Unfortunately, there are many pitfalls, and the methodology doesn't quite deliver the promised benefit—at least, as it is implemented in the wild.

Consider the idea of centralizing business logic. First, the benefits of having all the logic in one place—the business layer—are somewhat reduced when that "one place" is several hundred thousand lines of code. In practice, such a large business layer will result in duplication—or, worse, attempted duplication. When the business logic layer is bloated, it's hard to find a function that does exactly what one wants—as a result, often, real-world business logic is implemented in different ways in different methods, with different results.

Second, this business logic may be available to additional end user interfaces, but it is not available to other business uses that interact directly with the database—most crucially, reporting. Thus, report writers end up duplicating application logic code, perhaps in a data warehouse or, worse yet, in individual reports, with no guarantee of equivalence with application logic.

Additionally, with this approach, communication with the persistence layer is typically limited to individual objects or even single scalar values, effectively disabling the power of the database engine. The end user interface might know all the different data elements that it needs, but because it doesn't communicate directly with the persistence layer, requests for data are mediated by the business logic layer.

A typical implementation of the persistence layer has data access classes that correspond one-to-one with business object classes. It is straightforward to write basic database DML functions (INSERT, UPDATE, DELETE), but what happens when operations must be performed on a set of objects of this class? There are two paths: The developer can create another set of methods that implement the same functions for a set of

221

objects. However, this would violate the principle of code reuse. Alternately, and more commonly, the developer simply iterates through the collection, calling the functions that have already been defined to handle each individual object in turn.

Imagine an application interface that lists all passengers departing from O'Hare airport. A database developer would assume that to list all passengers departing from O'Hare airport, they need to join the table `flight` with the table `boarding_pass`. All the information is returned in one go. For an application developer, the task might be trickier. They might have a method like `get_flight_by_departure_airport()` that takes an airport code as a parameter and returns a collection of flights. Then, they can iterate through the flights, returning all boarding passes for the flight. In effect, they are implementing a nested loop join algorithm inside the application.

To avoid this, they might use a few different solutions. They could add a departure airport attribute to the boarding pass object. However, this would open the door to data integrity problems: what if the flight departure time is updated in the flight record but not all boarding passes? Alternately, a method could be defined to retrieve boarding passes given a flight departure airport, but this would violate the precept of objects being ignorant of one another. In a pure layered approach, the boarding pass object is ignorant of the flight object, and the flight object is ignorant of the boarding pass. A method that pulls data for both wouldn't belong in either object.

"Shopping List Problem"

Stephane Faroult[2] describes the situation described previously as the "shopping list problem."

Suppose you have a shopping list for the grocery store. In real life, you would go to the grocery store, get a cart, pick up all the items on your list, check out, pack the items up, go home, bring them inside, and put them into your fridge. Now imagine that instead, you go to the store, go inside, pick up just the first item from your shopping list, go back home, put the item in the fridge, and head to the store again! And you would continue in this fashion for every item on your list.

Does this sound ridiculous? Yes, but that's exactly what many applications do when it comes to their interaction with databases.

---

[2] Stephane Faroult and Peter Robson, *The Art of SQL*

Now imagine that in order to speed up the grocery run, experts suggested increasing the width of the aisles in the grocery store or building better roads to get there or devising a new sort of shopping cart.

Some of these suggestions could, indeed, help. But even if the shopping time was reduced by 30%, it would be a drop in the bucket compared to one simple process improvement: picking up all groceries in a single trip.

How can the shopping list problem be translated to application behavior? Most performance problems are caused by **too many queries that are too small.** And just as better highways can't improve the shopping experience if we continue to take an extra trip for each item on our list, the following popular suggestions do not help application performance:

- *More powerful computers* do not help much, as both the application and the database are in a wait state for 99% of time.

- *Higher network bandwidth* does not help either. High-bandwidth networks are efficient for transfer of bulk amounts of data but cannot significantly improve the time needed for roundtrips. Time depends on the number of hops and the number of messages but does not depend significantly on message size. Furthermore, the size of the packet header does not depend on the message size; hence, the fraction of bandwidth used for payload is small for very short messages.

- *Distributed servers* might improve throughput, but not response time, as the application sends requests for data sequentially.

The anti-pattern of "too many too small queries" has been a known problem for several decades. About 20 years ago, one of us had to analyze an application that needed five to seven minutes to generate an HTML form containing about 100 fields. The application code was perfectly structured into small, well-commented methods with nice formatting. However, the database trace showed that to produce this form, the application issued about 16,000 queries—more than the characters on the form being generated. Further analysis showed that a few thousand of the queries were coming from the method GetObjectIdByName. Each of these calls was followed by a query from the method GetNameByObjectId that was invoked from another part of the application, probably written by another developer. The values of name were unique; therefore, the second call always returned the parameter of the first. A single query extracting all data needed to build the form returned the output in less than 200 milliseconds.

In the face of these predictable issues, many companies attempt many of the same, failed remedies to improve performance. Even if initially they are able to achieve some improvement, it does not last long. For example, we observed the optimization efforts of one company for several years.

Since the PostgreSQL optimizer is always trying to take advantage of available RAM, this company kept increasing hardware resources, making sure that the whole database could fit into main memory. They migrated from machines with 512 GB of RAM to 1 TB, 2 TB, and then 4 TB of main memory, when the only limiting factor was the availability of the respective configuration. Following each migration, after a short period of relative satisfaction, the problem would re-emerge: the database would grow bigger and stop fitting into main memory.

Another remedy that is often implemented is to use a key-value store instead of a full-featured DBMS. The argument usually goes something like "the application only uses primary keys to access data, so a query engine is not needed." And, in fact, this approach may improve response time for a single data access. However, this cannot improve the time needed to complete a business function. In one extreme case, a record retrieval using a primary key value would take about ten milliseconds on average. At the same time, the number of database calls performed in one application controller action was nearly a thousand, with predictable overall performance impacts.

Interfaces

Yet another reason for suboptimal interactions between an application and a database is at the level of interfaces. Typically, applications use a generalized interface such as ODBC or JDBC. These interfaces provide an oversimplified view of a database as a set of flat tables. Actually, both the application and the database can operate in terms of complex structured objects; however, there is no way to transfer such high-level structures through the interface. Thus, an application cannot benefit from the high-level model even if it is maintained in the database.

To transfer a complex database object, an application is forced to use separate queries for each part of a database object or, alternately, to use a custom parsing method for deserializing the flat representation as returned over the interface into the complex objects themselves.

The imperfections of dominant development practices are well known to professionals. Why are these practices so common?

The reasons are not technical. Application developers almost always work under time pressure. A new product or a new feature has a release deadline, which is often "as soon as possible." The financial gain of early delivery is significantly higher than that with later delivery and better quality.

Welcome to the World of ORM

The desire to isolate the database language (i.e., SQL) from application developers and thus simplify their task (and also reduce the need for the database skills) leads to the introduction of software that converts database functions into object methods.

An *object-relational mapper* (ORM) is software that maps a database object to an in-memory application object.

Some ORM developers have claimed that the impedance mismatch problem is solved. Objects are mapped one-to-one to database tables, and the underlying structure of the database, as well as the generated SQL used to interact with it, is of no concern to the application developer. Unfortunately, the cost of this solution is unacceptable performance degradation.

How does ORM work? The process is shown in Figure 11-1.

1. The application disassembles an object into undivisible (scalar) parts.

2. The parts are sent to/from the database separately.

3. In the database, the complex data structure is present, but all queries run separately.

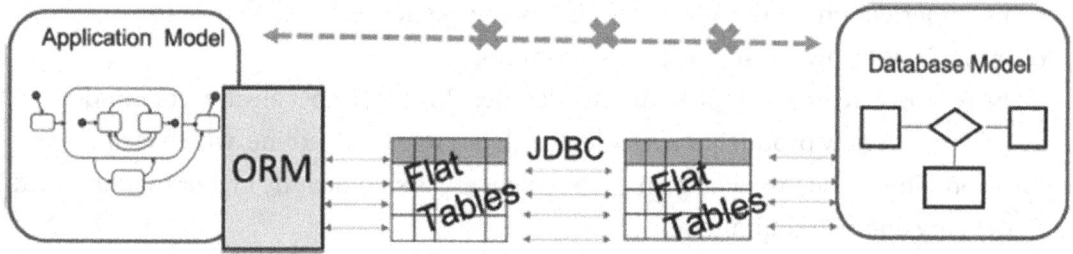

Figure 11-1. *How ORM works*

Theoretically, an ORM does not prevent the application from running arbitrary database queries; an ORM usually provides methods for that. However, in practice, generated queries are almost always used due to time pressures and the simplicity with which they are created in the application.

Because the actual database code is obscured from the developer, database operations on sets of objects end up happening very similarly to the non-ORM solution: an ORM method returns a list of object IDs from the database, and then each object is extracted from the database with a separate query (also generated in the ORM). Thus, to process N objects, an ORM issues N + 1 database queries, effectively implementing the shopping list pattern described in the previous section.

Such mapping solves the problem of abstraction from details of data storage but does not provide effective means to manipulate datasets.

In addition, the ORM might hide important implementation details. Take one example, observed in a production system: an IsActive flag on a Customer object to denote whether the customer had recent activity. A developer might think that this was just an attribute stored in the customer table of the database, but in actuality, it depended on a complex set of criteria based on customer behavior, and this query was run every time the attribute was invoked. Even worse, this attribute was used and frequently checked in the code for control flow and visual components that displayed differently based on the customer's status. As a result, this complex query ran multiple times to render a single page.

In Search of a Better Solution

To summarize the preceding, in the application layer, classes and methods for tables and sets should be integrated with the database to work effectively (methods should be executed by the DB engine). However, most architectures do not allow this kind of integration, which leads to reimplementation of database operations at the application layer.

This particular case of impedance mismatch is called *ORIM—object-relational impedance mismatch*.

Consequently, conventional ways of architecting communication between applications and databases are the most significant source of application slowness. There is no ill will here: application and database developers are doing the best they can with the tools they have.

To address this problem, we need to find a way to *transfer collections of complex objects*. Note that in fact, we are looking for a solution for two closely related problems. The first problem is inability to transfer "all the data at once," that is, to think and operate in sets. The second problem is inability to transfer complex objects without disassembling them before the data transfer to and from the application.

In order to illustrate the desired outcome, let's look at an example of how a web application may interact with the `postgres_air` database. When a user logs into the online booking system, the first thing they will see is most likely their existing bookings. When they select a specific booking, they will see a screen that looks something like the screenshot in Figure 11-2.

Your flight to Chicago (ORD) Jul 2 2023

Flight 3013 Munich (MUC) – New York (JFK) 4:10 PM
Flight 3014 New York (JFK) – Chicago (ORD) 12:10 PM – next day

Return flight – Jul 9 2023

Flight 3317 Chicago (ORD) – New York (LGA) 7:00 PM
Flight 3012 New York (JFK) – Munich (MUC) 5:05 AM – next day

Passengers
Passenger1: Kathleen Smith
Passenger 2: Doug White
Passenger 3; Martha White

Figure 11-2. *Your reservation screen*

The information that is displayed on your screen is drawn from several different tables: booking, booking_leg, flight, passenger, and airport. After check-in, you will also see the boarding passes.

A web application developed using a traditional approach would access the database 17 times to display these results: first, to select a booking_id list for the current user, then select booking details from the booking table, then select details for each booking leg (four in total), then select flight details for each flight (four more), and then select airport details (another four), and then passenger details (another three). However, an application developer knows exactly what objects to build to display booking results. On the database side, a database developer similarly knows how to select every piece of information needed to build this object. The structure of the object should look something like Figure 11-3.

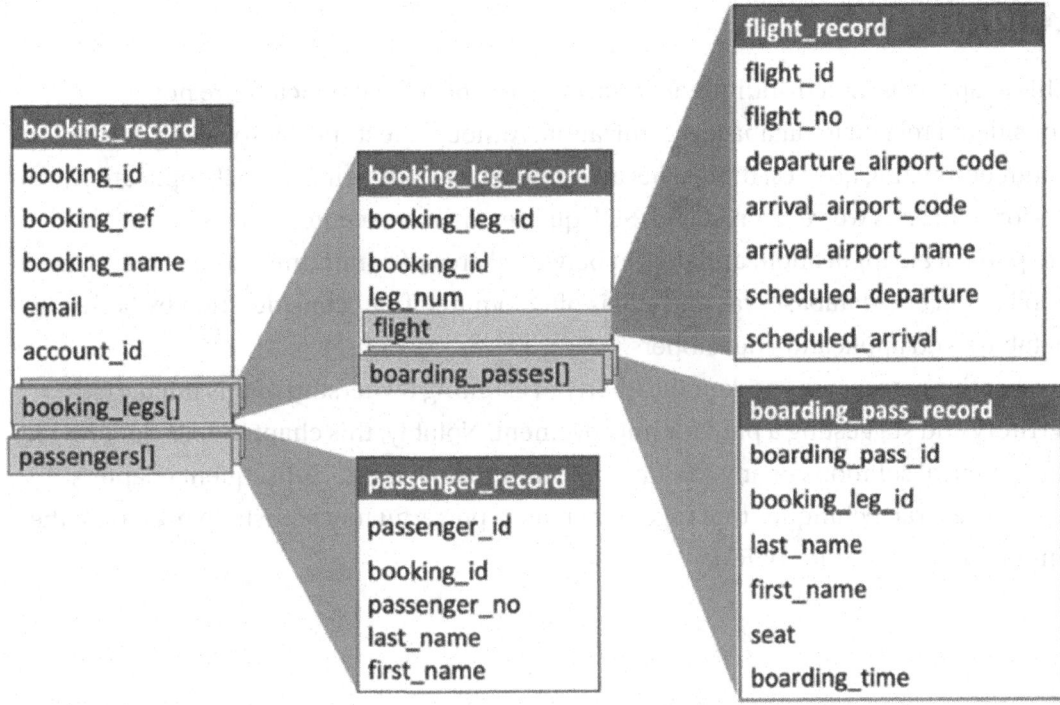

Figure 11-3. *Mapping complex objects*

If we could package data on the database side as such an object and send it to the application with one command, the number of database calls would decrease dramatically. And fortunately, PostgreSQL can build complex objects. The following PostgreSQL features make it possible:

- PostgreSQL is an object-relational database.

- PostgreSQL supports the creation of custom types.

- PostgreSQL functions can return sets, including sets of records.

Subsequent chapters will discuss functions that return sets of records and support of JSON/JSONB data types and custom data types and will show examples of how to create these functions and use them in applications.

Summary

This chapter discussed additional performance aspects that typically are not considered related to database optimization. Although, technically speaking, it is not about optimizing queries, it presents an approach to optimizing overall application performance. As we've often stated, SQL queries are not executed in a vacuum; they are parts of an application, and the "in between" area of communication between the application and database was and still is often omitted from consideration by both database and application developers.

For this reason, we've taken the liberty of claiming ownership of this uncharted territory and suggesting a path for improvement. Notably, this chapter does not provide any practical solutions or any examples of "how to do it right." Subsequent chapters discuss several techniques that together create a powerful mechanism to overcome the limitations of traditional ORMs.

CHAPTER 12

Functions

This chapter focuses on the most underused and misused features of PostgreSQL, objects—functions. Since all modern programming languages include user-defined functions, people often assume that database functions are cut from the same cloth and if you know how and when to write functions in an application programming language, you can apply this directly to PostgreSQL. This could not be further from truth.

This chapter discusses how PostgreSQL functions are different from functions in other programming languages, when functions should be created and when they should not, how using functions can improve performance, and how it can lead to a major performance degradation.

Before proceeding, let's address the widespread belief that using functions decreases portability. This is true as it goes, but consider the following:

- Neither SQL statements nor ORMs are 100% portable; some (hopefully minor) work will always be required.

- Swapping databases for an existing production system is always a major project and is never done on the fly. Some changes to the application itself are unavoidable. Converting functions adds relatively small overhead to the project.

Function Creation

PostgreSQL has both built-in (internal) functions and user-defined functions. In this respect, it is not any different from other programming languages.

© Henrietta Dombrovskaya, Boris Novikov, Anna Bailliekova 2024
H. Dombrovskaya et al., *PostgreSQL Query Optimization*, https://doi.org/10.1007/979-8-8688-0069-6_12

Internal Functions

Internal functions are written in the C language and are integrated with the PostgreSQL server. For each data type supported by PostgreSQL, there are a number of functions that perform different operations with variables or column values of that type. Similar to imperative languages, there are functions for mathematical operations, functions to operate on strings, functions to operate on date/time, and many others. The list of available functions and supported types expands with each new release.

Some examples of built-in functions are shown in Listing 12-1.

Listing 12-1. Examples of built-in functions

```
sin(x);
substr(first_name,1,1);
now();
```

User-Defined Functions

User-defined functions are functions created by users. PostgreSQL supports three kinds of user-defined functions:

- Query language functions, that is, functions written in SQL

- C functions (written in C or C-like languages, like C++)

- Procedural language functions, written in a supported procedural language (referred to as PL)

A CREATE FUNCTION command is shown in Listing 12-2.

Listing 12-2. CREATE FUNCTION command

```
CREATE FUNCTION function_name (par_name1 par_type1, ...)
RETURNS return_type
AS
<function body>
LANGUAGE function_language;
```

From a PostgreSQL perspective, the database engine captures only the function signature—the name of the function and the list of parameters (which may be empty), the type of return value (which may be void), and some specifications, such as the language in which it is written. For all procedural languages except for SQL, the function body is packaged into a string literal, which is passed to a special handler that knows the details of the language. The handler can either do all the work of parsing, syntax analysis, execution, and so on itself, or it can serve as the "glue" between PostgreSQL and an existing implementation of a programming language. The standard PostgreSQL distribution supports four procedural languages: PL/pgSQL, PL/Tcl, PL/Perl, and PL/Python. In this book, we will discuss only functions written in PL/pgSQL.

Introducing Procedural Language

Since we're covering functions, it seems like a good idea to formally introduce the language (or languages) in which these functions can be written.

So far in this book, the only language that has been used is SQL, and the only operator used in code snippets, other than CREATE operators, was SELECT. Now, it is time to introduce procedural languages. In this book, we discuss only the PostgreSQL native procedural language PL/pgSQL.

A function written in PL/pgSQL can include any SQL operators (potentially with some modifications) and control structures (IF THEN ELSE, CASE, LOOP) and calls to other functions.

Listing 12-3 shows an example of a function written in PL/pgSQL that converts a text string to numeric, if possible, and returns null if the string does not represent a number.

Listing 12-3. Function converting text to numeric

```
CREATE OR REPLACE FUNCTION text_to_numeric(input_text text)
RETURNS numeric AS
$BODY$
BEGIN
    RETURN replace(input_text, ',', '')::numeric;
EXCEPTION WHEN OTHERS THEN
    RETURN NULL::numeric;
END;
$BODY$
LANGUAGE plpgsql;
```

Using the information in Listing 12-2, we can identify the parts common to all user-defined functions. The function name is text_to_numeric, and it has only one parameter, input_text, of type text.

The RETURNS clause defines the type of value the function returns (numeric), and the LANGUAGE clause specifies the language in which the function is written, plpgsql.

Now, let's take a closer look at the function body.

Dollar Quoting

In the previous section, we stated that a function body is represented as a string literal; however, instead of quotes, it starts and ends with $BODY$. This notation in PostgreSQL is called dollar quoting, and it is especially useful when you create a function. Indeed, if you have a relatively large text of a function, chances are you will need to use single quotes or backslashes, and then you will need to double them at each occurrence. With dollar quoting, you can use two dollar signs, possibly with some tag between them to define a string literal.

Tagging makes this way of defining string constants especially convenient, because you can nest strings with different tags. For example, the beginning of a function body can look like Listing 12-4.

Listing 12-4. The usage of nested dollar quoting

```
$function$
DECLARE
V_error_message text:='Error:';
V_record_id integer;
BEGIN
...
v_error_message:=v_error_message||$em$Record can't be updated,
#$em$||quote_literal(v_record_id);
...
END;
$function$
```

Here, we use dollar quoting with the tag function for a function body. Note that there are no rules limiting which tags can be used for the function body, including the empty tag; the only requirement is that the string literal ends with the same tag as the tag that started it. The examples here will use different tags as a reminder that tags are not predefined.

The function body starts with a DECLARE clause, which is optional and can be excluded if no variables are needed. BEGIN (without a semicolon) denotes the start of the statements section, and the END keyword should be the last statement in the function body.

Please note this section is not a comprehensive guide to function creation. Please refer to PostgreSQL documentation for more details.

More details are discussed as they are introduced in future examples.

Function Parameters and Function Output: Void Functions

Most often, a function will have one or more parameters, but it might have none. For example, the internal function now(), which returns the current timestamp, does not have any parameters. We can assign default values to any function parameter, to be used if no specific value is explicitly passed.

In addition, there are multiple ways to define function parameters. In the example in Listing 12-3, parameters are named, but they can also be positioned ($1, $2, etc.). Some parameters may be defined as OUT or INOUT, instead of specifying a return type. Again, this chapter doesn't intend to cover every possible specification, because function performance does not depend on all these specification variations.

Finally, it's important to note that a function may return no value; in this case, a function is specified as RETURNS VOID. This option exists because previously, PostgreSQL did not have support for stored procedures, so the only way to package multiple statements together was inside a function.

Function Overloading

Similar to other programming languages, functions in PostgreSQL can be polymorphic, that is, multiple functions can use the same name with a different signature. This feature is called *function overloading*. As mentioned earlier, a function is defined by its name and its input parameter set; the return type may be different for different sets of input parameters, but for obvious reasons, two functions cannot share both the same name and same set of input parameters.

Let's take a look at the examples in Listing 12-5. In case #1, a function that calculates the number of passengers on a specific flight is created. In case #2, a function with the same name, which calculates the number of passengers departing on a specific date from a specific airport, is created.

However, if you try to run snippet #3 to create a function that calculates the number of passengers on a specific flight number on a specific date, you will get an error:

```
ERROR: cannot change name of input parameter "p_airport_code".
```

You can create a function with the same name and with a different set of parameters and a different return type; thereby, you can create another function with the same name, as shown in case #4. However, if you try to create a function with the same name and with a different return type but the same parameters (case #5), the database will throw an error:

```
ERROR: cannot change return type of existing function
```

Listing 12-5. Function overloading

```
#1
CREATE OR REPLACE FUNCTION num_passengers(p_flight_id int) RETURNS integer;
#2
CREATE OR REPLACE FUNCTION num_passengers(p_airport_code text, p_departure
date) RETURNS integer;
#3
CREATE OR REPLACE FUNCTION num_passengers(p_flight_no text, p_departure
date) RETURNS integer;
#4
CREATE OR REPLACE FUNCTION num_passengers(p_flight_no text) RETURNS
numeric;
#5
CREATE OR REPLACE FUNCTION num_passengers(p_flight_id int) RETURNS numeric;
```

Note that the source code of these functions differs significantly. Listing 12-6 shows the source code of the num_passengers(integer) function, and Listing 12-7 shows the code of the num_passengers(text, date) function.

Listing 12-6. Source code of num_passengers(int)

```
CREATE OR REPLACE FUNCTION num_passengers(p_flight_id int) RETURNS integer
AS
$$BEGIN
RETURN (
      SELECT count(*)
      FROM booking_leg bl
      JOIN booking b USING (booking_id)
      JOIN passenger p USING (booking_id)
      WHERE flight_id=p_flight_id);
END;
$$ LANGUAGE plpgsql;
```

Listing 12-7. Source code of num_passengers(text, date)

```
CREATE OR REPLACE FUNCTION num_passengers(
      p_airport_code text,
       p_departure date) RETURNS integer
AS
$$BEGIN
RETURN (
      SELECT count(*)
      FROM booking_leg bl
      JOIN booking b USING (booking_id)
      JOIN passenger p USING (booking_id)
      JOIN flight f USING (flight_id)
      WHERE departure_airport=p_airport_code
      AND scheduled_departure BETWEEN p_departure AND p_departure +1)
;
END;
$$ LANGUAGE plpgsql;
```

Function Execution

To execute a function, we use the SELECT operator. Listing 12-8 demonstrates two possible ways to execute the function num_passengers with the p_flight_id parameter set to 13.

Listing 12-8. Function execution

```
SELECT num_passengers(13);
SELECT * FROM num_passengers(13);
```

For functions that return scalar values, either syntax will produce identical results. Complex types are covered later in this chapter.

It is also worth noting that user-defined scalar functions can be used in SELECT statements, just like internal functions. Recall the function text_to_numeric in Listing 12-3. You might wonder why somebody would need to create a user-defined conversion function when PostgreSQL already has three different ways to convert a string to an integer. For the record, these three ways are

- CAST (text_value AS numeric)

- text_value::numeric (this is alternative syntax for CAST)

- to_number(text_value, '999999999999')—using an internal function

Why is a custom conversion function needed? For any of the methods listed in the preceding list, if the input text string contains symbols other than numerals, the attempted conversion results in an error.

To make sure that the conversion function does not fail, we include the *exception processing section* in the function body. The section starts with the EXCEPTION keyword; the WHEN keyword may identify specific exception types. In this chapter, we will use it only in the form WHEN OTHERS, which means all exception types not included in previous WHEN conditions. If, as in Listing 12-3, WHEN OTHERS is used by itself, it means all exceptions should be processed in the same way.

In Listing 12-3, this means that any conversion error (or, actually, any error) should not fail the function, but instead return NULL. Why is it so critical for a function not to fail when a "bad" parameter is passed? Because this function is being used in a SELECT list.

In Chapter 7, we created the materialized view passenger_passport (see Listing 7-11). Different columns of this materialized view should contain different data types, but since in the source data, all these fields are text fields, there is not much we can do. Now, if you want to select the passport_num as a numeric type, your SELECT might look like this:

```
SELECT
    passenger_id,
    passport_num::numeric AS passport_number
FROM passenger_passport
```

If, in even one instance, the `passport_num` column contains a non-numeric value (e.g., a blank or an empty string), then the whole SELECT statement will fail. Instead, we can use the custom function `text_to_integer`:

```
SELECT
     passenger_id,
     text_to_numeric(passport_num) AS passport_number
FROM passenger_passport
```

Let's create one more user-defined function, `text_to_date`, which will transform a string that contains a date to type date—see Listing 12-9.

Listing 12-9. Function converting text to date

```
CREATE OR REPLACE FUNCTION text_to_date(input_text text)
  RETURNS date AS
$BODY$
BEGIN
    RETURN input_text::date;
EXCEPTION WHEN OTHERS THEN
  RETURN null::date;
END;
$BODY$
  LANGUAGE plpgsql;
```

Now, we can use both functions in Listing 12-10.

Listing 12-10. Using functions in a SELECT list

```
SELECT
     passenger_id,
     text_to_integer(passport_num) AS passport_num,
     text_to_date(passport_exp_date) AS passport_exp_date
FROM passenger_passport
```

Although this example seems like a perfect use case for functions in PostgreSQL, in reality it represents a far from ideal solution when it comes to performance—as discussed in the following.

Function Execution Internals

This section explains some specifics of function execution that are unique to PostgreSQL. If you have previous experience with a DBMS like Oracle or MS SQL Server, you might assume a thing or two about function execution that are not true in PostgreSQL.

The first surprise might come when you execute a CREATE FUNCTION statement and receive a completion message that looks something like this:

```
CREATE FUNCTION
Query returned successfully in 127 msec.
```

Reading this, you might assume your function does not contain any errors. To illustrate what may go wrong afterward, let's compile the code in Listing 12-11. If you copy and execute this statement, you will receive a successful creation message.

Listing 12-11. Create a function that will complete with no errors

```
CREATE OR REPLACE FUNCTION num_passengers(
      p_airport_code text,
      p_departure date) RETURNS integer
AS $$
BEGIN
RETURN (
     SELECT
            count(*)
     FROM booking_leg bl
     JOIN booking b USING (booking_id)
     JOIN passenger p  USING (booking_id)
     JOIN flight f USING (flight_id)
     WHERE airport_code=p_airport_code
            AND scheduled_departure BETWEEN p_date AND p_date +1);
END;
$$ LANGUAGE plpgsql;
```

However, when you try to execute this function

```
SELECT num_passengers('ORD', '2020-07-05')
```

...you will receive an error message:

```
ERROR: column "airport_code" does not exist
```

What went wrong? The function uses `airport_code` instead of `departure_airport`. This is an easy mistake to make, but you might not expect that PostgreSQL would never inform you that you made this mistake in the first place, when you created the function.

Now, if you correct this mistake and run a new `CREATE FUNCTION` statement (see Listing 12-12), you will get yet another error:

```
ERROR: column "p_date" does not exist
```

Listing 12-12. Create a function: one error corrected, one more still there

```
CREATE OR REPLACE FUNCTION num_passengers(
      p_airport_code text,
      p_departure date) RETURNS integer
AS $$
BEGIN
RETURN (
      SELECT
              count(*)
      FROM booking_leg bl
      JOIN booking b USING (booking_id)
      JOIN passenger p  USING (booking_id)
      JOIN flight f USING (flight_id)
      WHERE departure_airport =p_airport_code
            AND scheduled_departure BETWEEN p_date AND p_date +1);
END;
$$ LANGUAGE plpgsql;
```

And PostgreSQL is right, since the name of the parameter is `p_departure_date`, not `p_date`. Still, why wasn't this error reported earlier?

During function creation, PostgreSQL performs only an initial parsing pass, during which only trivial syntax errors are detected. Anything deeper will not be detected until execution. If you are fresh from Oracle and assume that when you create a function, it is compiled by the database engine and stored compiled, this is bad news. Not only are functions stored in the form of source code but moreover, in contrast to other DBMSs, functions are interpreted, not compiled.

The PL/pgSQL interpreter parses the function's source text and produces an (internal) instruction tree the first time the function is called within each session. Even then, individual SQL expressions and commands used in the function are not translated immediately. Only when the execution path reaches a specific command is it analyzed and a *prepared statement* is created. It will be reused if the same function is executed again in the same session. One of the implications of this is that if your function contains some conditional code (i.e., `IF THEN ELSE` or `CASE` statements), you may not even discover the syntax errors in your code, if this portion was not reached during execution. We've seen these kinds of unpleasant discoveries made long after the function went into production. To summarize, when you create a PL/pgSQL function

1. No execution plan is saved.

2. No checks for existence of tables, columns, or other functions are performed.

3. You do not know whether your function works or not, until you execute it (often more than one time, if there are multiple code paths).

Another important thing to know about PostgreSQL functions, which can be concluded from the preceding explanation, is that functions are "atomic" in several different ways. First (to the dismay of Oracle users), you can't initiate transactions inside PostgreSQL functions, so in the case of DML statements, it's always "all or nothing." Second, the PostgreSQL optimizer knows nothing about function execution when it optimizes an execution plan, which includes invocations of user-defined functions. For example, if you execute

```
EXPLAIN SELECT num_passengers(13)
```

...the execution plan will look something like this:

```
"Result  (cost=0.00..0.26 rows=1 width=4)"
```

If you need to find out what execution plans are used to execute the SELECT statements inside the function, you will need to supply some actual values in place of parameters and run the EXPLAIN command for each of them.

One of the keywords in the `CREATE FUNCTION` operator (remember, we didn't list all of them!) is `COST`. It allows a developer to explicitly set the cost of function execution to be used by the optimizer. The default value is 100, and we do not recommend changing it, unless you have a really compelling reason to do so.

Functions and Performance

With that brief introduction out of the way, it's time to address this book's central concern. How do functions affect performance? Chapter 7 addressed the topic of code factoring and outlined the different implications of code factoring in imperative languages and in SQL. Several possible techniques were covered, and functions were mentioned as deserving a more detailed discussion, which follows.

Why create functions in PostgreSQL? In imperative languages, using functions is the obvious choice: functions increase code readability, facilitate code reuse, and have no negative impact on performance. By contrast, functions in PostgreSQL may increase code readability, but may also decrease code readability and may significantly worsen performance. Note the word "may"; the rest of the chapter concerns ways to use user-defined functions wisely, so that they provide performance benefits rather than performance disaster.

How Using Functions Can Worsen Performance

In a previous section, we created the function num_passengers(int), which calculates the number of passengers on a flight specified by a function parameter. This function works great for a single flight, returning a result within 150 ms.

Let's take a look at what happens if this function is included in a SELECT list. Listing 12-13 selects all flights that departed from ORD between June 13 and July 13 and, for each of these flights, calculates a total number of passengers.

Listing 12-13. Using a function in the SELECT list decreases performance

```
SELECT
        flight_id,
        num_passengers(flight_id) AS num_pass
FROM flight f
WHERE departure_airport='ORD'
        AND scheduled_departure BETWEEN '2023-07-05' AND '2023-07-13'
```

The execution time for this statement is 13 sec. Now, if instead of using a function, a SQL statement performing the exact same calculations is used (Listing 12-14), the execution time will be only 165 ms.

Listing 12-14. The same results without using a function

```
SELECT
        f.flight_id,
        count(*) AS num_pass
FROM booking_leg bl
JOIN booking b USING (booking_id)
JOIN n passenger p USING (booking_id)
JOIN flight f  USING (flight_id)
WHERE departure_airport='ORD'
        AND scheduled_departure BETWEEN '2023-07-05' AND '2023-07-13'
GROUP BY 1
```

Why such a big difference? In Chapter 7, we explained how views and CTEs can work as an optimization fence. The effect is even more pronounced with functions. Since a function is a true black box for the surrounding SQL statement, the only option for PostgreSQL is to execute each function as many times as many rows are selected.

To be precise, some time is saved because for the subsequent function calls from the same session, PostgreSQL uses a prepared statement, but that fact can both speed up and slow down the execution, because the execution plan won't take into account the differences in statistics between function calls.

Even when the difference is not that drastic, and one might argue that a moderate slowdown can be tolerated for ease of code maintenance, we are crossing a threshold of how long a user is willing to wait. And in this case, the SQL inside the function is pretty light and takes milliseconds to be executed.

Fine, we understand that it is not the greatest idea to execute SELECT statements embedded into the SELECT list of another statement. But what about functions, which perform simple data transformations? Like the ones we created for type conversion? In this case, the difference may not be so dramatic until the output size becomes really big, but it is still visible.

Let's compare the execution time for the statement from Listing 12-10 with the execution time for the statement in Listing 12-15.

Listing 12-15. Selecting passport information without type conversion

```
SELECT
      passenger_id,
      passport_num,
      passport_exp_date
FROM passenger_passport
```

Both of them select data from one single table and do not apply any filters, so the only time overhead will be the one incurred from executing the functions in the SELECT list. The `passenger_passport` materialized view contains over 16 million rows. The execution time for the statement in Listing 12-15 is seven seconds. If we apply type casting without calling the function (Listing 12-16)

Listing 12-16. Selecting passport information with type casting

```
SELECT
      passenger_id,
      passport_num::numeric,
      passport_exp_date::date
FROM passenger_passport
```

...the execution time will be nine seconds. Running the statement in Listing 12-10, the execution time will be 40 seconds! Note that in this case the significant execution time increase is a result of exception processing, which creates an implicit checkpoint.

In this particular case, not much can be done to improve performance, except to come up with a better design in the first place, but later in this book, we will review other examples, where some performance improvements are possible.

Any Chance Functions Can Improve Performance?

Having reviewed so many examples where functions affected performance negatively, one might wonder whether there are ever conditions under which functions can improve performance. As in many other cases, it depends.

If we are talking about improving an individual SQL statement's performance, wrapping it in a function can't make it run faster. However, functions can be extremely helpful when what is being optimized is a process.

Functions and User-Defined Types

In all of the function examples so far, the functions we built returned scalar values. Now, let's see what some additional benefits are provided by functions that return user-defined data types.

User-Defined Data Types

In addition to its own rich collection of data types, PostgreSQL allows the creation of a virtually unlimited number of user-defined data types.

User-defined types can be simple or composite. Simple user-defined types include the following categories: domain, enum, and range.

The following are examples of simple type creation:

```
CREATE DOMAIN timeperiod  AS tstzrange;
CREATE TYPE mood AS ENUM ('sad', 'ok', 'happy');
CREATE TYPE mood_range AS RANGE...
CREATE TYPE <base type>
```

Just as we can define *arrays* of base types, we can define arrays of user-defined types:

```
DECLARE
v_moods_set mood[];
```

Even more options are available when we create a *composite type*.

A composite type represents a row, or a record. A type definition consists of the sequence of field names and their respective data types. For example, Listing 12-17 defines the type boarding_pass_record.

Listing 12-17. Type boarding_pass_record

```
CREATE TYPE boarding_pass_record AS (
    boarding_pass_id int,
    booking_leg_id bigint,
    flight_no text,
    departure_airport text,
    arrival_airport text,
    last_name text,
    first_name text,
```

```
    seat text,
    boarding_time timestamptz
);
```

Now that the type boarding_pass_record is defined, we can declare variables of this type, the same as we can declare variables of base types:

```
DECLARE
v_new_boarding_pass_record boarding_pass_record;
```

And moreover, we can create functions, which return *sets of composite types*.

Functions Returning Composite Types

Why is the fact that functions can return sets of composite types so crucial? Why would we want to do it? Recall from Chapter 9 that we need to be able to retrieve the whole object from the database, not just one component after another. Now, everything previously discussed can be put together.

Let's build an example. In Listing 12-18, we present a function that returns all boarding passes for a specified flight.

Listing 12-18. Function returning all boarding passes for the flight

```
CREATE OR REPLACE FUNCTION boarding_passes_flight (p_flight_id int)
RETURNS SETOF boarding_pass_record
AS
$body$
BEGIN
    RETURN QUERY
        SELECT
                pass_id,
                bp.booking_leg_id,
                flight_no,
                departure_airport::text ,
                arrival_airport ::text,
                last_name ,
                first_name ,
                seat,
```

```
                boarding_time
        FROM flight f
        JOIN booking_leg bl USING (flight_id)
        JOIN boarding_pass bp USING(booking_leg_id)
        JOIN passenger USING (passenger_id)
        WHERE bl.flight_id=p_flight_id;
END;
$body$
LANGUAGE plpgsql;
```

To execute this function, run the following:

```
SELECT * FROM boarding_passes_flight(13);
```

The result of this SELECT is presented in Figure 12-1.

	boarding_pass_id integer	booking_leg_id bigint	flight_no text	departure_airport text	arrival_airport text	last_name text	first_name text	seat text	boarding_time timestamp with time zone
1	215158	15576	1699	KTM	CTU	BLAND	IZAIAH	0B	2023-05-29 23:40:00-05
2	215159	15578	1699	KTM	CTU	JOSEPH	AMELIA	0C	2023-05-29 23:40:00-05
3	215160	15580	1699	KTM	CTU	PETERS	ARIAH	0D	2023-05-29 23:40:00-05
4	215161	15582	1699	KTM	CTU	MC DONALD	EVERLY	0E	2023-05-29 23:40:00-05
5	215162	15584	1699	KTM	CTU	Pi	Liam	0F	2023-05-29 23:40:00-05

***Figure 12-1.** Result of the execution of the function boarding_passes_flight*

Now, let's create another function, which will select just one boarding pass by the pass_id. Note that since both functions accept a single integer parameter, overloading won't be possible in this case. The new function is shown in Listing 12-19.

***Listing 12-19.** Function that returns one boarding pass*

```
CREATE OR REPLACE FUNCTION boarding_passes_pass (p_pass_id int)
RETURNS SETOF boarding_pass_record
AS
$body$
BEGIN
    RETURN QUERY
        SELECT
                pass_id,
                bp.booking_leg_id,
                flight_no,
```

```
                    departure_airport::text ,
                    arrival_airport ::text,
                    last_name ,
                    first_name ,
                    seat,
                    boarding_time
            FROM flight f
            JOIN booking_leg bl USING (flight_id)
            JOIN boarding_pass bp USING(booking_leg_id)
            JOIN passenger USING (passenger_id)
            WHERE pass_id=p_pass_id;
END;
$body$
LANGUAGE plpgsql;
```

When we execute this function

```
SELECT * FROM boarding_passes_pass(215158);
```

...the result will be a set that consists of only one row, but its structure will be the same (see Figure 12-2).

	boarding_pass_id integer	booking_leg_id bigint	flight_no text	departure_airport text	arrival_airport text	last_name text	first_name text	seat text	boarding_time timestamp with time zone
1	215158	15576	1699	KTM	CTU	BLAND	IZAIAH	0B	2023-05-29 23:40:00-05

Figure 12-2. *Result of the execution of the function boarding_passes_pass*

Why would using these functions improve performance? As we discussed in Chapter 10, applications rarely execute SQL statements directly; instead, they often use SQL statements generated behind the scenes by ORMs. In this case, there is a high likelihood that boarding passes, passengers, and flights are accessible using different methods. That means that most likely, to select the same data returned by the function boarding_passes_flight, we will need one method to select departure airport, arrival airport, and scheduled departure for a flight, which is passed as a parameter to this function, another method to select all booking legs for that flight, another method for boarding passes, and yet another for passenger information. If the application developers can be convinced, consolidating this into a single function will be a huge performance improvement.

Selecting all boarding passes for a flight that has 600 passengers with the boarding pass function takes 220 ms, running `SELECT * FROM boarding_passes_flight(13650)`. On the other hand, any individual SELECT from any table takes around 150 ms. Since each process returns data to the application, making a roundtrip, the execution time is summed up—using multiple calls will very quickly exceed the execution time of the function.

Previously, we learned that for scalar functions there is no difference between the syntaxes `SELECT * FROM function_name` and `SELECT function name`. But when a function returns a composite type, there is a difference.

Figure 12-1 shows the results when running

`SELECT * FROM boarding_passes_flight(13)`

Figure 12-3 shows the results of

`SELECT boarding_passes_flight(13)`

	boarding_passes_flight boarding_pass_record 🔒
1	(215158,15576,1699,KTM,CTU,BLAND,IZAIAH,0B,"2023-05-29 23:40:00-05")
2	(215159,15578,1699,KTM,CTU,JOSEPH,AMELIA,0C,"2023-05-29 23:40:00-05")
3	(215160,15580,1699,KTM,CTU,PETERS,ARIAH,0D,"2023-05-29 23:40:00-05")
4	(215161,15582,1699,KTM,CTU,"MC DONALD",EVERLY,0E,"2023-05-29 23:40:00-0...
5	(215162,15584,1699,KTM,CTU,Pi,Liam,0F,"2023-05-29 23:40:00-05")

Figure 12-3. *Function results as a set of records*

Using Composite Types with Nested Structure

Can we use composite types as elements of other composite types? Yes, PostgreSQL allows it.

In Figure 11-4, we presented the structure of a complex object `booking_record`. One of its components is a complex object `booking_leg_record`. To build the representation of this object as a composite type, begin by creating a `flight_record` type and a `boarding_pass_record` type, and then proceed with creating a `booking_leg_record` type, as shown in Listing 12-20.

Listing 12-20. More record type definitions

```
CREATE TYPE flight_record AS(
        flight_id int,
        flight_no text,
     departure_airport_code text,
     departure_airport_name text,
     arrival_airport_code text,
     arrival_airport_name text,
     scheduled_departure timestamptz,
     scheduled_arrival timestamptz
);
CREATE TYPE booking_leg_record AS(
 booking_leg_id int,
 leg_num int,
 booking_id int,
 flight flight_record,
 boarding_passes boarding_pass_record[]
);
```

The booking_leg_record type contains as one of its elements a composite type flight_record and as another component the array of boarding_pass_record elements.

Looks like we solved the problem stated in Chapter 11: we can create composite types with nested structure and create functions that return such objects. However, there are still plenty of problems to solve.

To illustrate the remaining problems, let's create a function that will return the whole object booking_leg_record using booking_leg_id. The code for this function is presented in Listing 12-21.

Listing 12-21. Function returning a complex object with nested structure

```
CREATE OR REPLACE FUNCTION booking_leg_select (p_booking_leg_id int)
RETURNS SETOF booking_leg_record
AS
$body$
BEGIN
    RETURN QUERY
        SELECT
```

```
                bl.booking_leg_id,
                leg_num,
                bl.booking_id,
              (SELECT row(
                      flight_id,
                      flight_no,
                      departure_airport,
                      da.airport_name,
                      arrival_airport,
                      aa.airport_name ,
                      scheduled_departure,
                      scheduled_arrival)::flight_record
            FROM flight f
            JOIN airport da on da.airport_code=departure_airport
                JOIN airport aa on aa.airport_code=arrival_airport
                WHERE flight_id=bl.flight_id
                  ),
                (SELECT array_agg (row(
                        pass_id,
                        bp.booking_leg_id,
                        flight_no,
                        departure_airport ,
                        arrival_airport,
                        last_name ,
                        first_name ,
                        seat,
                        boarding_time)::boarding_pass_record)
              FROM flight f1
              JOIN  boarding_pass bp ON f1.flight_id=bl.flight_id
                      AND bp.booking_leg_id=bl.booking_leg_id
              JOIN passenger p ON p.passenger_id=bp.passenger_id)
          FROM booking_leg bl
          WHERE bl.booking_leg_id=p_booking_leg_id
;
END;
$body$ language plpgsql;
```

Don't be put off by the preceding massive function—it is long, but not too complex. Let's take a closer look.

The main SELECT extracts data from the booking_leg table, using the value of the function parameter as a search criterion. The first three elements of the record–booking_leg_id, leg_num, booking_id—come directly from the table booking_leg. The next element of the record is flight_record, where flight_id is the flight_id from the selected booking leg. This condition is set in the WHERE clause of the inner SELECT:

```
WHERE flight_id=bl.flight_id
```

We select the information about the flight, which is referenced in the selected booking leg.

The internal function row() builds the row from the set of elements, and this row is cast to the type flight_record, which is the type expected in the booking_leg_record.

The last element of the booking_leg_record is an array of boarding passes—as many passes as there are passengers in this reservation. Let's take a closer look at this inner SELECT:

```
(SELECT array_agg (row(
                        pass_id,
                        bp.booking_leg_id,
                        flight_no,
                        departure_airport ,
                        arrival_airport,
                        last_name ,
                        first_name ,
                        seat,
                        boarding_time)::boarding_pass_record)
            FROM flight f1
            JOIN  boarding_pass bp ON f1.flight_id=bl.flight_id
                        AND bp.booking_leg_id=bl.booking_leg_id
            JOIN passenger p ON p.passenger_id=bp.passenger_id)
```

The first thing you notice about this select is that it is essentially the same select as we used in the boarding_pass_flight function. The differences are the following:

- There is no need to join with the booking_leg table, since it was already selected in the outer SELECT. We still need information from the flight table, but we can use the flight_id from the selected booking leg. This way, there is a Cartesian product with one line from the table flight.

- Similarly, for the boarding pass, there is no join with the booking_leg table; we just use the booking_leg_id, which is already there.

Finally, we use the internal function array_agg() to create a single *array of records* that is expected as the last element of the booking_leg_record.

Note The preceding is only one of multiple ways to build an object with nested structure. In subsequent chapters, we will present alternative ways, which might be more useful in other circumstances.

And now, here is the bad news. We put in so much effort to create this function, and now, when we execute it, the results are somewhat disappointing. Execute

```
SELECT * FROM booking_leg_select (17564910)
```

The result is shown in Figure 12-4.

booking_leg_id integer	leg_num integer	booking_id integer	flight flight_record	
1	17564910	2	232346	(13650,1245,JFK,"John F Kennedy International Airport",CDG,"Charles de Gaulle International Airport","2023-06-02 00:20:00-05","2023-06-02 06:15:00...

Figure 12-4. *Returned complex object with nested structure*

The result set looks exactly as we wanted it to look, but notice one important detail. For the scalar elements, PostgreSQL retains the element names (same as if we would select from a table), but when it comes to the elements that are complex objects themselves, their structure is not revealed. Note that, internally, PostgreSQL still retains the notion of what is the structure of the inner type, but it does not communicate it to the upper level.

Why is this a problem? Chapter 11 covered ORM pitfalls and sketched out a hypothetical solution in Figure 11-3. At that time, we did not discuss any specifics of how this goal could be achieved, but with functions that can return complex types, a solution seems to be reachable. However, when neither an element name nor its type can be identified by the application, the function output becomes useless, at least for the purpose of being called from an application directly.

The solution is in Chapter 14, but for now, let's focus on functions that return records without nested structure.

Functions and Type Dependencies

Chapter 7 mentioned dependencies in the context of views and materialized views. For materialized views, the definition cannot be altered without dropping the object first. This, in turn, means all dependent objects must be dropped and recreated, even if the names and the number of columns in the materialized view didn't change. If these dependent objects are, in turn, used in other views or materialized views, their dependent objects have to be dropped as well.

This may result in some highly undesirable consequences. We've observed situations in production systems where one change resulted in a cascade drop of over 60 dependent objects, which had to be rebuilt following a particular order.

Fortunately, we do not have this problem with functions. Since SQL statements in the function body are not parsed during function creation, there are no dependencies on tables, views or materialized views, or other functions and stored procedures, which are used in the function body. For this reason, functions need only be recreated when needed as the result of an actual change, not simply due to a cascade drop.

However, functions create a new type of dependencies: functions depend on their returned types, including user-defined types. Just as with materialized views, user-defined data types cannot be modified without being dropped first. To drop a type, all other user-defined types that include it as an element and all functions that depend on that type must be dropped. This might sound like an even worse problem, but actually, it is exactly the right problem to have. If a user-defined type is modified, some of its elements must have been added, removed, or changed. That, in turn, means that SELECT statements that return that type of record must be revised, so the functions should be dropped.

In addition, unlike the creation of a materialized view, which may take some time, creating a function is nearly instantaneous.

Data Manipulation with Functions

So far, this chapter has only considered functions that select data. But PL/pgSQL functions allow any SQL command, including DML functions.

Listing 12-22 is a function that issues a new boarding pass to a passenger.

Listing 12-22. Create a new boarding pass

```
CREATE OR REPLACE FUNCTION issue_boarding_pass(
    p_booking_leg_id int,
    p_passenger_id int,
    p_seat text,
    p_boarding_time timestamptz)
RETURNS SETOF boarding_pass_record
AS
$body$
DECLARE
      v_pass_id int;
BEGIN
      INSERT INTO boarding_pass
            (passenger_id,
              booking_leg_id,
              seat,
              boarding_time,
              update_ts)
        VALUES (
              p_passenger_id,
              p_booking_leg_id,
              p_seat,
              p_boarding_time,
              now()) RETURNING pass_id INTO v_pass_id;
   RETURN QUERY
      SELECT  * FROM boarding_passes_pass(v_pass_id);
END;
$body$
LANGUAGE plpgsql;
```

Note the call to the function boarding_passes_pass in this function body. This
function was created earlier, but even if it didn't exist, the CREATE FUNCTION operator
wouldn't signal an error until this function is executed. There are pros and cons to
this behavior. It gives more flexibility during development, but it can also create issues
because the fact that the embedded function was removed or is not working properly
might go unnoticed. Executing this function is the same as other functions:

```
SELECT * FROM issue_boarding_pass(175820,462972, '22C', '2023-06-16
21:45'::timestamptz)
```

Note that this execution does not make much sense because the flight departed in the past, so it is present here for illustrative purposes only. Figure 12-5 presents the result of this execution—the data has the same format as for other functions that return boarding passes.

boarding_pass_id integer	booking_leg_id bigint	flight_no text	departure_airport text	arrival_airport text	last_name text	first_name text	seat text	boarding_time timestamp with time zone
1	25293500	175820	68	AMS	FRA	WOOD	KAITLYN	22C	2023-06-16 21:45:00-05

Figure 12-5. *DML function returning a user-defined type*

When creating this function, we made some assumptions that we would not hold up in real life. For example, the function doesn't check whether a boarding pass for that passenger and that flight was already issued, doesn't check seat availability against the seat chart, and does not capture possible errors on INSERT. In a production environment, this function would be much more complex.

Functions and Security

In this book, we do not cover data access control/permissions in PostgreSQL, mostly because this topic is not related to performance. However, we will cover a little bit about setting up security for PostgreSQL functions and a surprising link between function security settings and performance.

One of the parameters in the CREATE FUNCTION operator that was not covered earlier is SECURITY. This parameter has only two allowed values: INVOKER and DEFINER. The former is a default value; it indicates that the function will be executed using the set of privileges of the user who calls the function. That means that in order to be able to execute a function, a user should have relevant access to all the database objects that are used in the function body. If we explicitly specify SECURITY DEFINER, a function will be executed with the permissions of the user who created the function. Note that in contrast to other database object permissions, the execution privilege for any function is granted by default to PUBLIC.

Many of you (as well as us, your authors) have been in a situation where a power business user needs to have access to some critical data, but you do not want to give them READ ALL access, because you are not entirely sure about their SQL skills and whether their queries might bring the whole system down.

In this case, a compromise might be in order—you would create a function that pulls all the necessary data using a performant query, create this function with the SECURITY DEFINER parameter, remove execution permission from everybody (from PUBLIC), and then give this power user the execution permission. The sequence of actions is presented in Listing 12-23.

Listing 12-23. Usage of the SECURITY DEFINER function

```
CREATE FUNCTION critical_function (par1 ...)
RETURNING SETOF...
AS $FUNC$
...
END:
$FUNC$
LANGUAGE plpgsql
SECURITY DEFINER;
--
REVOKE EXECUTE ON critical_function (par1 ...)
FROM public;
GRANT EXECUTE ON critical_function (par1 ...)
TO powerbusinessuser;
```

What About Business Logic?

In cases when you can convince your application developers to use functions to communicate with the database, the performance gains are dramatic. The sheer fact of eliminating multiple roundtrips can easily improve application performance tens or even hundreds of times, when we measure the application response time rather than the database response time.

One of the most serious blockers on this road to success is the concept of *business logic*. One of the definitions (from Investopedia.com) reads like this:

> *Business logic is the custom rules or algorithms that handle the exchange of information between a database and user interface. Business logic is essentially the part of a computer program that contains the information (in the form of business rules) that defines or constrains how a business operates.*

Business logic is often considered a separate application layer, and when we put "too much logic" into database functions, it makes application developers unhappy. We spent a considerable amount of time trying to find common ground with business and application developers alike. The result of these discussions can be summarized as follows:

- We need some business logic to execute joins and selects.

- Selected result transformations and manipulations do not have to be executed on the database side.

In practice, this means that when deciding what can go to the database and what has to stay in the application, a decisive factor is whether bringing the dependencies into the database would improve performance (facilitate joins or enable the use of indexes). If so, the logic is moved into a function and considered "database logic"; otherwise, data is returned to the application for further processing of business logic.

For example, for the airline reservation application, a function can be created to return available trips, that is, potential bookings. The parameters of this function include the departure city, the destination, the trip start date, and the return date. To be able to retrieve all possible trips efficiently, the function needs to know how the tables `airport` and `flight` can be joined and how to calculate the duration of the flight. All this information belongs to database logic.

However, we do not want the function to make a final decision regarding which trip to select. Final selection criteria may vary and are processed by the application; they belong to business logic.

Applying this criterion consistently can be quickly incorporated into the regular development cycle and encourages developing applications "right right away."

Functions in OLAP Systems

By this time, we hope that we convinced you that using PostgreSQL functions in OLTP systems is beneficial. What about OLAP?

Unless you've tried it, you might not know that many reporting tools, including Cognos, Business Objects, and Looker, can present the results of a function. In fact, executing a function that returns a set of records is similar to performing `SELECT * FROM <some table>`.

However, the fact that software can do something doesn't means that it should. So when should you use functions in an OLAP environment?

Parameterizing

A view or materialized view can't be parameterized. This might not pose any problem if we want to run a report for the most recent date, for yesterday, for last week, and so on, because we can utilize such internal functions as CURRENT_DATE or CURRENT_TIMESTEMP, but if we need to rerun any report for any of the past time intervals, it won't be an easy task without making some changes to the view. For example, we might have a view

```
    CREATE VIEW recent_flights_v AS
    SELECT flight_id,
           departure_airport,
           arrival_airport,
           scheduled_departure
   FROM flight
WHERE scheduled_departure BETWEEN CURRENT_DATE-7
AND CURRENT_DATE
```

If you need to run the same query for a different date interval, you will need to create another view (or recreate the existing view). But if this SELECT is packaged into the function

```
CREATE OR REPLACE FUNCTION recent_flights(p_date date)
RETURNS SETTOF recent_flights_record AS
$BODY$
BEGIN
  RETURN QUERY
          SELECT flight_id,
            departure_airport,
            arrival_airport,
            scheduled_departure
  FROM flight
WHERE scheduled_departure BETWEEN p_date-7
AND p_date;
END; $BODY$;
```

...you can simply execute it with different parameters:

```
SELECT * FROM recent_flights(CURRENT_DAY)
SELECT * FROM recent_flights('2023-08-01')
```

No Explicit Dependency on Tables and Views

If a report is executed as a call to a function, it can be optimized without the necessity to drop and recreate it. Moreover, the underlying tables can be modified, or we can end up using completely different tables, all invisible to the end user.

Ability to Execute Dynamic SQL

Functions allow building SQL statements based on the values of parameters. The SQL language does not have an option of building the statement on the fly and then executing it. You can build the SQL statement in the application and then send it to the database to execute, or you can build it inside the plpgsql function. This is another exceptionally powerful feature of PostgreSQL, which is often underused and which is discussed in more detail in Chapter 13.

Stored Procedures

In contrast to other DBMSs, PostgreSQL didn't have stored procedures for some time, much to the disappointment of early adopters coming from commercial systems. As for us, your authors, we were especially frustrated with the atomic nature of functions, which does not allow any transaction management, including committing of intermediate results.

Functions with No Results

For a while, PostgreSQL developers had no option rather than to use functions in place of store procedures. You could do it using functions that return VOID, like

```
CREATE OR REPLACE function cancel_flight (p_filght_id int) RETURNS VOID
AS <...>
```

Also, there is an alternative way to execute functions when calling them from another function or procedure:

```
PERFORM issue_boarding_pass(175820,462972, '22C', '2020-06-16
21:45'::timestamptz)
```

The preceding way will execute the function and create a boarding pass, but it won't return the result.

Functions and Stored Procedures

The difference between functions and stored procedures is that procedures do not return any values; thereby, we do not specify a return type. Listing 12-24 presents the CREATE PROCEDURE command, which is very similar to the CREATE FUNCTION command.

Listing 12-24. CREATE PROCEDURE command

```
CREATE PROCEDURE procedure_name (par_name1 par_type1, ...)
AS
<procedure body>
LANGUAGE procedure language;
```

The syntax of the procedure body is the same as that of the function, except there is not a need for a RETURN type. Also, all the preceding sections on function internals apply to stored procedures, as well. To execute a stored procedure, the CALL command is used:

```
CALL cancel_flight(13);
```

Transaction Management

The most important difference between how functions and stored procedures are executed is that you can commit or roll back a transaction within a procedure body.

At the start of the procedure execution, a new transaction starts, and any COMMIT or ROLLBACK command within a function body will terminate the current transaction and start a new one. One of the use cases is the bulk data load. We find it beneficial to commit changes in reasonably sized portions, for example, every 50,000 records. The structure of the stored procedure might look like Listing 12-25.

Listing 12-25. Example of a stored procedure with transactions

```
CREATE PROCEDURE load_with_transform()
AS $load$
DECLARE
     v_cnt int:=0;
     v_record record;
BEGIN
     FOR v_record IN (SELECT * FROM data_source) LOOP
```

```
            PERFORM transform (v_rec.id);
            CALL insert_data (v_rec.*);
            v_cnt:=v_cnt+1;
          IF v_cnt>=50000 THEN
              COMMIT;
              v_cnt:=0;
        END IF;
END LOOP;
COMMIT;
END;
$load$ LANGUAGE plpgsql;
```

In this example, data is processed before loading and COMMIT when we process 50,000 records. An additional commit upon exiting the loop is necessary for the remaining records, processed after the last in-loop commit.

Exception Processing

Same as with functions, you can include instructions on what to do if certain processing exceptions occur. In Listing 12-3, we provided an example of exception processing in a function. Similar exception processing can be performed in procedures.

In addition, it is possible to create inner blocks inside of a function or procedure body and to have a different exception processing in each of them. The procedure body structure for this case is shown in Listing 12-26.

Listing 12-26. Nested blocks in the procedure body

```
CREATE PROCEDURE multiple_blocks AS
$mult$
BEGIN
---case #1
  BEGIN
  <...>
  EXCEPTION WHEN OTHERS THEN
    RAISE NOTICE 'CASE#1";
  END; --case #1
```

```
  ---case #2
 BEGIN
 <...>
 EXCEPTION WHEN OTHERS THEN
   RAISE NOTICE 'CASE#2";
 END; --case #2
---case #3
 BEGIN
 <...>
 EXCEPTION WHEN OTHERS THEN
   RAISE NOTICE 'CASE#3";
 END; --case #3
END; ---proc
$mult$ LANGUAGE plpbsql;
```

Note that BEGIN in the procedure body is different from the BEGIN command that starts a transaction.

Summary

Functions and stored procedures in PostgreSQL are exceptionally powerful tools that are all but ignored by many database developers. They can both drastically improve and drastically worsen performance and can be successfully used in both OLTP and OLAP environments. Chapter 14 will provide more guidance on making decisions regarding the function usage.

This chapter serves as a sneak peek of various ways functions can be used. Consult PostgreSQL documentation for more details on how to define and use functions and stored procedures.

CHAPTER 13

Dynamic SQL

What Is Dynamic SQL

Dynamic SQL is any SQL statement that is first built as a text string and then executed using the EXECUTE command. An example of dynamic SQL is shown in Listing 13-1. Dynamic SQL is underused in most RDBMSs, but especially in PostgreSQL. The recommendations in this chapter go against the grain of many database textbooks, but all suggestions are based strictly on our practical experience.

Listing 13-1. Dynamic SQL

```
DECLARE
     v_sql text;
     cnt int;
BEGIN
     v_sql:=$$SELECT count(*)
                    FROM booking
                    WHERE booking_ref='0Y7W22'$$;
   EXECUTE v_sql into cnt;
   <...>
```

Why Dynamic SQL Works Better in Postgres

What is so special about PostgreSQL relative to other DBMSs, to make the recommendations here stray so far from conventional wisdom? Consider the following.

First, in PostgreSQL, execution plans are not cached even for *prepared queries* (i.e., queries that are preparsed, analyzed, and rewritten using the PREPARE command). That means that optimization always happens immediately before execution.

© Henrietta Dombrovskaya, Boris Novikov, Anna Bailliekova 2024
H. Dombrovskaya et al., *PostgreSQL Query Optimization*, https://doi.org/10.1007/979-8-8688-0069-6_13

Second, the optimization step in PostgreSQL happens later than in other systems. For example, in Oracle, the execution plan for a parameterized query is always prepared for a generic query, even if the specific values are there. Moreover, a plan with binding variables is cached for future usage if the same query with different values is executed. The optimizer takes table and index statistics into account but does not take into account the specific values of parameters. PostgreSQL does the opposite. The execution plan is generated for specific values.

As mentioned earlier, dynamic queries are unfairly neglected in other DBMSs as well. That's primarily because for long-running queries (dozens of seconds or more), the overhead mostly is negligible.

What About SQL Injection?

Often, the suggestion to use dynamic SQL for better performance is met with alarm: What about SQL injection? Of course, we've all heard horror stories about stolen passwords and deleted data, because a malicious actor passed a dangerous command instead of data into a form. Of course, this is a real risk, and there's more than one way for hackers to get access to data they should not have access to. However, there are guardrails available to using dynamic SQL that minimize risks.

In cases when parameter values for a function call are obtained from the database directly (e.g., referencing IDs), SQL injection is impossible. Values obtained from user input must be sanitized with PostgreSQL functions (`quote_literal`, `quote_indent`, etc. or `format`)—examples of this are demonstrated later in this chapter. User inputs can also benefit from validation on the application side.

How to Use Dynamic SQL for an Optimal Execution Plan

As mentioned in Chapter 12, PostgreSQL may reuse execution plans for parametrized SQL statements issued from functions, which in some cases may cause poor performance. To ensure that the execution plan is built optimally, we can build dynamic SQL inside a function and then execute it rather than pass parameter values as binding variables. Let's look at an example.

Recall the query in Listing 6-6, which has two selection criteria: departure airport country and the last time the booking was updated. Chapter 6 demonstrated how PostgreSQL modifies the execution plan depending on specific values of these parameters.

In this chapter, we see what happens with this query if it is executed inside a function.

Let's start by creating a return type (see Listing 13-2).

Listing 13-2. Create a return type

```
DROP TYPE IF EXISTS booking_leg_part ;
CREATE TYPE booking_leg_part AS(
       departure_airport char (3),
       booking_id int,
       is_returning boolean
);
```

Now, let's create a function with two parameters: ISO country code and the timestamp of the last update. This function is shown in Listing 13-3.

Listing 13-3. SQL from Listing 6-6, packaged in a function

```
CREATE OR REPLACE FUNCTION select_booking_leg_country (
       p_country text,
       p_updated timestamptz)
RETURNS SETOF booking_leg_part
AS
$body$
BEGIN
RETURN QUERY
 SELECT
       departure_airport,
       booking_id,
       is_returning
FROM booking_leg bl
JOIN flight f USING (flight_id)
WHERE departure_airport IN
```

```
                    (SELECT
                                airport_code
                      FROM airport
                      WHERE iso_country=p_country
                      )
          AND bl.booking_id IN
                    (SELECT
                                booking_id
                        FROM booking
                        WHERE update_ts>p_updated
                      )
 ;
END; $body$
LANGUAGE plpgsql;
```

Chapter 6 demonstrated how PostgreSQL chooses different execution plans depending on the values for country and timestamp search parameters and how this influences execution time.

Since functions in PostgreSQL (just as in other systems) are atomic, we can't run the EXPLAIN command to see the execution plan for the function (to be precise, the EXPLAIN will be executed, but the only thing it will show will be the execution itself), but since the expected response time for the query is known, we can get a good idea what's going on under the hood.

Recall that previously, executing the statement in Listing 13-4 resulted in an execution time of about 9.5 seconds, with two hash joins executed.

Listing 13-4. SELECT with two hash joins

```
SELECT
      departure_airport,
      booking_id,
      is_returning
FROM booking_leg bl
JOIN flight f USING (flight_id)
WHERE departure_airport IN
            (SELECT
                        airport_code
```

```
            FROM airport WHERE iso_country='US'
         )
   AND bl.booking_id IN
         (SELECT
                booking_id
         FROM booking
         WHERE update_ts>'2023-07-01'
         )
```

Recall also that by moving the bound on update_ts closer to the dataset's "current date" of August 17, initially, the execution time doesn't change significantly. Execution time with update_ts>'2023-08-01 will still be about 7.9 seconds, with a reduction attributable to a smaller intermediate dataset. The execution plan for that case is shown in Figure 13-1.

	QUERY PLAN text	🔒
1	Hash Join (cost=169581.38..630554.84 rows=286036 width=9)	
2	Hash Cond: (bl.booking_id = booking.booking_id)	
3	-> Hash Join (cost=18963.54..433030.38 rows=3645943 width=9)	
4	Hash Cond: (bl.flight_id = f.flight_id)	
5	-> Seq Scan on booking_leg bl (cost=0.00..310506.66 rows=17893566 width=9)	
6	-> Hash (cost=17223.52..17223.52 rows=139202 width=8)	
7	-> Hash Join (cost=20.41..17223.52 rows=139202 width=8)	
8	Hash Cond: (f.departure_airport = airport.airport_code)	
9	-> Seq Scan on flight f (cost=0.00..15398.78 rows=683178 width=8)	
10	-> Hash (cost=18.65..18.65 rows=141 width=4)	
11	-> Seq Scan on airport (cost=0.00..18.65 rows=141 width=4)	
12	Filter: (iso_country = 'US'::text)	
13	-> Hash (cost=143353.65..143353.65 rows=442735 width=8)	
14	-> Bitmap Heap Scan on booking (cost=8291.63..143353.65 rows=442735 width=8)	
15	Recheck Cond: (update_ts > '2023-08-01 00:00:00-05'::timestamp with time zone)	
16	-> Bitmap Index Scan on booking_update_ts (cost=0.00..8180.94 rows=442735 width...	
17	Index Cond: (update_ts > '2023-08-01 00:00:00-05'::timestamp with time zone)	

Figure 13-1. *Execution plan with two hash joins*

Eventually, as the value of update_ts approaches August 17, PostgreSQL will choose index access, and for the query in Listing 13-5, the execution time is 1.8 seconds.

Listing 13-5. One hash join is replaced with a nested loop

```
SELECT departure_airport, booking_id, is_returning
  FROM booking_leg bl
  JOIN flight f USING (flight_id)
  WHERE departure_airport IN
           (SELECT airport_code
                    FROM airport WHERE iso_country='US')
        AND bl.booking_id IN
           (SELECT booking_id FROM booking
                    WHERE update_ts>'2023-08-14')
```

The execution plan for this case is shown in Figure 13-2.

1	Hash Join (cost=29828.94..401980.77 rows=6682 width=9)
2	Hash Cond: (f.departure_airport = airport.airport_code)
3	-> Nested Loop (cost=29808.52..401873.75 rows=32795 width=9)
4	-> Hash Join (cost=29808.10..387285.40 rows=32795 width=9)
5	Hash Cond: (bl.booking_id = booking.booking_id)
6	-> Seq Scan on booking_leg bl (cost=0.00..310506.66 rows=17893566 width=9)
7	-> Hash (cost=29678.81..29678.81 rows=10343 width=8)
8	-> Bitmap Heap Scan on booking (cost=196.59..29678.81 rows=10343 width=8)
9	Recheck Cond: (update_ts > '2023-08-14 00:00:00-05'::timestamp with time zo...
10	-> Bitmap Index Scan on booking_update_ts (cost=0.00..194.00 rows=10343 ...
11	Index Cond: (update_ts > '2023-08-14 00:00:00-05'::timestamp with time zo...
12	-> Index Scan using flight_pkey on flight f (cost=0.42..0.44 rows=1 width=8)
13	Index Cond: (flight_id = bl.flight_id)
14	-> Hash (cost=18.65..18.65 rows=141 width=4)
15	-> Seq Scan on airport (cost=0.00..18.65 rows=141 width=4)
16	Filter: (iso_country = 'US'::text)

Figure 13-2. *Execution plan with one hash join and one nested loop*

Also, if we run the same SELECT with the iso_country='CZ', PostgreSQL will produce yet another differing execution plan, as shown in Figure 13-3. In this case, the execution time will be around 200 ms.

	QUERY PLAN text	🔒
1	Nested Loop (cost=13.49..18917.18 rows=8349 width=9)	
2	-> Nested Loop (cost=13.06..6615.00 rows=25858 width=9)	
3	-> Nested Loop (cost=12.62..3022.73 rows=987 width=8)	
4	-> Seq Scan on airport (cost=0.00..18.65 rows=1 width=4)	
5	Filter: (iso_country = 'CZ'::text)	
6	-> Bitmap Heap Scan on flight f (cost=12.62..2993.50 rows=1058 width=8)	
7	Recheck Cond: (departure_airport = airport.airport_code)	
8	-> Bitmap Index Scan on flight_departure_airport (cost=0.00..12.36 rows=1058 width...	
9	Index Cond: (departure_airport = airport.airport_code)	
10	-> Index Scan using booking_leg_flight_id on booking_leg bl (cost=0.44..2.79 rows=85 widt...	
11	Index Cond: (flight_id = f.flight_id)	
12	-> Index Scan using booking_pkey on booking (cost=0.43..0.48 rows=1 width=8)	
13	Index Cond: (booking_id = bl.booking_id)	
14	Filter: (update_ts > '2023-07-01 00:00:00-05'::timestamp with time zone)	

Figure 13-3. *Execution plan with nested loops only*

With these figures as a reference, let's examine how the function version of the query performs.

Let's try to replicate the same behavior observed in Chapter 6 for a long query with different search conditions and execute the statements shown in Listing 13-6.

Listing 13-6. Examples of function calls

```
#1
SELECT * FROM select_booking_leg_country('US', '2023-07-01');
#2
SELECT * FROM select_booking_leg_country('US', '2023-08-01');
```

```
#3
SELECT * FROM select_booking_leg_country('US', '2023-08-14');
#4
SELECT * FROM select_booking_leg_country('CZ', '2020-08-01');
```

The execution times observed will differ depending on what parameters are passed to the function during the first three to five calls. As a result, the execution time for statement #1, which should take around nine seconds, may vary from nine seconds up to one minute, depending on the sequence of calls. You can even open two or three connections to your local PostgreSQL and try to execute these calls in different orders.

Why is the behavior of the function so inconsistent? Recall Chapter 12, which stated that PostgreSQL *may* save the execution plan of the prepared statement and when a function is called for the first time in a session, each SQL statement that it reaches during the execution will be evaluated and the execution plan will be optimized and then it *may* be cached for subsequent executions.

We are purposely not describing a specific behavior with each sequence of calls, because it is not guaranteed. And while "not guaranteed" may be acceptable for a training database, it is definitely not acceptable in a production environment, especially when an OLTP system implements a policy that caps maximum wait time and aborts transactions when the wait time exceeds that limit. Also, let's not forget about connection pools. Practically any web application initiates a certain number of connections, called a connection pool, and these connections are used by application users' processes, most often, for a single SQL statement. As a result, one PostgreSQL session will almost certainly execute each function with very different sets of parameters.

To guarantee that each time a function is executed *the execution plan will be evaluated and optimized for the specific values it's called with,* we create functions that execute dynamic SQL.

Listing 13-7 shows the function select_booking_leg_country_dynamic that executes the same SQL as the select_booking_leg_country function. The only difference is that the former function constructs a SELECT statement inside the function and then executes it.

Listing 13-7. A function that executes dynamic SQL

```
CREATE OR REPLACE FUNCTION select_booking_leg_country_dynamic(
      p_country text,
      p_updated timestamptz)
RETURNS setof booking_leg_part
```

CHAPTER 13 DYNAMIC SQL

```
AS
$body$
BEGIN
RETURN QUERY
EXECUTE $$
SELECT
    departure_airport,
    booking_id,
    is_returning
FROM booking_leg bl
JOIN flight f USING (flight_id)
WHERE departure_airport IN
          (SELECT
                  airport_code
             FROM airport
            WHERE iso_country=$$|| quote_literal(p_country) ||
     $$ )
    AND bl.booking_id IN
          (SELECT
                  booking_id
             FROM booking
                 WHERE update_ts>$$|| quote_literal(p_updated)||$$)$$;
END;
$body$ LANGUAGE plpgsql;
```

This function accepts the same set of parameters as select_booking_leg_country and returns the same result. But observe that its execution time for each set of parameters is consistent, which is exactly what we want in production systems.

Why did this behavior change? Since the SQL is built immediately prior to execution, the optimizer does not use a cached plan. Instead, it evaluates the execution plan for each execution. It may seem that this would take extra time, but in practice, the opposite happens. Planning time is under 100 ms, and it pays off with a better execution plan, which saves significantly more time.

Also note that this function uses the quote_literal() function to guard against SQL injection.

This is the first but not the only reason to use dynamic SQL in functions. More cases in support of this practice follow later in this chapter.

How to Use Dynamic SQL in OLAP Systems

The title of this section may be misleading. The technique demonstrated in the following can be used in any system; however, the most impressive results are observed when the result set is large. The larger the result set is, the more pronounced the benefits.

Let's assume that for statistical analysis, we need to sort passengers by age. A function to define age categories is defined in Listing 13-8.

Listing 13-8. A function that assigns the age category

```
CREATE OR REPLACE FUNCTION age_category (p_age int)
RETURNS TEXT language plpgsql AS
$body$
BEGIN
    RETURN (CASE
            WHEN p_age <= 2 then 'Infant'
            WHEN p_age <=12 then 'Child'
            WHEN p_age < 65 then 'Adult'
            ELSE 'Senior'
        END);
END; $body$;
```

If this function is used for statistical reports, we might need to calculate an age category for every passenger. In Chapter 12, we mentioned that executing functions in the SELECT list may slow things down, but the functions were more complex. The age_category function performs a very simple substitution. Still, function invocation takes time. Thus,

```
SELECT
    passenger_id,
    age_category(age)
FROM passenger
```

takes 6.5 seconds to execute, while

```
SELECT passenger_id,
        CASE
            WHEN age <= 2 then 'Infant'
```

```
    WHEN age <=12 then 'Child'
    WHEN age < 65 then 'Adult'
    ELSE 'Senior'
END from passenger
```

takes 3.5 seconds.

In this particular case, using a function is not really imperative, because it is used only once, and even one of the biggest tables in Postgres Air, `passenger`, has only 16 million rows. In real analytical queries, the number of rows to process might be hundreds of millions, and multiple category-assigning functions might be needed. In one real-life scenario, execution time with functions was four hours, while execution time with just one function substituted by a direct CASE operator was less than 1.5 hours.

Does this mean we want to avoid using functions in the SELECT list at all costs? There may be a reason our analytics team wants to package the age category assignment in the function. Most likely, they are going to use this function in multiple selects and with different tables and want their queries to be resilient and consistent if age categories ever change.

A more performant solution that retains the maintainability of the function is to create a different function, which contains *part of the code as text,* as in Listing 13-9.

Listing 13-9. A function that builds dynamic SQL

```
CREATE OR REPLACE FUNCTION age_category_dyn (p_age text)
RETURNS text language plpgsql AS
$body$
BEGIN
    RETURN ($$CASE
            WHEN $$||p_age ||$$ <= 2 THEN 'Infant'
            WHEN $$||p_age ||$$<= 12 THEN 'Child'
            WHEN $$||p_age ||$$< 65 THEN 'Adult'
            ELSE 'Senior'
END$$);
END; $body$;
```

Notice the difference: when we execute

```
SELECT age_category(25)
```

…it will return the value 'Adult.'

If you execute

```
SELECT age_category_dyn('age')
```

...it will return a text line that contains the part of code

```
CASE
      WHEN age <= 2 THEN 'Infant'
      WHEN age<= 12 THEN 'Child'
      WHEN age< 65 THEN 'Adult'
      ELSE 'Senior'
END
```

To use this function, you will need to package the SELECT statement into a function, but we already know how to do that—see Listing 13-10.

Listing 13-10. Using the age_category_dyn function to build a dynamic SQL query

```
CREATE TYPE passenger_age_cat_record AS (
passenger_id int,
age_category text
);
CREATE OR REPLACE FUNCTION passenger_age_category_select ()
RETURNS setof passenger_age_cat_record
AS
$body$
BEGIN
RETURN QUERY
EXECUTE $$SELECT
        passenger_id,
     $$||age_category_dyn('age')||$$ AS age_category
FROM passenger $$
;
END;
$body$ LANGUAGE plpgsql;
```

Now, we can execute the following statement:

```
SELECT * FROM passenger_age_category_select ()
```

This will take about five seconds to execute, which is more than a statement without any function calls, but still less than when we choose to execute the original version of the age_category function. And once again, when we are dealing with real analytical queries, the effect will be more visible. In fact, using a larger table (e.g., by building the passenger_large table, similarly to how boarding_pass_large was built in Chapter 7), we can observe similar behavior with a more pronounced difference in execution time.

Some might argue that going to the trouble of creating functions that generate code is not worth the performance gains. To reiterate, there is no universal principle for whether or not creating functions is beneficial—either for performance, code factoring, or portability. Chapter 11 mentioned that code factoring does not work for PG/PL SQL functions the way it works for object-oriented programming languages and promised to provide some examples. This section gives one of those examples. Here, the function age_category_dyn helps code factoring, because updates to the age category assignment must be made in only one place. At the same time, it has less impact on performance than a more traditional function with parameters. Most of the time, building a function that executes dynamic SQL takes some time in the beginning, because debugging is more difficult. However, when the function is already in place, it takes little time to make changes. Deciding which time is more critical—the initial development time or average execution time—can only be done by application and/or database developers.

Using Dynamic SQL for Flexibility

The technique described here is most commonly used in OLTP systems, although, once again, it's not strictly limited to one type of environment.

Often, a system allows a user to select an arbitrary list of search criteria, perhaps using some drop-down lists or other graphical means to construct a query.

The user does not (and should not) know anything about the way the data is stored in the database. However, the search fields may be located in different tables, search criteria may have different selectivity, and, in general, the SELECT statement may look very different depending on the selection criteria.

Let's look at an example. Suppose a function is needed to search for a booking using any combination of the following values:

- Email (or the beginning portion of email)

- Departure airport

- Arrival airport

- Departure date

- Flight ID

Is there any way to implement this function efficiently without defaulting to Elasticsearch?!

A common approach to this problem is something like Listing 13-11.

Listing 13-11. Function supporting search using different combinations of parameters

```
CREATE TYPE booking_record_basic AS(
        booking_id bigint,
      booking_ref text,
      booking_name text ,
      account_id integer,
      email text );
CREATE OR REPLACE FUNCTION select_booking (
     p_email text,
     p_dep_airport text,
     p_arr_airport text,
     p_dep_date date,
     p_flight_id int)
RETURNS SETOF booking_record_basic
AS
$func$
BEGIN
RETURN QUERY
SELECT DISTINCT
        b.booking_id,
        b.booking_ref,
```

```
            booking_name,
            account_id,
            email
FROM booking b
JOIN booking_leg bl USING (booking_id)
JOIN flight f USING (flight_id)
WHERE (p_email IS NULL OR lower(email) LIKE p_email||'%')
AND (p_dep_airport IS NULL OR departure_airport=p_dep_airport)
AND (p_arr_airport IS NULL OR arrival_airport=p_arr_airport)
AND (p_flight_id IS NULL OR bl.flight_id=p_flight_id);
END;
$func$ LANGUAGE plpgsql;
```

This function will always return the correct result, but from a performance standpoint, its behavior will be, at minimum, difficult to predict. Note that when searching by email address, the joins to the booking_leg and flight tables are not needed, but they will be still present.

In the following, we recoded one possible sequence of calls and the execution times we observed for these executions.

#1. Search on email.

```
SELECT DISTINCT
        b.booking_id,
        b.booking_ref,
        b.booking_name,
        b.email
FROM booking b
WHERE lower(email) like 'lawton52%'
```

As a SELECT, this takes 2.1 seconds.

```
SELECT * FROM select_booking ('lawton52',
NULL,
NULL,
NULL,
NULL
 )
```

A comparable function execution takes 3.5 seconds.

#2. Filter on email and flight_id.

```
SELECT DISTINCT
        b.booking_id,
        b.booking_ref,
        b.booking_name,
        b.email
FROM booking b
JOIN booking_leg bl USING (booking_id)
WHERE lower(email) like 'lawton52%'
AND flight_id= 2605
```

The SELECT takes 80 ms.

```
SELECT * FROM select_booking (
    'lawton52',
    NULL,
    NULL,
    NULL,
    2605
    )
```

Function execution takes the same 80 ms.

#3. Criteria on email, departure airport, and arrival airport.

```
SELECT DISTINCT
        b.booking_id,
        b.booking_ref,
        b.booking_name,
        b.email
FROM booking b
JOIN booking_leg bl USING (booking_id)
JOIN flight f USING (flight_id)
WHERE lower(email) like 'lawton52%'
AND departure_airport='ORD'
AND arrival_airport='JFK'
```

The SELECT takes 80 ms.

```
SELECT * FROM select_booking (
        'lawton52',
        'ORD',
        'JFK',
         NULL,
         NULL
        )
```

Function execution with the same parameters takes 200 ms.

#4. Criteria on email, departure airport, arrival airport, and scheduled departure.

```
SELECT DISTINCT
        b.booking_id,
        b.booking_ref,
        b.booking_name,
        b.email
FROM booking b
JOIN booking_leg bl USING (booking_id)
JOIN flight f USING (flight_id)
WHERE lower(email) like 'lawton52%'
AND departure_airport='ORD'
AND arrival_airport='JFK'
AND scheduled_departure BETWEEN '07-26-2023' AND '07-27-2023'
```

SELECT takes 46 ms.

```
SELECT * FROM select_booking (
        'lawton52',
        'ORD',
        'JFK',
        '2023-07-26',
         NULL
        )
```

Function execution takes 155 ms.

#5. Search on email and scheduled departure.

```
SELECT DISTINCT
       b.booking_id,
       b.booking_ref,
       b.booking_name,
       b.email
FROM booking b
JOIN booking_leg bl USING (booking_id)
JOIN flight f USING (flight_id)
WHERE lower(email) like 'lawton52%'
AND scheduled_departure BETWEEN '07-30-2023' AND '07-31-2023'
```

SELECT takes 1.3 seconds.

```
SELECT * FROM select_booking (
      'lawton52',
      NULL,
      NULL,
      '2023-07-30',
      NULL
      )
```

Function execution takes **35** seconds.

#6. Search on flight_id.

```
SELECT DISTINCT
       b.booking_id,
       b.booking_ref,
       b.booking_name,
       b.email
FROM booking b
JOIN booking_leg bl USING (booking_id)
WHERE flight_id= 27191
```

SELECT takes 56 ms.

```
SELECT * FROM select_booking (
      NULL,
      NULL,
      NULL,
      NULL,
       27191
       )
```

Function execution takes **10** seconds.

As we discussed previously, execution times for different function invocations could be even longer if the first five function executions in the current session produce an execution plan that is suboptimal for subsequent executions. While experimenting with this function, we managed to find a sequence of function invocations that made the last example run for three minutes. But even a ten-second execution time in a situation where the expected response time is under 100 ms can cause an application timeout. Even if such situations are extremely rare, they are unacceptable in production systems.

Can we find an alternative solution? Like the previous example, it's possible to write a function that builds a SELECT dynamically depending on which parameters are passed. In addition, it benefits from being analyzed before each execution.

The source code for the new function is shown in Listing 13-12.

Listing 13-12. A function that builds dynamic SQL to search by different criteria

```
CREATE OR REPLACE FUNCTION select_booking_dyn (
      p_email text,
      p_dep_airport text,
      p_arr_airport text,
      p_dep_date date,
      p_flight_id int)
returns setof booking_record_basic
AS
$func$
DECLARE
v_sql text:=
'SELECT DISTINCT
        b.booking_id,
        b.booking_ref,
```

```
        booking_name,
        account_id,
        email
FROM   booking b ';
v_where_booking text;
v_where_booking_leg text;
v_where_flight text;
BEGIN
IF p_email IS NOT NULL
    THEN v_where_booking :=$$ lower(email) like $$ ||quote_literal(p_
email||'%'); END IF;
IF p_flight_id IS NOT NULL
    THEN v_where_booking_leg:= $$ flight_id=$$||p_flight_id::text;
END IF;
IF p_dep_airport IS NOT NULL
    THEN v_where_flight:=concat_ws($$ AND $$, v_where_flight,
                                        $$departure_airport=$$||
                                        quote_literal
                                        (p_dep_airport));
END IF;
IF p_arr_airport IS NOT NULL
    THEN v_where_flight:=concat_ws($$ AND $$,v_where_flight,
                                        $$arrival_airport=$$||
                                        quote_literal
                                        (p_arr_airport));
END IF;
IF p_dep_date IS NOT NULL
    THEN v_where_flight:=concat_ws($$ AND $$,v_where_flight,
                                    $$scheduled_departure BETWEEN $$||
                                    quote_literal(p_dep_date)
                                    ||$$::date AND
                                      $$||quote_literal(p_dep_date)||
                                                $$::date+1$$);
END IF;
```

```
IF v_where_flight IS NOT NULL  OR v_where_booking_leg IS NOT NULL
    THEN v_sql:=v_sql||$$ JOIN booking_leg bl USING (booking_id) $$;
END IF;
IF v_where_flight IS NOT NULL
    THEN v_sql:=v_sql ||$$ JOIN flight f USING (flight_id) $$;
END IF;
v_sql:=v_sql ||$$ WHERE $$||concat_ws($$ AND $$,v_where_booking, v_where_
booking_leg, v_where_flight);
return query EXECUTE (v_sql);
END;
$func$ LANGUAGE plpgsql;
```

This is a lot of code to read! Let's walk through it and review what, exactly, is going on here.

The parameters of the new function are exactly the same as those of the old function, and the result type is also the same, but the function body is completely different. At a high level, this function builds a statement to be executed later in the v_sql text variable.

Building the query dynamically means that we have the option to only include the joins that are needed. The booking table is always needed, which is why the initial value of v_sql is set to

```
'SELECT DISTINCT
       b.booking_id,
       b.booking_ref,
       booking_name,
       account_id,
       email
FROM  booking b ';
```

Then, depending on what other parameters are passed as NOT NULL, the function determines which other tables are needed. It may only be the table booking_leg. This is the case if the p_flight_id parameter is null, that is, flight-related parameters are not used. Alternately, it might be both tables: booking_leg and flight.

After adding all necessary tables, the full search criteria are built by concatenating all conditions with the separator 'AND'. With the search criteria, the v_sql statement is finalized and executed. To see what the final query is for different invocations of the function, uncomment the RAISE NOTICE statement.

Is this too much work for a performance improvement? Try to compile this function and execute it with the same parameters from the preceding examples. It'll become clear quickly that the select_booking_dyn() function execution times do not exceed the execution times of the corresponding SQL statements for every set of parameters—this is especially evident in cases #5 and #6. Moreover, the execution time is predictable and does not depend on the first execution in the current session.

Once again, dynamic functions are not easy to debug, and you may need to include a lot of debugging printouts, but if performance in your production system is critical, the results are well worth the effort.

Using Dynamic SQL to Aid the Optimizer

Since this whole chapter is dedicated to ways to improve query performance by using dynamic SQL, this section header might be puzzling. However, this section concerns a different cause of performance issues. In these examples, dynamic SQL is not used to construct case-specific SQL, but to nudge the optimizer to choose a better execution plan.

Looking closely at all the examples in the previous section, one combination of the search criteria is performing notably poorly, even though the result set is small: the case when the search is on the email on the booking and the departure airport. Even in cases when email is restrictive enough, the optimizer fails to use the index on booking_id in the second join. If we execute the query in Listing 13-13, the execution plan shows hash joins—see Figure 13-4.

Listing 13-13. Selecting booking by email and departure airport

```
SELECT DISTINCT
        b.booking_id,
        b.booking_ref,
        b.booking_name,
        b.account_id,
        b.email
FROM booking b
JOIN  booking_leg bl USING (booking_id)
JOIN flight f USING (flight_id)
WHERE lower(email) like 'lawton510%'
     AND departure_airport='JFK'
```

The execution time for this query is about four seconds, and the result contains only 16 rows, so this is a small query, and the execution time should be faster.

The reason for this suboptimal plan has been mentioned before—the PostgreSQL optimizer does not estimate the size of intermediate result sets correctly. The actual number of rows filtered by the pattern index is 3941, while the estimate in the plan is 28219.

| | QUERY PLAN |
	text
1	Unique (cost=427531.98..427549.21 rows=1378 width=64) (actual time=1513.733..1513.745 rows=16 loops=1)
2	-> Sort (cost=427531.98..427535.43 rows=1378 width=64) (actual time=1513.732..1513.739 rows=25 loops=1)
3	Sort Key: b.booking_id, b.booking_ref, b.booking_name, b.email
4	Sort Method: quicksort Memory: 27kB
5	-> Hash Join (cost=69747.98..427460.13 rows=1378 width=64) (actual time=237.830..1513.670 rows=25 loops=1)
6	Hash Cond: (bl.flight_id = f.flight_id)
7	-> Hash Join (cost=60346.96..417824.26 rows=89468 width=68) (actual time=9.850..1365.625 rows=665 loops=1)
8	Hash Cond: (bl.booking_id = b.booking_id)
9	-> Seq Scan on booking_leg bl (cost=0.00..310506.66 rows=17893566 width=8) (actual time=0.314..734.995 rows=17893566 loops=1)
10	-> Hash (cost=59994.26..59994.26 rows=28216 width=64) (actual time=8.011..8.015 rows=222 loops=1)
11	Buckets: 32768 Batches: 1 Memory Usage: 277kB
12	-> Bitmap Heap Scan on booking b (cost=489.65..59994.26 rows=28216 width=64) (actual time=0.059..7.953 rows=222 loops=1)
13	Filter: (lower(email) ~~ 'lawton510%'::text)
14	Heap Blocks: exact=215
15	-> Bitmap Index Scan on booking_email_lower_pattern (cost=0.00..482.59 rows=28216 width=0) (actual time=0.034..0.034 rows=222 loo...
16	Index Cond: ((lower(email) ~>=~ 'lawton510'::text) AND (lower(email) ~<~ 'lawton511'::text))
17	-> Hash (cost=9269.50..9269.50 rows=10521 width=4) (actual time=147.605..147.605 rows=10530 loops=1)
18	Buckets: 16384 Batches: 1 Memory Usage: 499kB
19	-> Bitmap Heap Scan on flight f (cost=121.96..9269.50 rows=10521 width=4) (actual time=2.908..146.103 rows=10530 loops=1)
20	Recheck Cond: (departure_airport = 'JFK'::bpchar)
21	Heap Blocks: exact=4085
22	-> Bitmap Index Scan on flight_departure_airport (cost=0.00..119.33 rows=10521 width=0) (actual time=1.597..1.597 rows=10530 loops=1)
23	Index Cond: (departure_airport = 'JFK'::bpchar)

Figure 13-4. *Execution plan for Listing 13-13 with hash joins*

The technique to optimize this query is literally to help the optimizer do its job and remove the need to estimate the size of the result set. How? First, find the booking IDs that correspond to the email address that is being searched for, and then pass the list of booking_ids to the main SELECT statement. Note: The function that we use to illustrate this case is very case-specific and used for illustrative purposes only (Listing 13-14). A function with a more generalized approach closer to what would be used in a production system would be massive.

Listing 13-14. Dynamic SQL to improve the code from Listing 13-13

```
CREATE OR REPLACE FUNCTION select_booking_email_departure(
      p_email text,
      p_dep_airport text)
RETURNS SETOF booking_record_basic AS
$body$
DECLARE
   v_sql text;
   v_booking_ids text;
BEGIN
   EXECUTE $$SELECT array_to_string(array_agg(booking_id), ',')
            FROM booking
            WHERE lower(email) like $$||quote_literal(p_email||'%')
   INTO v_booking_ids;
   v_sql=
   $$SELECT DISTINCT
            b.booking_id,
            b.booking_ref,
            b.booking_name,
            b.account_id,
            b.email
      FROM booking b
      JOIN  booking_leg bl USING(booking_id)
      JOIN flight f USING (flight_id)
      WHERE b.booking_id IN ($$||v_booking_ids||$$)
            AND departure_airport=$$||quote_literal(p_dep_airport);
   RETURN QUERY EXECUTE v_sql;
END;

$body$ LANGUAGE plpgsql;
```

Why does this work? We know that the search by email is going to be relatively restrictive, because what is passed is nearly the whole email address or, at least, the essential part of it. So, in the first step, the relatively small number of bookings with this email is preselected and saved in the text variable v_booking_ids. Then, the SELECT is constructed with an explicit list of booking_ids.

Executing this new function

```
SELECT * FROM select_booking_email_departure('lawton510','JFK')
```

...the execution time will be just 200 ms. Examine the EXPLAIN command output for the generated SQL, including the execution plan as it appears in Figure 13-5.

	QUERY PLAN text
1	Unique (cost=14591.09..14591.25 rows=11 width=68) (actual time=5.429..5.442 rows=16 loops=1)
2	-> Sort (cost=14591.09..14591.11 rows=11 width=68) (actual time=5.428..5.431 rows=25 loops=1)
3	Sort Key: b.booking_id, b.booking_ref, b.booking_name, b.account_id, b.email
4	Sort Method: quicksort Memory: 27kB
5	-> Nested Loop (cost=1.29..14590.89 rows=11 width=68) (actual time=0.656..5.398 rows=25 loops=1)
6	-> Nested Loop (cost=0.87..14275.97 rows=704 width=72) (actual time=0.051..2.419 rows=665 loops=1)
7	-> Index Scan using booking_pkey on booking b (cost=0.43..1845.30 rows=222 width=68) (actual time=0.039..1.014 rows=222 loops=1)
8	Index Cond: (booking_id = ANY ('{3613355,957543,1111315,1253518,628907,629954,5183078,5184235,5376394,5406828,5454800,5582121,7213
9	-> Index Scan using booking_leg_booking_id on booking_leg bl (cost=0.44..55.86 rows=13 width=8) (actual time=0.005..0.006 rows=3 loops=222)
10	Index Cond: (booking_id = b.booking_id)
11	-> Index Scan using flight_pkey on flight f (cost=0.42..0.45 rows=1 width=4) (actual time=0.004..0.004 rows=0 loops=665)
12	Index Cond: (flight_id = bl.flight_id)
13	Filter: (departure_airport = 'JFK'::bpchar)
14	Rows Removed by Filter: 1
15	Planning Time: 0.816 ms
16	Execution Time: 5.483 ms

Figure 13-5. *Execution plan for dynamic SQL with the list of booking_ids*

Even with several thousand IDs, the index-based access proves more efficient.

FDWs and Dynamic SQL

As mentioned in the Introduction, detailed discussion of distributed queries is out of the scope of this book. However, since dynamic SQL is covered, this is a good opportunity to make a few remarks about working with *foreign data wrappers (FDWs)*.

A foreign data wrapper is a library that can communicate with an external data source (i.e., data that resides outside your PostgreSQL server), hiding the details of connecting to the data source and obtaining data from it.

An FDW is a very powerful tool, and more and more foreign data wrappers for different types of databases are becoming available. PostgreSQL does an outstanding job optimizing queries that include *foreign tables*, that is, mappings of the tables from the external systems. However, since the access to external statistics may be limited, especially when the external systems are not PostgreSQL based, the optimization may be not so precise. We have found it very helpful to use the techniques described in the previous section.

The first way to optimize would be to run the local part of the query identifying which records are needed from the remote server and then access a remote table. An alternative way is to send a query with constant-defined conditions (e.g., `WHERE update_ts> CURRENT_DATE -3`) to the remote site, pull the remote data to the local site, and then execute the rest of the query. Using one of these two techniques helps minimize inconsistencies in the execution time.

Summary

Dynamic SQL is an exceptionally powerful tool in PostgreSQL, which is not utilized enough by database developers. Using dynamic SQL can improve performance in situations where all other optimization techniques fail.

Dynamic SQL works best within functions; a SQL statement is generated based on function input parameters and then executed. It can be used both in OLTP and OLAP environments.

If you choose to use dynamic SQL for your project, be ready for extensive and time-consuming debugging. It might feel discouraging in the beginning, but the performance improvements are well worth it.

CHAPTER 14

Avoiding the Pitfalls of Object-Relational Mapping

Chapter 11 discussed a typical interaction between an application and a database and explained ORIM (object-relational impedance mismatch) and how it affects performance. It also stated that any potential solution should allow operating with large objects (i.e., datasets) and should support the exchange of complex objects. This chapter introduces an approach developed by us and successfully utilized in a production environment. This approach is called NORM (No-ORM).

We are by no means pioneers in the quest to overcome object-relational impedance mismatch, nor are we the first to propose an alternative to ORM. NORM is only one of many possible solutions. However, one feature that makes NORM stand out among other tools is the ease of use by application developers.

The NORM GitHub repo (`https://github.com/hettie-d/NORM`) contains some documentation on the approach and an example of the code built according to the NORM methodology. Most importantly, it contains the set of procedures that allow to automate the function code generation. More details will be provided later in this chapter.

© Henrietta Dombrovskaya, Boris Novikov, Anna Bailliekova 2024
H. Dombrovskaya et al., *PostgreSQL Query Optimization*, https://doi.org/10.1007/979-8-8688-0069-6_14

Why Application Developers Like NORM

Often, new development methodologies require application developers to make significant changes to the development process, which inevitably leads to lower productivity. It is not unusual for potential performance gains to fail to justify the increase in development time. After all, developer time is the most expensive resource in any project.

In Chapter 12, the benefits of using functions were preceded by the caveat "if you can convince application developers." And often, you can't convince them, because of the difficulties of adapting to a new programming style. That is not the case with NORM. In the following sections, we will explain the appeal of this approach for both application developers and database developers.

ORM vs. NORM

Chapter 11 discussed a bottleneck in data exchange created by ORM. Figure 14-1 is a copy of Figure 11-1 from Chapter 11, and it represents the dataflow between an application and a database.

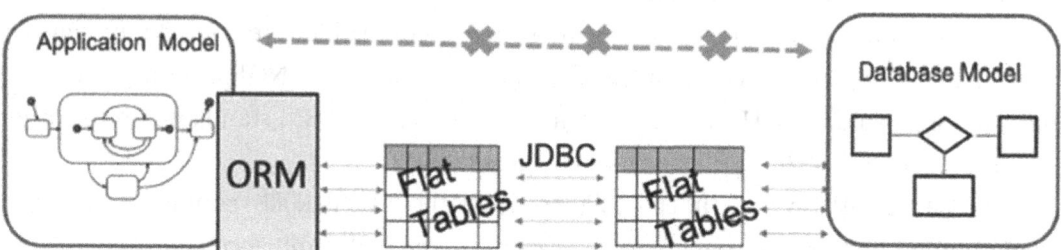

Figure 14-1. *How ORM works*

The major problem is that complex objects from the application model are disassembled into atomic objects before communicating with the database, generating too many too small queries, which bring down system performance. An even more important problem is that the correspondence between application complex objects and database complex data structures is lost.

The approach proposed by NORM is presented in Figure 14-2.

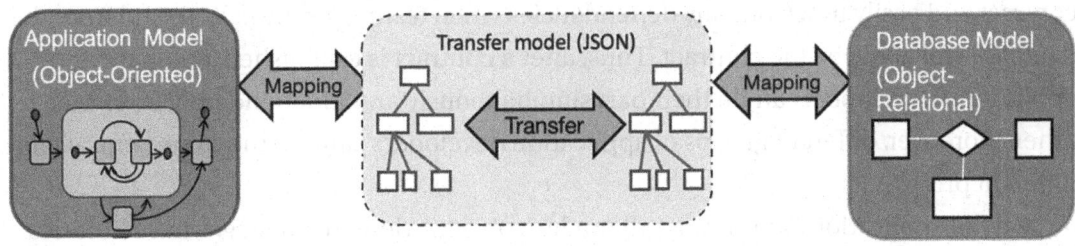

Figure 14-2. *How NORM works*

In this figure, A-Model is an application model, D-Model is a database model, and T-Model is a *transfer model*. The presence of the T-Model is a unique feature of the NORM approach, which makes the mapping *symmetrical*. We are not trying to build a database model based on an application model, nor are we insisting on creating database objects first.

Instead, we call for *a contract* to be established between the application layer and the database, like the way you would see a contract over a RESTful web service. The NORM contract requires that an application controller performs at most two accesses to the database: one to obtain all data needed for the function and another to send request for data modification. Since the whole complex hierarchical object is sent or received as a minimal unit of transfer, it is extremely important to properly define it for each case (or choose the right class/hierarchy from the ones already defined). Different implementations of NORM may use different means to represent hierarchies. Our implementation uses one of the most popular notations, namely, JSON.

The contract, or a T-Model, comes in a form of a JSON schema describing the structure of complex objects, their relationships in a hierarchy, and mapping of these objects to the database objects (tables and columns).

Through this contract, it is possible to simplify the persistence of objects by serializing the objects into JSON payloads that the database can consume. This results in one database call to persist an object regardless of its structure or complexity.

Likewise, when retrieving objects, the application can deserialize the result coming back from the database to a model in a single database call. It can also pass additional parameters as a part of the contract to tell the database that it needs additional pieces of the model, similar to an ODATA web service request.

Many application developers love the simplified implementation of the data access layer on the application side. The fact that NORM uses a contract to determine the inputs and outputs of every call to the database allows application developers to code to the contract and easily mock out any dependencies when testing, as the calls to and from the database will abide by the contract. Thus, after a contract is established, database and application developers can do their part simultaneously and independently from each other. Moreover, different groups of application developers can use the same contract for different projects.

On the application side, almost all modern object-oriented languages have libraries for serializing and deserializing objects. As each new database interaction occurs, it is possible to reuse the same pattern for implementation.

This allows application developers to spend more time designing the JSON payload to ensure it meets the current and future needs of the business. Reusing the same pattern of interactions also reduces implementation time, minimizes the likelihood of defects, and allows minimal code changes to impact the entire database access implementation. More importantly, an application usually needs different complex objects and thus requires multiple contracts, although these complex objects can be built from the same database.

NORM Explained

To illustrate how NORM works, let's get back to the example in Chapter 11.

Figure 14-3 represents a subset of the `postgres_air` Entity-Relationship diagram used to build the example.

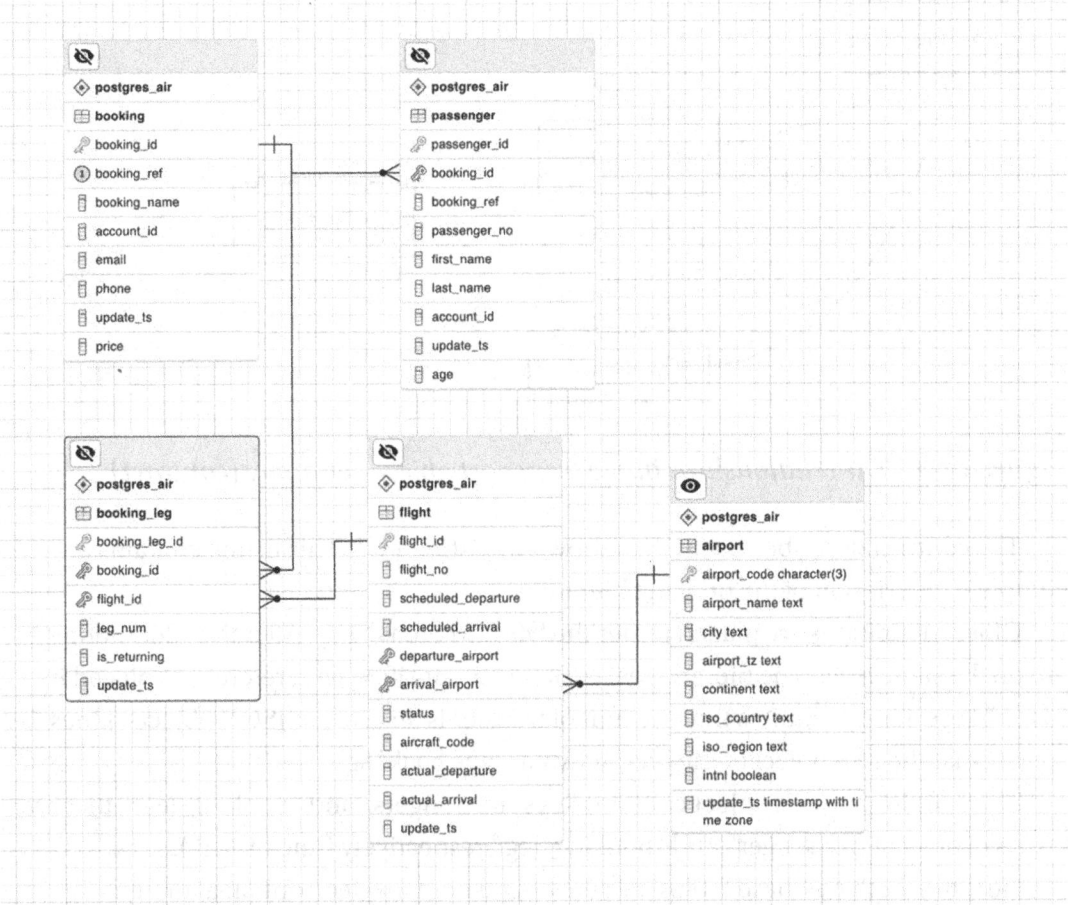

Figure 14-3. *ERD for the case study*

In Chapter 11, discussing the interaction between the application and the database, we drafted an object (which we can now call a T-object hierarchy) that represented all the information related to a booking. From the airline passenger perspective, a booking represents their travel itinerary. To keep the code sample readable, we eliminated some details that can usually be found on an itinerary. Specifically, we include airport codes, but not cities where airports are located, avoiding the need to include mapping of the airport table.

The ERD in Figure 14-3 presents all tables and relationships needed to build the mapping from a database object to a transfer object hierarchy. The relationships of transfer objects in the hierarchy are presented in Figure 14-4.

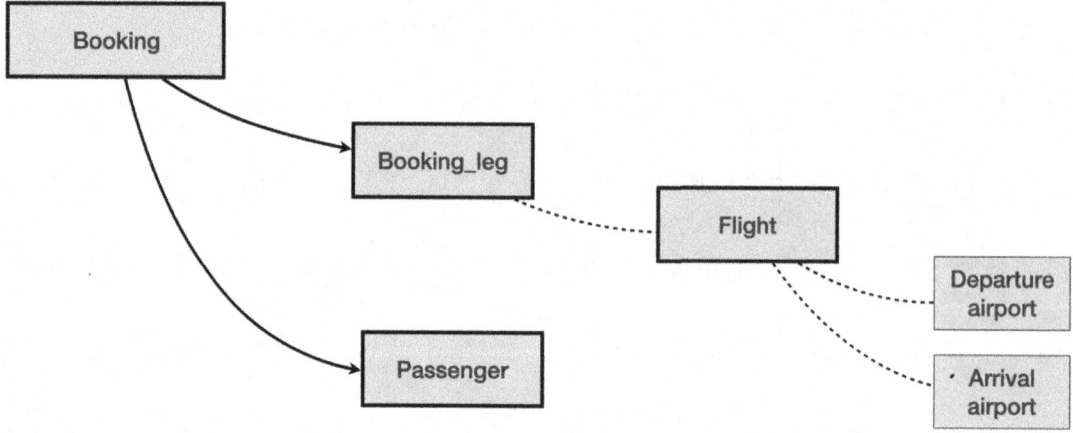

Figure 14-4. *The relationships in the transport object hierarchy (contract)*

The contract described as JSON is shown in Listing 14-1. This listing contains a complete description of the booking hierarchy.

Object definitions are placed under the "definitions" key. All object definitions are on the same level. The hierarchical structure is specified with references placed in "$ref" keys. Line 2 requires that the unit of transfer is an array of JSON objects. Lines 5–7 specify that the root object of the hierarchy has type booking.

The definition of this object contains keys "passengers" and "booking_legs" that are arrays of objects "passenger" and "booking_leg," respectively (lines 15–25).

Note that both database tables passenger and booking_leg contain a foreign key column booking_id. This field is not included to JSON as the relationships are represented with hierarchical structure of JSON.

Another method to build a hierarchy is used in the definition of "booking_leg." This object contains a single embedded object of type "flight." The important difference is that field flight_id is contained in the booking_leg object.

The flight data cannot be updated through this hierarchy (as such update would affect other bookings on the same flight).

Instead, the booking_leg.flight_id (lines 88–90) can be modified if rebooking is needed.

Similarly, the flight JSON object contains name and city of departure and arrival airports. These fields cannot be updated through this hierarchy because changes in the booking cannot affect properties of an airport.

Listing 14-1. The contract in the form of a JSON schema

```
1    {
2        "type": "array",
3        "title": "booking_hierarchy",
4        "description": "all booking details",
5        "items": {
6            "$ref": "#/definitions/booking"
7        },
8        "definitions": {
9            "booking": {
10               "type": "object",
11               "properties": {
12                   "booking_id": {
13                       "type": "number"
14                   },
15                   "passengers": {
16                       "type": "array",
17                       "items": {
18                           "$ref": "#/definitions/passenger"
19                       }
20                   },
21                   "booking_legs": {
22                       "type": "array",
23                       "items": {
24                           "$ref": "#/definitions/booking_leg"
25                       }
26                   },
27                   "booking_reference": {
28                       "type": "string"
29                   }
30               }
31           },
32           "flight": {
33               "type": "object",
34               "properties": {
```

```
35                      "flight_no": {
36                          "type": "string"
37                      },
38                      "arrival_city": {
39                          "type": "string"
40                      },
41                      "departure_city": {
42                          "type": "string"
43                      },
44                      "scheduled_arrival": {
45                          "type": "string"
46
47                      },
48                      "scheduled_departure": {
49                          "type": "string"
50                      },
51                      "arrival_airport_code": {
52                          "type": "string"
53                      },
54                      "arrival_airport_name": {
55                          "type": "string"
56                      },
57                      "departure_airport_code": {
58                          "type": "string"
59                      },
60                      "departure_airport_name": {
61                          "type": "string"
62                      }
63                  }
64              },
65          "passenger": {
66              "type": "object",
67              "properties": {
68                  "last_name": {
69                      "type": "string"
70                  },
```

```
 71                     "account_id": {
 72                         "type": "number"
 73                     },
 74                     "first_name": {
 75                         "type": "string"
 76                     },
 77                     "passenger_id": {
 78                         "type": "number"
 79                     },
 80                     "passenger_no": {
 81                         "type": "number"
 82                     }
 83                 }
 84             },
 85             "booking_leg": {
 86                 "type": "object",
 87                 "properties": {
 88                     "flight_id": {
 89                         "type": "number"
 90                     },
 91                     "flight": {
 92                         "type": "object",
 93                         "items": {
 94                             "$ref": "#/definitions/flight"
 95                         }
 96                     },
 97                     "leg_num": {
 98                         "type": "number"
 99                     },
100                     "booking_leg_id": {
101                         "type": "number"
102                     }
103                 }
104             }
105         }
106     }
```

Note that this schema represents the contract, that is, the object structure that the application expects to receive. It differs significantly from how the data is stored in the database, and the most important part is that the database implementation has no impact on how the application interacts with it, as long as the database response remains in accordance with the contract.

An example JSON object following this contract is shown in Figure 14-5.

```
1    {
2         "booking_id": 10679,
3         "passengers": [
4             {
5                 "last_name": "CHARLES",
6                 "account_id": 193770,
7                 "first_name": "ARYA",
8                 "passenger_id": 34482,
9                 "passenger_no": null
10            }
11        ],
12        "booking_legs": [
13            {
14                "flight": {
15                    "flight_no": "36",
16                    "arrival_city": "FRANKFURT",
17                    "departure_city": "ADDIS ABABA",
18                    "scheduled_arrival": "2023-06-03T12:10:00-05:00",
19                    "scheduled_departure": "2023-06-03T05:15:00-05:00",
20                    "arrival_airport_code": "FRA",
21                    "arrival_airport_name": "Frankfurt am Main Airport",
22                    "departure_airport_code": "ADD",
23                    "departure_airport_name": "Addis Ababa Bole International Airport"
24                },
25                "leg_num": 1,
26                "flight_id": 6392,
27                "booking_leg_id": 16734488
28            },
29            {
30                "flight": {
31                    "flight_no": "37",
32                    "arrival_city": "ADDIS ABABA",
33                    "departure_city": "FRANKFURT",
34                    "scheduled_arrival": "2023-06-10T21:00:00-05:00",
35                    "scheduled_departure": "2023-06-10T14:05:00-05:00",
36                    "arrival_airport_code": "ADD",
37                    "arrival_airport_name": "Addis Ababa Bole International Airport",
38                    "departure_airport_code": "FRA",
39                    "departure_airport_name": "Frankfurt am Main Airport"
40                },
41                "leg_num": 2,
42                "flight_id": 32604,
43                "booking_leg_id": 16734489
44            }
45        ],
46        "booking_reference": "EN6B12"
47    }
48
```

Figure 14-5. *Transfer object as JSON*

In short, the interaction between the application and the database can be summarized as follows:

1. The application serializes data into JSON format and sends it to the database by calling a corresponding database function.

2. A database function parses the JSON that was passed as a parameter and executes whatever the function is supposed to do: either a search or data transformation. PostgreSQL has a very well-developed JSON support with a rich set of functions, which makes it easy to manipulate JSON on the database side.

3. The result set is converted to JSON and passed to the application, where it is deserialized and is ready to be consumed by the application.

NORM in the Application Perspective

On the application side, the Python classes in Listing 14-2 are mapped to the same transfer object.

Listing 14-2. Postgres Air application classes

```python
from typing import List
from pydantic import BaseModel, Field
from datetime.datetime import datetime, timezone
from phonenumber import PhoneNumber

class Booking(BaseModel):

    booking_id: int
    booking_ref: str
    booking_legs: List[BookingLeg]
    booking_name: str
    account_id: int
    email: str
    phone: PhoneNumber
    update_ts: datetime
    price: decimal

class BookingLeg(BaseModel):

    booking_leg_id: int
    flight: Flight
    is_returning: bool
    update_ts: datetime
```

```python
class Flight(BaseModel):

    flight_id: int
    flight_no: int
    scheduled_departure: datetime
    scehduled_arrival: datetimee
    departure_airport: Airport
    arrival_airport: Airport
    status: str
    aircraft_code: str
    actual_departure: datetime
    actual_arrival: datetime
    update_ts=datetime

class Airport(BaseModel):

    airport_code: str = Field(min_length=3,max_length=3)
    airport_name: str
    airport_tz: timezone
    city: str
    continent: str
    iso_country: str
    iso_region: str
    intnl: bool
    update_ts: datetime

class Passenger(BaseModel):

    passenger_id: int
    booking: Booking
    passenger_no: int
    first_name: str
    last_name: str
    account_id: int
    update_ts: datetime
    age: int
```

It is worth mentioning that we can build completely different transfer objects using the same set of tables. For example, before any flight departs, a document that is called manifest has to be produced. This document lists all the passengers on the fight along with their seat assignments. The transfer object for the manifest is presented in Figure 14-6.

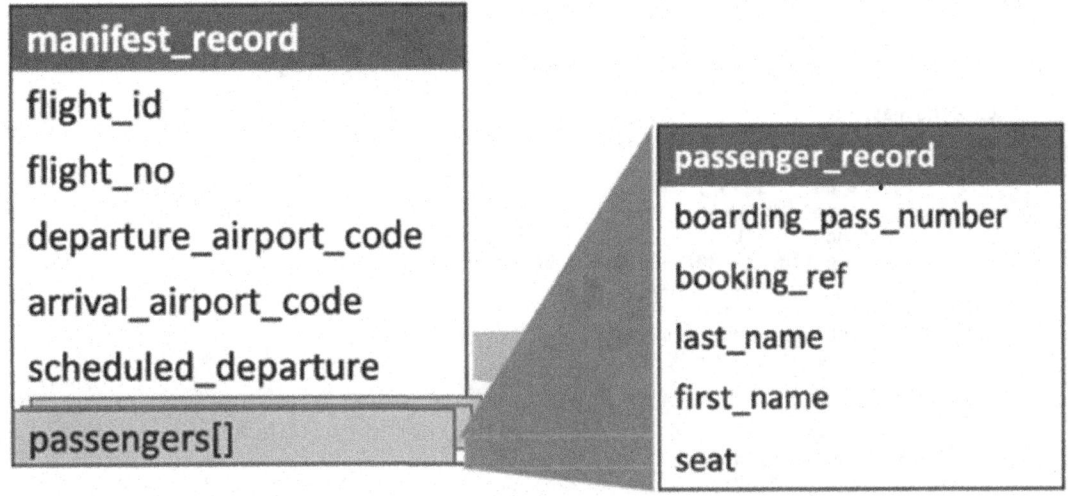

Figure 14-6. *Transfer object for the flight manifest*

The matching JSON is shown in Figure 14-7.

```json
{
    "flight": {
        "flight_id": 13650,
        "flight_no": "1245",
        "scheduled_arrival": "2020-06-05T02:45:00-05:00",
        "scheduled_departure": "2020-06-05T00:20:00-05:00",
        "arrival_airport_code": "CDG",
        "arrival_airport_name": "Charles de Gaulle International Airport",
        "departure_airport_code": "JFK",
        "departure_airport_name": "John F Kennedy International Airport"
    },
    "boarding_passes": [
        {
            "seat": "1E",
            "flight_no": "1245",
            "last_name": "LEWIS",
            "first_name": "ELIA",
            "boarding_time": "2020-06-04T23:50:00-05:00",
            "booking_leg_id": 17564910,
            "arrival_airport": "CDG",
            "boarding_pass_id": 1247796,
            "departure_airport": "JFK"
        },
        {

            "seat": "1F",
            "flight_no": "1245",
            "last_name": "LEVY",
            "first_name": "ALEXANDER",
            "boarding_time": "2020-06-04T23:50:00-05:00",
            "booking_leg_id": 17564910,
            "arrival_airport": "CDG",
            "boarding_pass_id": 1247797,
            "departure_airport": "JFK"
        },
        ...
    ]
}
```

Figure 14-7. *Manifest object as JSON*

NORM from a Database Perspective

In the early stages of the NORM project, the only serious objection to its adoption was the necessity of manually creating all data manipulation functions. Agile teams didn't want to spend time on writing additional code, especially when ORMs generate code with similar functionality (almost) without human interaction. Nor did they want to have an additional person (a database developer) on the team. To address these concerns, we added an auto-generation module to NORM, which we call NORM-GEN. In this section, we will explain how to generate types and functions on the database side, instead of creating them manually. To achieve this goal, we need to make one important change to our contract, that is, to find a way to define the mapping between application classes and database objects.

Mapping JSON to the Database

To enable the automatic generation of the database objects, we extend the JSON schema syntax with a db_mapping key that can be specified for the whole hierarchy, an object, or a key. The mapping specifies the database schema, table names and column names corresponding to the JSON object and keys, as well as primary and foreign key columns that define relationships between objects.

Listing 14-3 shows how the mapping is specified for a part of the contract, namely, for the passenger object. Lines 4–7 of this listing define the table corresponding to the JSON object, the primary key of the table, the primary key of the parent object, and the name of the complex data type that represents the object in the database before conversion to JSON. The explicit mapping of lower-level objects can be omitted when JSON key names coincide with the table column names.

Listing 14-3. Database mapping for the passenger object

```
1          "passenger": {
2             "type": "object",
3             "db_mapping": {
4                "pk_col": "passenger_id",
5                "db_table": "passenger",
6                "record_type": "passenger_record",
7                "parent_fk_col": "booking_id"
8             },
9             "properties": {
10               "last_name": {
11                  "type": "text"
12               },
13               "account_id": {
14                  "type": "number"
15               },
16               "first_name": {
17                  "type": "text"
```

```
18                    },
19                    "passenger_id": {
20                        "type": "number"
21                    },
22                    "passenger_no": {
23                        "type": "number"
24                    }
25                }
26            },
```

Generating Database Code

The contract is used to generate

- Database type definitions that represent the hierarchy in the form of nested complex objects and arrays.

- A function that selects full hierarchies from the database based on a list of primary keys of the root objects. The hierarchy is built as a database complex nested object, which is then converted into JSON format.

- A function returning a list of root object keys based on a search request specified as an input parameter.

- A function that performs modifications of specified objects or their sub-objects in the hierarchy. Multiple objects and/or sub-objects can be inserted, updated, or deleted in the same request.

Some of the interfaces that applications use to access the database, including JDBC, do not support JSON as a data type. To bypass this, the JSON is converted into a list of text strings right before the transfer and converted back to JSON immediately after transfer.

Now, let's get more specific and show how this is achieved.

Listing 14-4 shows generated type definitions for the booking hierarchy. These definitions are similar to definitions from Listings 12-17 and 12-20.

We define the types `passenger_record`, `flight_record`, and `booking_leg_record,` which includes a `flight_record` sub-object, and then `booking_record`, which has arrays of these types as components.

Listing 14-4. Booking type definitions

```
/* entering  : booking */
  /* entering  : passenger */
   drop type if exists norm.bh_passenger_record cascade;
   create type norm.bh_passenger_record as (
       last_name  text,
       account_id  int4,
       first_name  text,
       passenger_id  int4,
       passenger_no  int4
   );
   /* entering  : booking_leg */
  /* entering  : flight */
   drop type if exists norm.bh_flight_record cascade;
   create type norm.bh_flight_record as (
       flight_no  text,
       arrival_city  text,
       departure_city  text,
       scheduled_arrival  timestamptz,
       scheduled_departure  timestamptz,
       arrival_airport_code  bpchar,
       arrival_airport_name  text,
       departure_airport_code  bpchar,
       departure_airport_name  text
   );
   drop type if exists norm.bh_booking_leg_record cascade;
   create type norm.bh_booking_leg_record as (
       flight_id  int4,
       flight  norm.bh_flight_record,
       leg_num  int4,
       booking_leg_id  int4
   );
   drop type if exists norm.bh_booking_record cascade;
   create type norm.bh_booking_record as (
       booking_id  int8,
```

```
    passengers   norm.bh_passenger_record[],
    booking_legs   norm.bh_booking_leg_record[],
    booking_reference   text
);
```

Looking at these type definitions, it is clear they do indeed represent the transport object booking from Figure 14-4.

Getting Data from the Database

The contract requires that the application should receive all needed data with the smallest possible number of interactions with the database. Typically, an application should receive a set of complete hierarchies. This implies that the structure of returned data depends on the definition of the hierarchy, but not on the specific query. Listing 14-5 shows the SELECT clause generated for the booking hierarchy.

Listing 14-5. Generated SELECT clause

```
/* selecting booking_hierarchy booking */
select
            array_agg(
    /* Entering booking_record */
    row(top.booking_id  ,
        (
    select array_agg(  /* Entering passenger_record */
    row(passengers.last_name  ,
    passengers.account_id  ,
    passengers.first_name  ,
    passengers.passenger_id  ,
    passengers.passenger_no)::norm.bh_passenger_record)
 from  postgres_air.passenger  passengers
 where  top.booking_id = passengers.booking_id
)
  ,
        (
    select array_agg(  /* Entering booking_leg_record */
    row(booking_legs.flight_id  ,
```

```
       (
select  (  /* Entering flight_record */
    row(flight.flight_no  ,
    arrival.city  ,
    departure.city  ,
    flight.scheduled_arrival  ,
    flight.scheduled_departure  ,
    flight.arrival_airport  ,
    arrival.airport_name  ,
    flight.departure_airport  ,
    departure.airport_name)::norm.bh_flight_record)
from  postgres_air.flight  flight
    join postgres_air.airport departure on  departure.airport_code =
    flight.departure_airport
    join postgres_air.airport arrival on  arrival.airport_code = flight.
    arrival_airport
where  booking_legs.flight_id = flight.flight_id
)
   ,
    booking_legs.leg_num  ,
    booking_legs.booking_leg_id)::norm.bh_booking_leg_record)
from  postgres_air.booking_leg  booking_legs
where  top.booking_id = booking_legs.booking_id
)
   ,
    top.booking_ref)::norm.bh_booking_record)
from  postgres_air.booking  top
```

The SELECT clause shown in Listing 14-5 returns a PostgreSQL array of nested complex objects. This output is converted into JSON format with a single invocation of the to_json function.

In contrast with the SELECT clause, the filtering criteria depend on the specific needs of the application and therefore are needed for each query. NORM accepts search conditions in the JSON format that resembles a format found in some JSON-oriented systems. However, NORM provides neither the full power of these languages nor even a subset of them. Essentially, NORM supports basic comparison operations on any scalar keys in the JSON contact at any level of the hierarchy. An example of search conditions is shown in Listing 14-6.

Listing 14-6. Search conditions in JSON format

```
{
"booking_hierarchy":{
"departure_airport_code":"ORD",
"arrival_city":{"$like":"NEW%"},
"last_name":"Smith"}
}
```

This search will return all bookings that have a passenger with a last name of "Smith" and have a leg with flight from ORD to any city whose name starts with "NEW." For all these bookings, all passengers and all legs will be included in the result.

Note that search conditions cannot include any join operations because relationships between objects are defined in the hierarchy. If more relationships are needed, another hierarchy must be defined. Listing 14-7 shows the SQL code generated for this search.

Listing 14-7. Generated filtering conditions

```
  booking_id IN (
    select booking_id from postgres_air.booking_leg where
     flight_id IN (
    select flight_id from postgres_air.flight where
     arrival_airport IN (
    select airport_code from postgres_air.airport where
     city  LIKE  ('NEW%'::text) )
 AND  departure_airport  =  ('ORD'::bpchar) ) )
 AND  booking_id IN (
    select booking_id from postgres_air.passenger where
     last_name  =  (Smith::text) )
```

This generated code is wrapped in functions that construct a complete query and execute it. Notice that this generated code resembles the code discussed in Chapter 12 and shown in Listing 12-21.

Modifying Data in the Database

NORM can handle any data manipulation operation, that is, INSERT, UPDATE, and DELETE, which are collectively called update requests.

An update request is sent from the application as a complex object and, on the database level, may result in multiple update operations applied to different tables. Once again, database development is contract-driven. A database function receives a JSON object from the application, parses the object, and interprets the actions that are required on the database level.

The NORM approach aims to reduce the number of database operations. Of course, it is not possible to update multiple tables in a single SQL statement, so NORM needs to execute several SQL statements for an update request. However, it collects data from several sub-objects of the update request so that at most one DELETE, one UPDATE, and two INSERT statements are performed for each table that can be modified through the hierarchy, no matter how many hierarchies and sub-objects are modified by the update request.

The generated NORM code relies on the assumption that all tables have a single-column primary key and the values of primary keys are automatically assigned when new rows are inserted.

An update request is sent from the application as a JSON array of hierarchies conforming the contract schema and satisfying a few additional rules:

- If an object at any level of the hierarchy does not include the key mapped to the primary key, this object and all its sub-objects are inserted into the appropriate tables.

- If an object contains the value of the primary key and an additional key "cmd":"DELETE", then this object and all its sub-objects are deleted from the database.

- If an object contains a primary key and does not contain the "cmd" key, then the values of other keys of this object are used in the UPDATE operation.

An example of an update request is shown in Listing 14-8. The modifications specified in this request do not necessarily make sense from a business viewpoint; however, they illustrate how modifications are specified.

Listing 14-8. An example of an update request

```
1    [
2        {
3            "booking_id": 556470,
4            "cmd": "DELETE"
5        },
6        {
7            "passengers": [
8                {
9                    "last_name": "Jones",
10                   "account_id": 238648,
11                   "first_name": "Lucy"
12               }
13           ],
14           "booking_legs": [
15               {
16                   "leg_num": 1,
17                   "flight_id": 558238,
18               },
19               {
20                   "leg_num": 2,
21                   "flight_id": 563410
22               }
23           ],
24           "booking_reference": "IYZI42"
25       },
26       {
27           "booking_id": 3974917,
28           "passengers": [
29               {
30                   "cmd": "DELETE",
31                   "passenger_id": 11479596
32               },
33               {
34                   "last_name": "SCOTT",
```

```
35                    "first_name": "MILES",
36                    "passenger_id": 11479599
37                }
38            ],
39            "booking_legs": [
40                {
41                    "flight_id": 432724,
42                    "booking_leg_id": 11453272
43                },
44                {
45                    "flight_id": 427273,
46                    "booking_leg_id": 11453273
47                }
48            ]
49        },
50        {
51            "booking_id": 2733047,
52            "booking_reference": "Q8JX22"
53        }
54    ]
```

The update request shown in Listing 14-8 requests the following actions:

- Delete a whole booking (lines 2–5).

- Insert a new booking (lines 6–25).

- Delete one passenger, update first and last names of another
  passenger, and change the flight in two booking_leg entries
  (lines 26–49).

- Update the booking reference in a booking (lines 50–53).

To support update requests, NORM generates several functions that contain SQL
DML operations for each table and a function TO_DB that accepts update requests and
invokes all the other functions as needed to perform the requested modifications. This
function returns a list of primary keys of the top-level objects of all hierarchies that were
touched during the execution of the update request.

The generated code is too long to be included in this book, but is available in the NORM repository on GitHub.

Why Not Store JSON?!

At this point, you might wonder why we go into such trouble when PostgreSQL supports the JSON type? Why not store JSON "as is"?

Some reasons were previously discussed in Chapter 9. In particular, Chapter 9 discussed key-value and hierarchical models and explained their limitations. If a booking leg, as defined in this chapter, was stored as a JSON object, flight information would be duplicated, because it belongs to a different hierarchy. Another reason is that JSON is typeless and therefore unreliable in terms of providing a consistent interface to develop against.

In addition, although we can build indexes to facilitate search on specific JSON keys, their performance is worse than B-tree indexes on regular columns. Indexing JSON and related performance concerns are covered in Chapter 15.

Performance Gains

What is the effect of using NORM on performance? As discussed in Chapter 11, this kind of performance difference is difficult to benchmark. We need to measure overall application performance, rather than comparing the speed of separate operations, and the applications themselves in this case are written in very different programming styles. We are not providing any examples of application code in this chapter since it is out of scope of this book.

However, based on our industrial experience, this approach used in place of traditional ORM can improve the performance of application controllers by 10–50 *times*. Moreover, application performance appears to be more consistent, since it avoids the *N + 1 problem* (i.e., when the code needs to load the children of a parent-child relationship: most ORMs have lazy-loading enabled by default, so queries are issued for the parent record and then one query for *each* child record).

Working Together with Application Developers

As discussed many times, overall system performance is not limited to database performance, and optimization starts with gathering requirements. NORM is a very good illustration for this statement.

With NORM, development starts from defining a contract, which allows application and database developers to work in parallel on their tasks. In addition, this contract means that future performance improvements on the database side can be made without making any changes to the application.

Summary

NORM is an approach to application design and development, which allows seamless data exchange between a back end and a data layer eliminating the need for ORM. Applied consistently, it helps produce performant systems while simplifying application development.

NORM is one of several potential solutions; however, it has a proven record of success and can be used as a template for those who want to avoid the potential pitfalls of ORM.

CHAPTER 15

More Complex Filtering and Search

Previous chapters discussed several ways to support filtering and search with indexes in PostgreSQL. Why are more needed, and why haven't these indexes been covered yet? Prior discussion of this topic focused on the most common indexes, those that are needed in nearly any application. However, there are data types that cannot be efficiently supported with indexes such as B-trees.

Full Text Search

Everything discussed in previous chapters is applicable to structured data, and all queries considered so far are Boolean. That is, a row is either needed for computation of the result or not, and a computed row either belongs to the output or not. Nothing resides in between. SQL is a powerful language for structured data and lends itself well to this sort of analysis.

In this section, we consider unstructured data. The most common example of unstructured data is text written in natural language. This kind of text is usually called a *document*. In contrast with structured data, a search for documents is always imprecise, because we are typically interested in a document meaning that is not precisely expressed in the content of the document. However, the criteria must be precisely expressed in a query. Welcome to the world of uncertainty!

There are several different models for document search; the one implemented in PostgreSQL is called a Boolean model. Note that modern Internet search engines use more complex models.

H. Dombrovskaya et al., *PostgreSQL Query Optimization*, https://doi.org/10.1007/979-8-8688-0069-6_15

In a Boolean search model, a document is considered a list of *terms*. Each term usually corresponds to a word in the document transformed using certain linguistic tools. This conversion is needed to improve the quality of the search. For example, we expect that the words "word" and "words" should map to the same term. The transformations are not trivial: "a leaf" and "leaves" are the forms of the same word; however, "to leave" is different. And it's not just morphological transformations: meaning depends on context. For example, "host" and "computer" have the same meaning in a document describing network protocols, but these words are different in a document related to organizing a conference.

In PostgreSQL, the linguistic rules defining the transformations are encapsulated in a *configuration*. Several predefined configurations for different languages are available, and additional configurations may be defined. One of the predefined configurations does not depend on any language.

The output of this linguistic processing is represented as a value of type `ts_vector`. The values of `ts_vector` are lists of terms and not related to any language or even text. A `ts_vector` can be built from any list of values.

Why is text search called *full text search*? In the dark ages (the 1970s), when the capacity of hard drives was small, lists of terms were built from titles or abstracts. So full text means that all the words in the document are considered as a source of terms.

Similarly, a query for document search is represented as a value of type `ts_query`. These values are constructed from a textual representation of a query that can contain words and the logical operators AND, OR, and NOT. A simple query consists of words only (with an implicit AND between them).

A term (word) in a query yields true if it is present in the document and yields false otherwise. The Boolean values for the terms are combined into a single Boolean value using operators contained in the query. For simple queries that only contain terms, a document matches if all terms in the query are present in the `ts_vector` corresponding to the document.

The match operator @@ returns true if a document satisfies the query and false otherwise. It can be used in the `WHERE` clause of a SELECT statement or anywhere else where a Boolean expression is expected.

A Boolean search produces definite results: a document either matches a query or does not match. Is it still uncertain? Yes, it is. Some information is lost when a document is converted to ts_vector, and some information is lost when a query is converted into ts_query as well.

The text search features of PostgreSQL can work without any indexes. PostgreSQL also provides special types of indexes that can speed up text search. We discuss these index types later in this chapter.

Multidimensional and Spatial Search

Filtering conditions considered in previous chapters used scalar attributes. Some kinds of indexes, for example, compound indexes, may contain several attributes, but the ordering of the attributes is essential: the index is useless if the value of the first attribute is not specified.

A fixed ordering of attributes is not desirable for some applications and data types. These applications require that multiple attributes are treated symmetrically, without any preference to any attribute. Typical examples are objects on a plane or three-dimensional space with coordinates as attributes. These kinds of data are collectively called spatial.

More importantly, spatial data often requires different types of queries. The most common queries are

- *Range queries* – Find all objects located at a certain distance or closer to the specified point in space.

- *Nearest-neighbor queries* – Find the k objects closest to the specified point.

These queries cannot be supported with one-dimensional indexes even if multiple indexes are used.

Of course, this kind of search is not limited to space only. The coordinates might have timestamp values or even values in a discrete domain.

PostgreSQL provides index types suitable for spatial data. These indexes are briefly discussed in the next section.

Generalized Index Types in PostgreSQL

The CREATE INDEX operator includes an optional index type specified on index creation. So far, this hasn't been demonstrated in prior examples, because all of the previously created indexes were B-tree indexes, and B-tree is the default value for the index type. The other possible values are hash, GIST, spgist, GIN, BRIN, and user-defined type (if installed), at the time of writing.

This section discusses some of these types in more detail.

GIST Indexes

Some applications use multi-attribute objects like points with coordinates on a surface or a plane. Previously, we discussed compound indexes that include multiple attributes. However, compound indexes are not symmetric: the attributes are ordered. In contrast, the coordinates of a point should be treated symmetrically.

GIST is a family of index structures, each of which supports a certain data type and can be configured to implement several different tree-based index structures. Specifically, it implements index structure for spatial data known as an R-tree. Support for R-tree and a few other indexes is included in the PostgreSQL distribution; more types may be installed as extensions.

An R-tree implemented as the GIST index type does exactly what is needed here: it indexes spatial objects (such as points and rectangles). Objects that have more complex shape are represented in the index with rectangular bounding boxes. Search conditions are expressed with a rectangle. All objects that intersect with the search rectangle are returned as the result of the search.

Of course, the attributes included in a GIST index are not necessarily coordinates. Such attributes may represent time or other ordered data types.

Indexes for Full Text Search

PostgreSQL provides two kinds of indexes that can support text search. First, consider GIN indexes, where GIN stands for Generalized Inverted.

For the purpose of indexing, a document is considered as a list of terms (or tokens), for example, as a value of the ts_vector data type discussed previously.

For each term contained in at least one document, an inverted index contains a list of documents containing the term. Thus, the overall structure is symmetrical: a document has a list of terms, and a term has a list of documents. This symmetry explains why the index type is called inverted.

Inverted indexes can efficiently support text search. For example, to find documents containing all terms specified in a query, PostgreSQL scans all lists of documents for these terms and leaves only the documents that appear in the lists for all terms in the query. The lists are ordered, so a single pass over the lists is sufficient to produce the result set.

A GIN index can be created as a functional index with an expression converting the document being indexed into a ts_vector, or values of ts_vector can be stored as a separate column. The advantage of the former approach is that it uses less space, while the advantage of the latter is that the index does not depend on the configuration (as the configuration is needed only to compute the value of ts_vector). If the values of ts_vector are stored, an index can refer to documents written in different natural languages and converted into ts_vector with different configurations. Generally, pre-computed ts_vectors will perform better, but this can depend as always on the function used to generate the vectors and system configuration.

The structure of GIN is not derived from or related to a natural language; as noted earlier, it treats documents as lists. Thus, it can work with data other than documents—in fact, any attribute type containing multiple values, such as arrays. The GIN index will find all rows with multivalued attributes containing all values specified in a query, just as it finds all documents containing specified terms.

Documents (values of ts_vector type) can also be indexed with GIST. To build such an index, the values of ts_vector are converted into bitmaps of fixed length. To construct the bitmap, each term that appears in any of the documents being indexed is hashed to obtain a number that represents its position in the bitmap. Each term is a bitmap of the same length, with a single bit equal to 1 (representing the term) and all other bits set to zero. A bitmap for a document is a bitwise logical OR of all the bitmaps that represent terms in the document. Thus, the document bitmap has a bit equal to 1 in all positions corresponding to terms appearing in that document. A query bitmap is constructed similarly.

A search on this index is based on the following fact: a document satisfies the query if its bitmap contains 1 in every position that the query bitmap has a 1.

Different terms can be hashed into the same position. Therefore, a GIST index can return documents that are not relevant for the query; and usually, a recheck of ts_vector values is needed, but PostgreSQL can recognize this automatically.

The number of false matches grows as the number of different terms increases. Therefore, the GIST index is efficient for collections of documents where the total number of different terms is small. This is uncommon with texts in natural languages, so GIN indexes are usually more efficient in this case. GIST indexes for textual search are still useful in special cases.

Indexing Very Large Tables

Any index occupies some space, and indexes on large tables can be very large. Is it possible to reduce the size of an index?

Database textbooks distinguish between dense and sparse indexes. All the indexes covered so far are dense; that is, they contain all values of the indexed column (or columns). A sparse index contains only a fraction of all values but still reduces the number of reads needed to find any value of the indexed attribute. This differs from conditional indexes that do not speed up search of values not included in the index.

Some database systems always store table rows in the order of the (surrogate) primary key. The index on a primary key can then contain only one value per table block, and hence it can be a sparse index. More advanced database systems support ordering tables on values of other attributes, which do not necessarily need to be unique. This organization of tables also provides for sparse indexes. Sometimes these indexes are called cluster indexes as the rows with the same value of the indexed column are placed close to each other.

PostgreSQL does not provide any means for explicitly controlling row ordering. However, in many cases, rows are ordered naturally. For example, rows registering certain kinds of events will be, most likely, appended to the table and will be naturally ordered on the arrival timestamp, making sparse indexing possible.

A generalization of sparse indexes implemented in PostgreSQL is called BRIN (for Block Range Index). A table for which a BRIN index is created is considered a sequence of block ranges, where each range consists of a fixed number of adjacent blocks. For each range, a BRIN index entry contains a summary of column values contained in the block range. For example, a summary may contain the minimum and maximum values of the timestamp column in an event log table.

To find any value of the indexed attribute, it is sufficient to find an appropriate block range (using the index) and then scan all blocks in the range.

The structure of the summarization method depends on the type of the column being indexed. For intervals, a summary may be an interval containing all intervals contained in the block range. For spatial data, a summary can be a bounding box containing all boxes in the block range.

If the column values are not ordered or rows are not ordered in the table, a scan of a BRIN index will return multiple block ranges to be scanned.

The summarization is expensive. Therefore, PostgreSQL provides multiple choices for BRIN index maintenance: a BRIN index can be updated automatically with triggers; alternatively, delayed summarization can be done automatically together with vacuum or started manually.

Indexing JSON and JSONB

Sometimes developers looking for flexibility convert table rows into text or semistructured format (JSON or XML) and then use text search instead of more specific indexes. This approach definitely works better than external indexing tools, but is significantly slower than specific indexes.

Returning to the question we posed at the end of Chapter 14, why go to the trouble of building functions that transform search results into JSON when we can simply store the JSON type directly in the database?

Let's see how this approach would work in practice. To do so, let's build a table that stores bookings as JSON objects. The first problem we encounter is that we might need different JSON structures for different application endpoints (we already built several different record types in Chapters 12–14). But let's assume we can consolidate different requirements and store the data in a way that would satisfy most use cases. We can use the code in Listing 15-1.

Listing 15-1. Building a table with JSONB column type

```
--create simplifies booking leg type
CREATE TYPE booking_leg_record_2 AS
(booking_leg_id integer,
     leg_num integer,
     booking_id integer,
     flight flight_record);
--create simplified booking type
```

```
CREATE TYPE booking_record_2 AS
(       booking_id integer,
        booking_ref text,
        booking_name text,
        email text,
        account_id integer,
        booking_legs booking_leg_record_2[],
        passengers passenger_record[]
);
---create table
CREATE TABLE booking_jsonb AS
SELECT  b.booking_id,
to_jsonb ( row (
 b.booking_id,  b.booking_ref,  b.booking_name, b.email, b.account_id,
ls.legs,
ps.passengers
 ) :: booking_record_2 ) as cplx_booking
FROM booking b
JOIN
 (SELECT booking_id,     array_agg(row (
booking_leg_id, leg_num, booking_id,
 row(f.flight_id, flight_no, departure_airport,
 dep.airport_name,
arrival_airport,
arv.airport_name,
 scheduled_departure, scheduled_arrival
 )::flight_record
)::booking_leg_record_2)  legs
FROM  booking_leg l
JOIN flight  f   ON  f.flight_id = l.flight_id
JOIN    airport dep  ON dep.airport_code =  f.departure_airport
JOIN    airport arv  ON arv.airport_code =  f.arrival_airport
GROUP BY booking_id) ls
ON b.booking_id = ls.booking_id
JOIN
( SELECT     booking_id,
```

```
array_agg(
row(passenger_id, booking_id, passenger_no, last_name, first_name)::
passenger_record)  as passengers
 FROM passenger
 GROUP by booking_id) ps
 ON ls.booking_id = ps.booking_id
) ;
```

Note that we create the table with a column type of JSONB (JSON Binary), not JSON. The only difference between these types is that JSONB stores a binary representation of the JSON data, rather than a string. For the JSON type, the only indexes you can build are B-tree indexes on specific tags, and then you need to specify a full path, including the indexes in the arrays, which would make it impossible, for example, to index "any" booking leg.

If we want to build highly performant indexes on JSON columns, we need to use the JSONB type.

Building this table will take a while. And it will take a while to build a GIN index:

```
CREATE INDEX idxgin ON booking_jsonb USING GIN (cplx_booking);
```

However, after this index is created, it feels like all our problems are solved. Now we can retrieve all the data we need without any joins and any complex structure builds, using simple queries like the one shown in Listing 15-2.

Listing 15-2. Search using a GIN index on a JSONB column

```
SELECT  *
FROM  booking_jsonb
WHERE
cplx_booking @@ '$.**.departure_airport_code == "ORD" && $.**.arrival_
airport_code == "JFK"'
```

The execution plan in Figure 15-1 proves that the GIN index is used.

	QUERY PLAN
	text
1	Bitmap Heap Scan on booking_jsonb (cost=199.73..21438.53 rows=5643 width=1205)
2	Recheck Cond: (cplx_booking @@ '($.**."departure_airport_code" == "ORD" && $.**."arrival_airport_code" == "JFK")'::jsonpath)
3	-> Bitmap Index Scan on idxgin (cost=0.00..198.32 rows=5643 width=0)
4	Index Cond: (cplx_booking @@ '($.**."departure_airport_code" == "ORD" && $.**."arrival_airport_code" == "JFK")'::jsonpath)

Figure 15-1. *Execution plan with a GIN index*

There are several issues that make this approach less appealing than it looks at first glance. First, this search is still slower than the search that uses B-tree indexes. The search functions generated using techniques described in Chapter 14 produce the same result but two to five times faster.

Second, GIN indexes do not support searches on date-time attributes or searches using the like operator or searches on any transformed attribute values, like lower(). You can specify several complex search conditions with json_path expressions and JSONB operators and functions, including regular expressions, in the WHERE clause, but these will be checked with a heap scan. A good idea is to combine such conditions with others that are supported with indexes.

In fact, we saw a production system that was built this way: data from multiple tables/schemas was used to create "search documents" of type JSON, and then ts_vector columns were added and indexed.

However, there is a third problem with this approach. As already stated, one JSON structure would support only one hierarchy. If we built a booking_jsonb column as described earlier, we could relatively easily update a flight in the booking leg, but we couldn't update the actual departure time or flight status.

This means that the booking_jsonb table will have to be rebuilt periodically in order to remain useful. Indeed, the production system mentioned earlier had a complex sequence of triggers that rebuilt all potentially affected JSON data. In cases with a relatively low expected number of updates, this restriction might not be critical, but that is not the case with delayed flights and changing flight schedules.

Summary

PostgreSQL has a multitude of different indexes. This book covers many of them, but not all of them; new index types appear with nearly every new version. It would be unsurprising if new indexes are released between the writing of this chapter and this book's release.

Both Chapter 5 and this chapter provide a number of examples of how to choose the right indexes to support different searches. Choosing indexes that are best suited for your system, for specific searches, is not a straightforward task. Do not stop at creating B-tree indexes for individual columns. Do you need compound indexes? Functional indexes? Will a GIST index help solve your problem? How critical is response time for this particular query? How much does this particular index impact updates? Only you can answer these questions.

CHAPTER 16

Ultimate Optimization Algorithm

The preceding chapters covered a lot of optimization techniques: not only different ways to optimize SQL statements but also how database design affects performance, the importance of working together with application developers, the use of functions, and many other aspects of database performance.

Still, the question posed in the Introduction remains: Where to start, when you have a real-world problem, when your users see an hourglass and you have no idea why? A related but more challenging task is to figure out what to do from the start. You do not have a problem yet. You have a task, possibly a draft of a query, or maybe you are lucky enough to have detailed requirements. How do you make sure you are doing it right?

In this chapter, we will present a step-by-step guide that will help you write queries right right away and, when you have the option, choose the database design that is right for you.

Major Steps

Figure 16-1 presents a flowchart that we suggest you can use to identify the best strategy for your query in question. In the subsequent sections, we will discuss each step in more detail.

© Henrietta Dombrovskaya, Boris Novikov, Anna Bailliekova 2024
H. Dombrovskaya et al., *PostgreSQL Query Optimization*, https://doi.org/10.1007/979-8-8688-0069-6_16

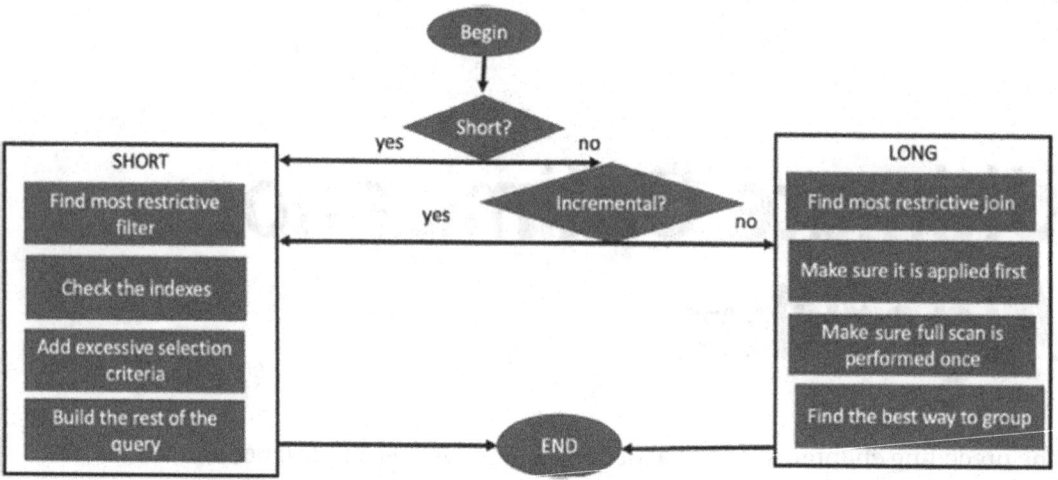

Figure 16-1. *Steps of the Ultimate Optimization Algorithm*

Step-by-Step Guide

Step 1: Short or Long?

The first step is to determine whether the query in question is short or long. As discussed in Chapters 5 and 6, looking at the query itself won't necessarily help you find the answer. Step 1 is a great time to recall that query optimization starts from gathering requirements, and it's important to work together with business owners and/or business analysts.

Check whether the business is interested in the most recent data or they need to follow historical trends and so on. The business might say that they need to see all canceled flights, but it would be a good idea to ask whether they want to see all canceled flights from the beginning of time or within the past 24 hours.

If you determine that the query in question is short, go to step 2; otherwise go, to step 3.

Step 2: Short

So your query is a short query. Which steps do you need to follow to make sure that not only is it written in the best possible way but also that query performance will be stable even when data volumes grow?

Step 2.1: The Most Restrictive Criteria

Find the most restrictive criteria for your query. Remember that often you can't tell which criteria this will be by just looking at the query. Query the tables to find the number of distinct values of attributes. Be aware of the value distribution (i.e., find out which values are the least frequent). When the most restrictive criteria are identified, proceed to the next step.

Step 2.2: Check the Indexes

In this step, you need to check whether there are indexes that support the search on the most restrictive condition. This includes the following:

- Check whether all search attributes for the most restrictive condition are indexed. If the index(es) is missing, request or create one.

- If more than one field is involved, check whether a compound index would perform better and whether the performance gains are enough to justify the creation of an additional index.

- Check whether you can use an index-only scan using either a compound or covering index.

Step 2.3: Add an Excessive Selection Criterion, If Applicable

If the most restrictive condition is based on a combination of attributes from different tables and thereby can't be indexed, consider adding an excessive selection criterion.

Step 2.4: Building (or Rebuilding) the Query

Start writing the query by applying the most restrictive criteria; this may mean starting from a select from a single table or a join that incorporates the most restrictive criteria.

Do not omit this step. Often, when database developers know the relationships between objects, they tend to write all the joins before applying filtering. While we are aware that this is an often-recommended approach, we believe that for complex queries with multiple joins, it might complicate development. We suggest starting from a SELECT that you know is executed efficiently and then adding one table at a time.

Check query performance and the execution plan each time you add a new join. Remember, optimizers tend to err in estimating the size of intermediate result sets more and more the further from the root of the execution tree they are. If the number of joins in the query is approaching ten, you may consider either using CTEs, if you are on version 12 or higher, or you may consider building dynamic SQL.

Step 3: Long

Your query is a long query. In this case, the first step would be to determine whether you can use incremental refresh. Once again, this is when you need to work together with the business owner and/or business analysts to understand better what the purpose of the query is. Often, requirements are formulated without considering data dynamics. When the results of a query are stored in a table and it is updated periodically, it can either be pulled fresh each time (a full refresh, pulling all data from the dawn of time to the most recently available data), or it can be pulled incrementally, bringing in only data that has changed since the last data pull. The latter is what we mean by incremental updates. In the vast majority of cases, it is possible to pull data incrementally. For example, instead of creating the `passenger_passport` materialized view as shown in Chapter 7, create it as the table `passenger_passport`, and add/update rows when new passport information is entered.

- If it is possible to use incremental updates, go to step 4.

- Otherwise, go to step 5.

Step 4: Incremental Updates

Treat the query to select recently added/updated records as a short query with time of update being the most restrictive criterion. Go to step 2 and follow the steps for optimizing short queries.

Step 5: Non-incremental Long Query

If running incremental updates is not possible, proceed with the following steps of long query optimization:

- Find the most restrictive join, semi-join, or anti-join, if applicable (refer to Chapter 6 for details), and make sure it is executed first.

- Keep adding tables to your join, one by one, and check the execution time and the execution plan each time.

- Make sure you do not scan any large tables multiple times. Plan your query to go through large tables only once, as described in Chapter 6.

- Pay attention to grouping. In the majority of cases, you need to postpone grouping to the last step, that is, you need to make sure that GROUP BY is the last statement in the execution plan. Be aware of some cases described in Chapter 6, when grouping should be performed earlier to minimize the size of intermediate datasets.

But Wait—There Is More!

Throughout this book, we've insisted that database optimization is not limited to optimizing individual queries; individual queries do not come from outer space. Still, the optimization algorithm described in the previous sections is a guide only to the process of optimizing an individual query or rather writing a query the right way from the start. However, we've covered several other techniques.

Here are other things to consider:

- *Parameters* – Most likely, the query you are optimizing is parameterized, that is, if you have a condition on `flight_id`, it won't be `flight_id=1234` all the time, but rather could be any arbitrary `flight_id`. As we discussed in Chapter 5, depending on particular filtering values, the most restrictive criterion may differ (e.g., "Canceled" flight status will be more restrictive than most other criteria).

- *Dynamic SQL* – In the latter situation, the right approach is to use dynamic SQL, which will be also the case when the selection criteria themselves vary.

- *Functions* – As discussed in Chapter 12, functions in and of themselves do not improve performance and may significantly degrade the execution times. However, if dynamic SQL is needed, it is difficult to avoid using functions.

- *Database design changes* – While working on queries, you might feel the need to make some DDL changes, from creating new indexes to changing the table schema. You will need to work with your DBAs and system architects to determine which changes can be implemented.

- *Interaction with the application* – If your query is executed by an application, query performance might be pretty good, while the overall application performance may not be. If you and your team choose to use NORM or another similar approach, you will need to work with application developers to determine what belongs to business logic and what belongs to database logic, as described in Chapters 11 and 13.

Summary

This chapter provided a step-by-step guide to help you navigate the process of writing queries right right away. We encourage you to give it a try and follow these steps when working on your next project.

CHAPTER 17

Conclusion

Like all good things must, this book is coming to an end.

In the Introduction, we shared that we wrote this book because we felt we could not *not* write it. Countless times, we've met the question: "Is there a book you can recommend for getting started with PostgreSQL?"

In the preponderance of cases, those asking this question were not database development novices. PostgreSQL is not yet the database of choice for most educational institutions, and a typical developer "new to PostgreSQL" already knows how to write syntactically correct SELECT statements, but is not familiar with the particulars of PostgreSQL. This includes not just any minor language differences, but more importantly, differences in how data is stored and how queries are processed.

Yes, of course, documentation is always available, but it is not always easy to find what you need, unless you already know exactly what you are looking for. Other resources include many excellent tutorials on various subjects, as well as the blogs of leading PostgreSQL experts. Most of the time, however, they are focused on specific topics, showing off numerous great features of PostgreSQL, but not necessarily indicating where exactly they fit into the big picture.

Of course, this book does not present the full picture either—PostgreSQL has a lot to offer, and we did not attempt to provide exhaustive coverage. Rather, we approach PostgreSQL from a different perspective: we demonstrate how to make these great features work.

That being said, we hope that this book will become a go-to book for database developers who are starting to explore PostgreSQL. We also hope that those who have already been using PostgreSQL for a while will also find some useful information, perhaps some techniques that they haven't used before.

Our goal is to give you a structure that you can use to navigate the challenges of database development and a resource you can consult in "what if" situations. Our hope is that having this book as a guide will make it easier for you to find more details in the PostgreSQL documentation.

© Henrietta Dombrovskaya, Boris Novikov, Anna Bailliekova 2024
H. Dombrovskaya et al., *PostgreSQL Query Optimization*, https://doi.org/10.1007/979-8-8688-0069-6_17

In addition to documentation, there are many other valuable resources available, including

- PostgreSQL Wiki, which contains thousands of helpful hints, usage patterns, and anti-patterns

- *The Art of PostgreSQL*, a great book to improve your SQL skills and learn about a variety of features for developing PostgreSQL-based applications

- Blogs by PostgreSQL experts (the Planet PostgreSQL aggregator is a great resource)

- PostgreSQL IRC chat

Throughout the book, we've tried to explain not only what to do but also why it works, because if you know the "why," you will be able to recognize other situations in which a similar solution could work. Understanding relational theory is a key to understanding these "whys," which is why this book began with a healthy portion of theory. For those who persevered through the theoretical chapters, your work will be rewarded. These theoretical foundations bring you one step closer to "thinking like a database," which allows you to write your queries right right away, rather than "write first and then optimize."

In addition, we've introduced the postgres_air schema, which is now open sourced and is available at `https://github.com/hettie-d/postgres_air`. We hope this realistic dataset will be helpful as a training, experimentation, and demonstration tool, as well as an educational resource.

In the Introduction, our target audience was described as IT professionals working in PostgreSQL who want to develop performant and scalable applications, anyone whose job title contains the words "database developer" or "database administrator," or anyone who is a backend developer charged with programming database calls. We hope that one of the takeaways from this book will be that collaboration between all these groups and business owners is key to developing performant applications.

Database queries do not run in a vacuum: the database is a service. Database work is invisible if everything works well, and it is extremely visible if something goes wrong. With that in mind, we hope that your work will remain mostly invisible!

And now have fun with PostgreSQL!

Index

© Henrietta Dombrovskaya, Boris Novikov, Anna Bailliekova 2024
H. Dombrovskaya et al., *PostgreSQL Query Optimization*, https://doi.org/10.1007/979-8-8688-0069-6